Gender and the Changing
Face of Higher Education

SRHE and Open University Press Imprint
General Editor: Heather Eggins

Current titles include:

Catherine Bargh *et al.*: *University Leadership*
Ronald Barnett: *Beyond all Reason*
Ronald Barnett: *Higher Education: A Critical Business*
Ronald Barnett: *Realizing the University in an age of supercomplexity*
Ronald Barnett & Kelly Coate: *Engaging the Curriculum in Higher Education*
Tony Becher and Paul R. Trowler: *Academic Tribes and Territories (2nd edn)*
John Biggs: *Teaching for Quality Learning at University (2nd edn)*
Richard Blackwell & Paul Blackmore (eds): *Towards Strategic Staff Development in Higher Education*
David Boud *et al.* (eds): *Using Experience for Learning*
David Boud and Nicky Solomon (eds): *Work-based Learning*
Tom Bourner *et al.* (eds): *New Directions in Professional Higher Education*
Anne Brockbank and Ian McGill: *Facilitating Reflective Learning in Higher Education*
Stephen D. Brookfield and Stephen Preskill: *Discussion as a way of teaching*
Ann Brooks and Alison Mackinnon (eds): *Gender and the Restructured University*
Sally Brown and Angela Glasner (eds): *Assessment Matters in Higher Education*
Burton R.Clark: *Sustaining Change in Universities*
James Cornford & Neil Pollock: *Putting the University Online*
John Cowan: *On Becoming an Innovative University Teacher*
Sara Delamont, Paul Atkinson and Odette Parry: *Supervising the Doctorate 2/e*
Sara Delamont & Paul Atkinson: *Successful Research Careers*
Gerard Delanty: *Challenging Knowledge*
Chris Duke: *Managing the Learning University*
Heather Eggins (ed): *Globalization and Reform in Higher Education*
Heather Eggins & Ranald Macdonald (eds): *The Scholarship of Academic Development*
Gillian Evans: *Academics and the Real World*
Merle Jacob and Tomas Hellström (eds): *The Future of Knowledge Production in the Academy*
Peter Knight: *Being a Teacher in Higher Education*
Peter Knight and Paul Trowler: *Departmental Leadership in Higher Education*
Peter Knight and Mantz Yorke: *Assessment, Learning and Employability*
Ray Land: *Educational Development*
John Lea *et al.*: *Working in Post-Compulsory Education*
Mary Lea and Barry Stierer (eds): *Student Writing in Higher Education*
Dina Lewis and Barbara Allan: *Virtual Learning Communities*
Ian McNay (ed.): *Beyond Mass Higher Education*
Elaine Martin: *Changing Academic Work*
Louise Morley: *Quality and Power in Higher Education*
Lynne Pearce: *How to Examine a Thesis*
Moira Peelo and Terry Wareham (eds): *Failing Students in Higher Education*
Craig Prichard: *Making Managers in Universities and Colleges*
Stephen Rowland: *The Enquiring University Teacher*
Maggi Savin-Baden: *Problem-based Learning in Higher Education*
Maggi Savin-Baden: *Facilitating Problem-based Learning*
Maggi Savin-Baden and Kay Wilkie: *Challenging Research in Problem-based Learning*
David Scott *et al.*: *Professional Doctorates*
Peter Scott: *The Meanings of Mass Higher Education*
Michael L Shattock: *Managing Successful Universities*
Maria Slowey and David Watson: *Higher Education and the Lifecourse*
Colin Symes and John McIntyre (eds): *Working Knowledge*
Richard Taylor, Jean Barr and Tom Steele: *For a Radical Higher Education*
Malcolm Tight: *Researching Higher Education*
Penny Tinkler and Carolyn Jackson: *The Doctoral Examination Process*
Susan Toohey: *Designing Courses for Higher Education*
Melanie Walker (ed.): *Reconstructing Professionalism in University Teaching*
Melanie Walker and Jon Nixon (eds): *Reclaiming Universities from a Runaway World*
Diana Woodward and Karen Ross: *Managing Equal Opportunities in Higher Education*
Mantz Yorke and Bernard Longden: *Retention and Student Success in Higher Education*

Gender and the Changing Face of Higher Education

A Feminized Future?

Carole Leathwood and Barbara Read

Society for Research into Higher Education
& Open University Press

Open University Press
McGraw-Hill Education
McGraw-Hill House
Shoppenhangers Road
Maidenhead
Berkshire
England
SL6 2QL

email: enquiries@openup.co.uk
world wide web: www.openup.co.uk

and Two Penn Plaza, New York, NY 10121–2289, USA

First published 2009

A catalogue record of this book is available from the British Library

ISBN-13: 978 0335 22713 6 (pbk)   978 0335 22714 3 (hbk)
ISBN-10: 0335 22713 9 (pbk)   0335 22714 7 (hbk)

Library of Congress Cataloging-in-Publication Data
CIP data applied for

Typeset by RefineCatch Limited, Bungay, Suffolk
Printed in the UK by Bell and Bain Ltd, Glasgow

The McGraw·Hill Companies

Contents

Acknowledgements   vi

1 Introduction   1
2 The feminization thesis   9
3 The global context: gender, feminization and
   higher education   26
4 Gender, participation and higher education in the UK   48
5 Institutional identities and representations of the university   71
6 Student identities, femininities and masculinities   95
7 Academic identities and gendered work   119
8 Academic practices: assessment, speaking and writing   141
9 Academic practices: curriculum, knowledge and skills   157
10 Conclusions: Re-visioning the academy   175

References   180
Index   209

Acknowledgements

Writing this book has been a challenging, engrossing and ultimately an incredibly rewarding experience. It was made incalculably easier by being a joint enterprise. Throughout the process of researching and writing we have been able to rely on each other for constant support and friendship (and, in the latter stages, much tea and cherry cake).

We have also relied on many others both in terms of academic support, emotional support, and friendship. We would both jointly like to thank: SRHE and in particular, Patrick Ainley and Joyce Canaan, for their help and support in the instigation of this project; Shona Mullen, Donna Edwards, Maureen Cox and everyone at Open UP; Middlesex University, Alverno College and University College Dublin for generously allowing us to reproduce images from their websites in Chapter 5; all the staff at IPSE; and Val Gillen, for putting up with our invasion of her house over many weekends.

Carole would also like to thank: all my family, friends and colleagues who have tolerated my obsession with this book (I will soon be able to talk about something else, honest!). In particular, I would like to give my heartfelt personal love and thanks to Val Gillen for ongoing support and encouragement, and for always being there. My love and thanks also to my (late) Mum and Dad who encouraged me in my studies from the beginning. I would like to dedicate this book to my Mum, Dorothy Leathwood, who sadly passed away before it was published. She would have loved to have had the chance to go to higher education and was thrilled at the idea of having her name in a book.

Barbara would also like especially to thank: all the members of my varied family tree; my wonderful and cherished friends both inside and outside of academia, and my current friends and colleagues at Roehampton University, especially Becky Francis, who has perhaps done more than anyone else to make me feel I could make a 'space of my own' in academia. Finally, I would like to dedicate this book to my Mum and my Dad, whose love and encouragement over the years has been immeasurable. Much love and thanks to you.

1

Introduction

'Ladies first: women take over universities' (*Guardian*, UK, 18 May, 2004)

'US colleges attempt to redress gender balance: men go missing on campus' (*The International Herald Tribune*, USA, 14 February, 2000)

'Growing gender gap risks turning universities into "male-free zones"' (*The Times*, UK, 15 February, 2007)

'Sudanese women winning gender war in education' (*PanAfrican News Agency*, 9 December, 1999)

'Pack it up, guys. The takeover is complete' (*Star Tribune*, Minneapolis, USA, 17 January, 2004).

If we believed the newspaper headlines, we would have to assume that the feminization of higher education is complete – that across the world, the forward march of women has succeeded in turning universities into spaces largely devoid of men.

In 1974, Adrienne Rich wrote:

The university is above all a hierarchy. At the top is a small cluster of highly paid and prestigious persons, chiefly men, whose careers entail the services of a very large base of ill-paid or unpaid persons, chiefly women: wives, research assistants, secretaries, teaching assistants, cleaning women, waitresses in the faculty club, lower-echelon administrators, and women students who are used in various ways to gratify the ego. (Rich, 1980: 136)

So have things changed dramatically since Rich wrote her account, or is it that reports of women's 'take-over' of the academy are, perhaps, exaggerated? In this book we investigate the extent to which higher education is a 'feminized' arena. Our intention is twofold, both to examine the feminization thesis itself, and to analyse the ways in which the academy might be considered a 'feminized' field. In undertaking this analysis, we explore the participation of women as students and academic staff in higher education across the world. We also examine the ways in which constructions of institutional, student and academic identities, and academic cultures, pedagogies and curricula, are gendered, classed and racialized.

The changing face of higher education

Higher education (HE) across the world is a rapidly changing field. As Brine (2001: 120) notes, 'the economic, cultural and political reality of globalization is the context within which supranational and national education policy is made'. Despite differences in the ways in which 'globalization' is conceptualized both theoretically and politically (Singh et al., 2005), there is general consensus that technological, economic and cultural developments, and the growing importance of the knowledge economy, have had a profound impact on higher education across the world. Naidoo (2003: 249) argues that governments have tended to use 'globalization' as a rationale for higher education reform, and highlights 'the attempt by governments to harness public universities in a relatively unmediated manner to economic productivity and to reposition higher education as a global commodity'. This has been supported by transnational organizations such as the World Trade Organization, with 'neoliberal globalism' or 'the ideology of rule by the world market' (Beck, 2000: 9) very evident. Key themes in higher education internationally have included a dramatic increase in participation as governments attempt to increase the skills base and enhance human capital, and the increasing marketization of higher education institutions, products and services. This has been accompanied by new managerialism and an audit culture of 'performativity', that is 'the use of targets and performance indicators to drive, evaluate and compare educational "products"' (Ball, 1999: 1). Knowledge has been increasingly commodified as it is packaged into smaller marketable units in a modularized curriculum. Despite a rhetoric of inclusion in many national and global higher education policy arenas, as Naidoo (2003: 250) notes:

> The perception of higher education as an industry for enhancing national competitiveness and as a lucrative service that can be sold in the global marketplace has begun to eclipse the social and cultural objectives of higher education generally encompassed in the conception of higher education as a 'public good'.

Naidoo argues that an increasing stratification is evident both within higher education in Western countries, but also between the industrialized and developing countries, as the west uses its economic and cultural capital to offer online and other for-profit education in 'developing' countries.

As Tomlinson notes, 'education within a competitive global economy can encourage new forms of racial and social exclusion' (2003: 213). However, there has been little attention to social inequalities, or to gender specifically, in both texts about processes of globalization and those discussing changes to the field of higher education (see, e.g. Blackmore, 2000; Stromquist, 2001), outside specifically feminist contributions. Indeed, as Blackmore and Sachs (2003a) note, an increased emphasis on the performative university has been accompanied by a reduction in attention to access and equity issues, and in this context, gender equity for women tends to be seen as a luxury.

Yet as will be seen, women's access to higher education has increased significantly since the 1990s in many parts of the world, and in a number of countries worldwide women now constitute a higher proportion of the undergraduate student population than men. Stories of women's educational achievements, along with examples of their presence in prominent positions in the public arena (such as successful business people or as political leaders), are often seen as signs that gender is no longer an issue. Indeed, the problem of gender equality today is often framed in terms of a concern that boys and men are 'losing out'. It is in this context that the feminization thesis has emerged in the contemporary arena.

It is not difficult to find accounts of women's advancement in many parts of the world. A newspaper article in the UK, for example, asked 'Will women rule the world?' noting that 'Germany is already governed by a woman' and, at the time the article was written, women were competing for the presidency in both France and America (Baxter, 2007). That such a question could be posed on the basis of one woman as leader of her country shows how rare such an event is in Europe. Yet there have been changes in gender identities and relations. In the UK, for example, economic restructuring and the decline of the manufacturing industry have been accompanied by new family and social relationships, as more women enter the paid workforce and 'feminine' skills are increasingly lauded, not only in the domestic arena but in business and other public arenas. As Walby (1997) noted, however, gender transformations have been accompanied by an increasing polarization of life opportunities between rich and poor, a claim supported by other research (see, for example, Walkerdine et al., 2001) – not all women have benefited, nor have they done so equally. Moreover, as Pereira (2007: 186) notes, 'It is much easier to increase access to university education for women than it is to change gendered power relations.'

The costs of capitalist globalization for women across the world have been spelt out by Mohanty:

> In fundamental ways, it is girls and women around the world, especially in the Third World/South, that bear the brunt of globalization. Poor women and girls are the hardest hit by the degradation of environmental conditions, wars, famines, privatization of services and deregulation of governments, the dismantling of welfare states, the restructuring

of paid and unpaid work, increasing surveillance and incarceration in prisons, and so on. (Mohanty 2002: 514)

Smith (2006) has also reported that 'according to the UN, at least one in every three women will be beaten, coerced into sex or otherwise abused in her lifetime; the organization describes violence against women as "a universal problem of epidemic proportions" and "perhaps the most pervasive human rights violation that we know today". Therefore, whilst women can be seen to be achieving educationally in ever increasing numbers in many parts of the world, this is not a simple, straightforward narrative of women's progress. As will be seen, in different places and at different times including the present, women's participation in higher education has declined as well as increased.

Perspectives and themes

What these different accounts highlight are the complexities of gender relations and transformations. In this book we draw on a range of feminist work that has contributed to an understanding of gender as socially constructed and hence subject to change, and as intermeshed with other social identities such as those of 'race'/ethnicity, social class, sexuality, disability or age (see, for example, Brewer, 1993; Yuval-Davis, 1997; Archer et al., 2001; Francis, 2001). We need to continually ask 'which women?' are participating in higher education in specific contexts, in recognition that women are not a homogenous group. As Hall notes, 'identities are never unified . . . never singular but multiply constructed across different, often intersecting and antagonistic discourses, practices and positions' (Hall, 1996: 4). Gender identities, and constructions of femininity and masculinity, change over time and in different social contexts, and reflect 'the complex nature of positionality faced by those who are at the interplay of a range of locations and dislocations in relation to gender, ethnicity, national belonging, class and racialization' (Anthias, 2001: 634).

Our position is that gender, and indeed sex, are socially constructed (see Butler, 1990). By this, we do not mean to deny embodied differences, but to recognize that the social significance and meanings attached to differently gendered (classed and racialized) bodies are discursively produced. Our theoretical focus combines both feminist post-structuralist and materialist analyses: we are interested in the material structures of inequality, privilege, exclusion and segregation, as well as in the complex negotiations, investments, fears and pleasures of subjects within the field of higher education.

Our central focus in the book is on gender, and we agree with Blackmore that:

despite the foregrounding of difference by post-structuralist feminist epistemologies, postcolonial and black feminisms, which put the category of 'woman' under question, it is both possible and desirable to speak of a normative feminist project, although one that is continually negotiated and contested. (Blackmore, 1999: 221)

We also recognize Mohanty's (2002) warnings of the dangers of ethnocentric scholarship. Our starting point is that of higher education in the UK – the context in which we work and know reasonably well – although we have included data and research from other countries across the world. What is clear, though, is that not only is there an absence of a linear narrative of progress, the narrative we have presented here is also not one of the 'progressive' West striding ahead in achieving gender equality, leaving the rest of the world behind – far from it. Whilst there are differences between women's participation in higher education in different regions of the world, in many cases there are larger differences *within* regions than *between* them.

There are however, some themes that have emerged strongly throughout our analysis, to which we return at different times throughout the book. These include:

- the persistence of the myth of the gender neutrality of the academy, something also noted by Morley (2005a);
- the evidence that universities are highly gendered organizations, both structurally and in terms of cultures and practices;
- the persistence of a gendered, racialized and classed division of labour globally – both in the academy and more widely, with implications for university graduates;
- the persistence of a gender binary which, although differently constructed in different contexts and relations, tends to identify the masculine with the rational/mind, and the woman with the emotional/body (see also Francis, 2000);
- the challenge, historically and in the contemporary context across the globe, to the possibility of the 'intellectual woman';[1]
- the importance of autonomy, and the ways in which women are denied it: as Pereira (2007: 148) noted, 'certain masculinist assumptions undermine women's capacity to engage in decision-making within the institution. One of the most fundamental is that men's autonomy is taken for granted, whilst women have to struggle for theirs.'

---

[1] An example of this emerged as we were completing our writing of this book. An exhibition of portraits at the National Portrait Gallery in London, entitled 'Brilliant Women: 18th-Century Bluestockings', was reviewed in a London newspaper. The reviewer derided the intellectual achievements of the women portrayed and disputed highly favourable reviews of their work by both their contemporaries in the late eighteenth century and the curators of the exhibition today, with the comment 'I am reminded of the adage: "A sow may whistle, though it has an ill mouth for it"' (Sewell, 2008). 'Bluestockings' was a term applied to women pursuing intellectual or literary interests – it has derogatory connotations.

As we conducted the research and analysis for the book, these themes emerged time and time again. It became increasingly clear to us that the feminization thesis is in many ways a myth – a product of a masculinist social imaginary – rather than a plausible account of the changing face of higher education in the contemporary arena.

Methodology

We have drawn on a range of primary and secondary data sources in the writing of this book. These include theoretical texts and accounts of empirical research, publicly available statistical resources, data from our own previous research, and an analysis of university websites that we undertook specifically for this book.

Our literature review of existing work in the field revealed an important body of work from feminist academics on gender in the academy. There is, as Morley (2005b) noted, a dominance of literature from the west, reflecting differential capitals and access to publishing opportunities (in English) in different parts of the world. We have, though, been able to find some literature about gender and higher education in a range of countries, reflecting some common concerns and interests. In her study and review of literature of gender and higher education in the Commonwealth, Morley (2005b) notes that although some research mentions social class, ethnicity or religion, there is little on how gender relates to other aspects of difference, and very little on sexuality or disability outside South Africa. We are also aware of the silences in this book about sexuality and disability – the absence of studies and texts that address these issues extends beyond the Commonwealth.

The statistical resources on which we have drawn have enabled us to provide an overview of patterns of gendered participation in the academy across the world. However, there are limitations to this data. In some cases, data for particular countries is unavailable, and where it is possible to find, direct comparability is often problematic due to differences in data collection methodology, as well as different educational systems and patterns of higher education study. We have focused predominantly on higher education study in universities (or their equivalent), and on students on predominantly theoretical degree courses – in terms of the international standard classification system (ISCED) these are level 5a (which includes both 'bachelor' and 'master' level courses) and level 6 (advanced research degrees such as the PhD).

In these analyses, we have tried to pay attention to both broad patterns and local contexts. Deem (2001) notes that in discussions of the globalization of higher education, similarities and convergences between universities in different countries may be emphasized at the expense of attention to more localized factors that affect higher education institutions. Silova and Magno (2004) also stress the importance of local context, giving the example of post-Soviet bloc democratization which has had different gender impacts in different countries. Where possible, we have combined an analysis of the broad statistical patterns of participation with reference to locally contextualized qualitative studies that offer more nuanced approaches.

A major problem is that statistical analyses tend to separate out identities and inequalities and to treat gender, for example, in isolation from ethnicity. The tendency, therefore, is to homogenize groups, rather than to explore differences within groups. There are particular difficulties, even when it is considered or attempted, in obtaining reliable data related to social class, ethnicity, disability or sexuality, including issues of conceptualization and respondent (non-)disclosure. The statistical accounts do, however, illustrate patterns of relative advantage and disadvantage and provide the broad context for the more nuanced analyses provided by qualitative studies. Given that the feminization thesis rests on an assumption that women are, numerically, 'taking over' the academy, attention to actual proportions of women at university is highly relevant. It is important to point out that whilst we have drawn on sources of published statistical data, the analyses and interpretations and we have conducted are our own. In some cases, for example, we have given mean scores in a table which we have calculated from the raw data – and obviously the responsibility for such analyses rests with us.

Outline of the book

In the next chapter, we explore the feminization thesis in detail. We draw on popular media representations and debates about the 'feminization' of society, education in general and higher education specifically to explore the underpinning assumptions about gender contained in these arguments. Consideration will be given to the feminization thesis as an example of a 'moral panic' and emblematic of a cultural anxiety about changing gender relations, as well as the association of feminization with discourses of the 'dumbing down' or devaluing of the academy.

In Chapters 3 and 4, we examine the evidence in relation to gender participation in HE. Chapter 3 provides a global overview, and Chapter 4 offers a more in-depth account of the situation in the UK. Both draw predominantly on statistical data. We examine gendered (and where possible, classed and racialized) patterns of access, participation, achievements and outcomes for students, as well as issues of subject 'choice' and institutional 'diversity'. We also consider the position of women as academic staff.

Chapters 5, 6 and 7 all focus on constructions of identities: of 'the university', 'the student' and 'the academic'. For Chapter 5, we conducted an original examination of a range of university websites from the UK and selected English-speaking countries. We consider the ways in which universities represent themselves and the extent to which these representations construct the university as a gendered (classed and racialized) space. In Chapter 6 we examine four different constructions of the higher education student: the independent learner, the 'needy' student, the 'student consumer' and the future graduate – all of which can be identified in the contemporary academy. We discuss whether this means that there are now many different ways of being a student, thereby making higher education more accessible than in the past. In Chapter 7, we turn our attention to academic identities, exploring gendered academic cultures and the changing nature of academic work.

Chapters 8 and 9 focus specifically on academic practices. In Chapter 8 we explore assessment, speaking and writing, considering the ways in which these practices are gendered and the implications for students. In Chapter 9 we move on to the curriculum, knowledge and skills. We discuss the kinds of knowledge that acquire status in the academy and the ways in which different disciplines are gendered, and move on to a consideration of the 'skills agenda' and its association with issues of feminization. Finally, in Chapter 10, we provide a summary of the key issues addressed in the book, and conclude with a discussion of the possibility of a feminist, rather than a 'feminized' future for the academy.

2
The feminization thesis

In this chapter we explore the feminization thesis in some detail, unpicking the different uses and meanings associated with the term 'feminization' in popular media representations and policy discourses. We are not concerned here with whether, or to what extent, feminization might be said to be occurring in HE (we discuss this in other chapters), but rather with the *discourses* of feminization, conceptualizing discourse in the Foucauldian sense as a system of statements, thoughts, rules and practices imbued with power. Discourses constitute meanings and knowledge, and they contain rules about what can be said and by whom. Such a focus on discourse directs our attention to examine taken for granted assumptions and 'truths' about feminization, and the ways in which these are constructed and maintained. It leads us to ask questions about why and how feminization has been identified, named and articulated as a problem demanding attention, and to consider the interests that such an articulation serves. It also leads us to consider how higher education, students and academics are constructed and positioned within the discursive framing of the feminization of the sector, and to reflect upon the relationship to other contemporary discourses of higher education, such as those concerned with mass participation, academic standards and allegations of 'dumbing down'.

We also consider the relationships between the discourses and practices of feminization and changing constructions of gender and gender relations. Through an identification of theoretical resources that have been used to understand processes of feminization in relation to other social fields, for example the labour market, we discuss the extent to which the feminization of higher education can be understood as indicative of, and/or productive of, changing constructions of gender and gender relations within society as a whole and specifically within the academy.

Contemporary discourses of 'feminization'

The term 'feminization' is now in common usage and regularly appears in popular debates and newspaper headlines, particularly in the UK and USA, but also in international and other national contexts. It is perhaps most commonly read as a description of a field in which women are in the majority, for example in the concept of 'the feminization of poverty'. 'Feminization' also often signifies a process of change, whereby women are seen to be increasing their numbers in relation to men – an example here might be changes relating to the medical profession in the UK. Traditionally, medically trained doctors were men, and women's struggle to enter the profession met with considerable resistance. Now, however, more women than men are training to be doctors – hence discussions about the feminization of the profession. Another example is the focus of a recent headline in a UK newspaper: 'It's arrived: the feminization of the net' (Allen, 2007: 3) which reported that women are now spending more time online than men – a notable change from the young male dominance of the internet at its inception in the early 1990s.

In addition to this concern with numbers, however, feminization is also used to signify cultural change or transformation, whereby 'feminine' values, concerns and practices are seen to be changing the culture of an organization, a field of practice or society as a whole. This is usually assumed to be a consequence of the numerical increase described above, so that more women entering a particular domain are thought to impact on the culture. Changes in cultural values towards a greater emphasis on cooperation, care, negotiation, and a 'feminine' aesthetics are seen as evidence of women's greater numbers and/or influence – and hence of feminization. In the UK, for example, the election of 120 women members of parliament in 1997 (from a mere 19 in 1979 when Margaret Thatcher became Prime Minister) prompted considerable debate about the extent to which the masculinist culture and practices of parliament would change – such as through a less adversarial style of debate, the introduction of more 'family-friendly' working hours, and a commitment to placing childcare higher on the government's agenda.[1] Another example is the rise of television talk shows which explore and expose family and personal relationships and which are seen as evidence of the feminization of culture in the UK and USA. Within such popular debates, the assumed synchronicity between specific constructions of femininity and greater numbers of women's bodies is rarely questioned. Indeed, Francis Fukuyama explicitly states that women's biological nature underpins his argument that as more women gain political power in different countries, these countries 'should become less aggressive, adventurous, competitive and violent' (Fukuyama, 1998: 27). Such a gender essentialism –

---

[1] For an account of the successes and difficulties faced by this new intake of women, see Sones et al., 2005.

that women are naturally/innately more cooperative, caring and so on than men – appears to implicitly underpin many of the arguments about feminization, something to which we will return.

But first, we want to note a third usage of the term 'feminization' to refer to changes in bodily characteristics. This is most frequently used to describe physical changes to animals, with, for example, the American Broadcasting Corporation reporting 'Feminized fish throughout Europe' as a result of 'gender-bending' chemicals (ABC, 2000), and Science News Online asking 'Are environmental "hormones" emasculating wildlife?' (Raloff, 1994). Comparable effects are being reported in humans, with reductions in male fertility rates (Cadbury, 1998), and a fall in the number of baby boys born in the Arctic region (Kirby, 2007).

Whilst cultural feminization and the production of feminized male bodies might initially appear to be distinct and separate uses of the term 'feminization', links have been made between the two. Some have suggested that an increasingly feminized culture is responsible for changing boys by making them more 'feminine', for example through disapproval and punishment of what is regarded as 'natural' boyish behaviour (see, for example, Sommers, 2000). What is being posited here, then, concerns a transformation of (embodied) identity or subjectivity which can be read as both suggesting that masculinity and femininity are socially constructed (and so can be changed) to implying a gender essentialism (that is, boys are naturally masculine – they are just being taught to repress it, but it will come out). Sax argues that both cultural feminization in the USA (in relation to psychology, men's magazines, politics and entertainment) and reductions in male sperm counts are consequences of oestrogens in the environment. He concludes that 'we should explore the possibility that our minds and bodies are being affected by environmental oestrogens in ways that we do not, as yet, fully understand' (Sax, 2003). Again, here there is an assumption that cultural constructions of femininity and masculinity are rooted in physical bodies – in this case in hormones. A renewed interest in brain science and assertions of gender differences in types of brain is also indicative of, and fuelling, a new gender essentialism. For example, Cohen has proposed a model of five brain types from 'extreme male' to 'extreme female', and whilst he suggests that some women have 'male' brains and some men have 'female' brains, he goes on to argue that people with 'female brains' make excellent counsellors because of their empathic skills, whilst those with 'male brains', indicative of systemizing skills, make excellent scientists and engineers (Newman, 2007). Cohen's work has been criticized for reinforcing stereotypes, failing to account for cultural differences in proportions of women scientists across countries, and contributing towards a naturalization of sex differences. Furthermore, a US review of studies on brain and hormonal differences concluded that there was no evidence that biological differences explained the under-representation of women in science and mathematics (Committee on Maximizing the Potential of Women in Academic Science and Engineering, 2006).

But to return to conceptualizations of feminization: whatever its assumed 'cause', discourses of feminization reinforce/reproduce a gender dichotomy. They tend to position boys and men as the victims – of feminising cultures, institutions, hormones and bodies, and of a cultural value system which, from this perspective, valorizes the feminine and derides the masculine. Michael Buerk, a UK newsreader, epitomized these views when he declared that 'Life is lived in accordance with women's rules', that 'almost all the big jobs in broadcasting are held by women' who 'decide what we see and hear', and that 'women aren't going to want an unemployable sperm donor loafing around and making the house look untidy' (BBC, 2005). He also argued that 'men are becoming more like women' (BBC, 2005). A similar theme was articulated in an edition of the US *Whistleblower* magazine on 'the war on fathers', subtitled 'How the "feminization" of America destroys boys, men – and women' (*Whistleblower*, 2006). This magazine used a wide range of 'evidence' for this, including boys' relative failure at school compared to girls, the fact that two thirds of all divorces in the US are instigated by women, that mothers are far more likely to get custody of their children than fathers, and that 'today, television virtually always portrays husbands as bumbling losers or contemptible, self-absorbed egomaniacs'. The managing editor of this magazine, David Kupelian, argues that feminists are the problem:

> [M]isguided feminists, intent on advancing a radically different world-view than the one on which this nation was founded, have succeeded in fomenting a revolution. And the revolution amounts to a powerful and pervasive campaign against masculinity, maleness, boys, men and patriarchy. (*Whistleblower*, 2006)

A 'young men in crisis' discourse, with men portrayed as the new 'underclass' and 'more at risk than girls of committing suicide, underperforming at school and turning to criminal behaviour' (Honigsbaum, 2006: 29), is frequently articulated in the Western media. A fear of men being 'left behind' was revealed in a study reporting on the numbers of women leaving the former East Germany, which highlighted fears of 'a demographic crisis' as women desert 'an underclass of poorly educated, jobless and disillusioned men' (Connolly, 2007: 18) for opportunities abroad. These men 'often have little chance of finding a job or a partner, and as a result they are typically drawn to far-right parties, such as the German Nationalists (NPD) or to neo-Nazi groups' (p. 18).

So not only are men constructed as the victims in this discourse, but also women, and in some cases feminists, are positioned as responsible for this. This relates to discourses of 'girl power' and to analyses that suggest that women have now achieved equality – indeed that feminism has gone 'too far'. It also relates to conceptualizations of the ideal neo-liberal subject as based on middle-class femininity (Walkerdine, 2003) – subjects who are self-reflexive, successful, mobile and able to 'remake' themselves to meet the demands of the new economy – Harris's (2004) 'can-do girl'.

This discursive framing of women as successful/men as victims homogenizes women and men, fails to recognize the inter-relationship of other social identities and inequalities, for example related to social class or 'race', (or the costs for middle-class women who try to meet these expectations, see Walkerdine et al., 2001) and continues to reinforce a gender binary. It also rests on a naturalization of heterosexuality, with a gender binary constructed of heterosexual 'girly' women and their complementary opposite, and equally heterosexual, 'manly' men.

Feminization: the case of education

Within these discourses of an increasingly feminized society, education is central. Education is positioned as both a feminized field per se and as a prime feminizing force for society as a whole. In a nutshell: increasing numbers of women teachers are assumed to be producing an increasingly feminized educational culture which then alienates and/or disadvantages boys and men – and indeed risks 'feminizing' them (see, for example, Skelton, 2002; Francis and Skelton, 2005; Read, forthcoming). Girls' and women's educational achievements and increased participation in post-compulsory and higher education are positioned against boys'/men's comparative 'underachievement' in a reconstruction of a gender binary in which the success of one group inevitably means the failure of the other (Jackson, 1998). In this context then, we can see all three uses of the term 'feminization' described above – an increase in the number of women (as both teachers and students), an assumed cultural feminization of pedagogy and the curriculum, and the potential/feared transformation of boys/men and masculine subjectivity.

One form that this debate has taken has been a particular focus on the lack of, and assumed need for, male teachers – especially in primary schools. This emerged as a particular concern in the 1990s, for example in the UK (Epstein et al., 1998a; Francis and Skelton, 2005; Francis et al., forthcoming), Australia (Lingard, n.d.) and Holland (Driessen, 2007), although it remains an issue today, with an article in the UK press reporting that men make up only 16 per cent of primary school teachers (Bawden, 2007). There has not been the same concern about the lack of women in senior education positions – for example as headteachers.

The concern is that women teachers are assumed to be imposing their 'feminine' values through their teaching, so that the culture of schooling, and indeed boys themselves, have been feminized. An article in a UK tabloid newspaper provides a prime example of this discourse:

> Boys are being failed by our schools because lessons have been 'feminized', a leading academic claimed yesterday. Dr Tony Sewell said boys fall behind in exams and the job market because teachers do not nurture male traits such as competitiveness and leadership. Instead,

schools celebrate qualities more closely associated with girls, such as methodical working and attentiveness in class. He said some boys become so alienated they turn to gang violence to vent their frustrated masculine side. (Clark 2006: 1)

We have challenged the 1950s patriarchy and rightly said this is not a man's world. But we have thrown the boy out with the bath water. . . . The school system does not value enough of the traditional male things like competition. . . . [Boys] have found the skills have been feminized. What seems to have been beaten out of them is any enthusiasm for anything. Some boys are resorting to gangs, which represent a world where basic male instincts hold sway. (Sewell, cited by Clark, 2006: 4)

Such views have not gone unchallenged (see, for example, Epstein et al., 1998a; Francis and Skelton, 2005; Francis et al., forthcoming). Marshall, for example, argued that not only is a competitive model of performance thriving in schools in pupil grouping practices such as 'setting',[2] but that school culture can hardly be described as feminine when almost all the key policy-makers and senior figures in education are men. She added: 'I'm not quite sure what annoys me more. The idea that the dead hand of the present male-imposed bureaucracy is feminine or that girls are so dull they don't mind being bored to death' (Marshall 2006: 3). In a study of the views of over 300 primary pupils in the UK, Francis and colleagues found no evidence to support the conception that boys preferred male teachers or saw them as 'role models' in terms of achievement or behaviour (Carrington et al., 2007; Hutchings et al., 2007; Francis et al., forthcoming). Neither did they find that primary school cultures are 'feminized' – indeed they found a complexly gendered variety of practices in relation to discipline and classroom talk that bore little relation to the embodied gender of specific teachers (Francis, 2008; Read, forthcoming).

The gender essentialism underpinning Sewell's argument – that boys have their natural male instincts which need satisfying/accommodating whilst girls are passive and compliant – is nontheless pervasive in this discourse of feminization. Similar arguments have been made in the USA, with Mercer arguing that in American schools:

girls are favoured over boys. When boys bubble over with unbridled testosterone, instead of challenging, disciplining and harnessing their energies, as teachers once did, they are emasculated or medicated. The former means being made over in the image of woman; the latter entails being diagnosed as 'learning disabled' and drugged with Ritalin. It is a

---

[2] Where pupils are grouped according to their educational achievement in particular subjects. So for example, a pupil might be in a top set for English, but a lower set for maths.

consequence of the demonization of male biopsychology. (Mercer, 2007)

So boys suffer, and are not only transformed but ultimately destroyed in this discursive framing; they are either feminized or demonized and women are to blame. This discourse has been evident in a number of countries since the early 1990s, with Bouchard et al. (2003) identifying similar examples in an analysis of media reports in 612 newspapers/magazines from Canada, Australia, US, France, Belgium and England between 1990 and 2000.

The case of higher education: feminized and devalued?

The feminization thesis is not only prevalent in discussions of schooling, but is also articulated in relation to higher education. The newspaper headlines with which we began this book are indicative of a public concern that women are taking over the universities. It is less easy to find media articles that celebrate women's considerable success in accessing higher education, or that point to men's continued dominance of academic posts – instead the focus is on the idea of men 'losing out'. The UK government stated that 'we are increasingly concerned about male participation' in HE (DfES, 2007), whilst 'the Iranian government is alarmed at the growing numbers of women in institutions of higher education' (Shavarini, 2005: 331). In Portugal, the heads of medical institutions were so concerned about the encroachment of women that they asked for measures to limit the number of women students in medical schools, with one arguing that:

> It isn't sexism. It's a reality that women get pregnant and have to avoid contagious diseases and definitely cannot perform microsurgery operations that can last up to 12 or 14 hours. . . . There are medical specialities that are not very attractive or suitable for women. For example, there is only one woman urologist in Portugal, because I believe a man feels embarrassed consulting a female doctor in that discipline (Sousa Pereira, President of the Institute of Biomedical Sciences, cited by Queiroz, 2004)

Obviously women never need to consult a urologist! Not only are women defined here purely by their bodies, but there is also an assumption that all women get pregnant and that they are permanently so. Presumably only gynaecology or paediatrics are likely to be thought as 'suitable' fields for women through this reasoning.

Reports do not only focus on more women than men entering universities as undergraduate students, but also that they doing better than men. 'Women take the lead in the contest for top degrees' reported *The Times* newspaper in the UK (Owen, 2004) as women for the first time not only achieved more degrees than men, but also achieved a higher proportion of the first class honours degrees awarded.[3]

In part these changes are seen as an inevitable consequence of (some) boys' relatively lower levels of achievement in school, although concerns about the assumed feminization of the cultures and practices of universities are still evident, for example in relation to claims that an increase in the use of coursework assessment favours women and effectively discriminates against men, a claim that is further discussed in some detail in Chapter 8. For now, however, it is worth noting that in contrast to schools, where discourses of feminization rest on the assumption that it is the predominance of women teachers that is causing 'the problem' and bringing about a feminized culture, in universities, women lecturers are not in a majority and hence cannot be blamed in the same way. Indeed men still dominate at all levels amongst university academics, from junior lecturers and researchers to professors and presidents/vice chancellors, as will be seen in the next chapter. Responsibility for the feminization of higher education therefore tends to be placed either on feminist academics, or on wider cultural changes in society. So, for example, Gilder (2005: 16) asks:

> Why would any self-respecting boy want to attend one of America's increasingly feminized universities? Most of these institutions have flounced through the last forty years fashioning a fluffy pink playpen of feminist studies and agitprop 'herstory', taught amid a green goo of eco-motherism and anti-industrial phobia.

This is a deeply conservative and misogynistic position, reflective of a particular form of 'masculinity politics' (Lingard, 2003) which ignores the persistence of male dominated and masculinist university cultures and curricula and lays the blame for this 'feminization' on women (in particular, single mothers) and a 'too generous' welfare state. Gilder's assumption that lone mothers are unable to effectively bring up and discipline boys reflects the feminization of schooling discourse about the lack of men primary teachers. Pointing to the lower incidence of 'fatherlessness' in Switzerland where men are about 60 per cent of the student population, Gilder does not question this imbalance in favour of men, presumably because he regards this as better reflecting the 'natural' order.

A rather different concern about changes in the cultures and practices of higher education has been articulated by some academics in the UK, drawing on Furedi's (2003) work on the 'therapy society', to criticize what is seen as a growing concern with emotion and feelings in universities (Ecclestone, 2004; Furedi, 2004; Ecclestone et al., 2005; Ecclestone and Hayes, 2007).

---

[3] This is because, however, increasing numbers of women are doing degrees. It is still the case that of all the men who graduate, a slightly higher proportion are awarded first class honours than the comparable figure for women – see Chapter 4.

This is not explicitly articulated in terms of the feminization debate, nor is gender specifically referenced. Given, however, the powerful tradition of a gendered rational/emotional binary in Western thought, the association of increased attention to emotion in popular culture in the US with feminization, and that 'it was quite common in the nineteenth century to exclude women from higher education and the professions on the grounds that they were swayed by their emotions and not, therefore, invested with the capacity to make rational judgements' (Walkerdine, 1994: 60), it is difficult to see this concern as gender neutral. The language used by some of these authors is also illustrative. Ecclestone and Hayes (2007: 2) for example, criticize what they see as an increasing tendency to provide 'comforting rather than challenging experiences' for students, whilst Hayes argues that a focus on 'the affective side of learning . . . undermines hard critical thinking' in his critique of 'the march of emotionalism through the UK's lecture theatres' (Hayes, 2005). This brings to mind Miller's observation that:

> a history of the last one hundred and twenty years or so reveals a recurring pattern of utopian ambitions amongst mainly women teachers for their working-class pupils, alternating with periods like the one we are currently living through, where a barrage of criticism is addressed at what are seen as the 'soft' centres of education. (Miller, 1992: 5)

The hard/soft, rational/emotional and highly gendered dichotomy discussed above persists.

The growth of a 'support culture' in universities has been associated with moves towards a mass higher education system, with the 'new', 'non-traditional' students perceived to need higher levels of academic and other support to enable them to succeed at university. Given that the main group to increase their representation in universities in a mass era has been (middle-class) women, the gendered associations of support and emotional need are again implicit, a discussion which we develop further in Chapter 6.

There has also been an increased emphasis on the development of personal skills and emotional literacy in HE, reflecting a neo-liberal concern to produce 'employable' graduates, and in particular, graduates with the kinds of 'people skills' required by a service economy. The assumption, notes Adkins, is that 'a form of mobility, specifically the transposition of a feminine habitus into the economic sphere of action, is understood to be key for these features of the economy' (Adkins, 2002: 6). Such developments have been assumed to benefit women, with femininity, rather than being seen as a disadvantage in the labour market, now perceived to be a highly valued resource. Such assumptions have been subject to critique by Adkins and others (see Chapter 6), but in a context in which human capital theory maintains its influence and where higher education is increasingly positioned as key to meeting the labour needs of the global economy, the personal skills and employability agenda has gained considerable ground. These developments are seen to provide a further example of an increasing feminization of higher education: of a feminized curriculum and academic culture that valorizes emotional literacy and 'people skills' and so produces feminized students.

A range of changes to the higher education curriculum, including modularization and the packaging of knowledge into easily marketable components, discussed further in Chapter 9, have accompanied this emphasis on skills development. In addition, a range of degree courses have been developed in new subjects/professional areas such as sports science or media studies, which were infamously labelled as 'Mickey Mouse degrees' by the UK Higher Education Minister of the time (Hodge, 2003). All of this has been associated with a devaluing of university education – with the higher education that the new students are receiving being seen as a poor replica of the serious intellectual work performed predominantly by (white, middle-class) men in a romanticized 'golden age' of higher education. This chimes with a dominant and persistent 'dumbing down' discourse in the media, where the annual publication of educational achievements in the UK is accompanied by claims of reduced academic rigour and a 'dumbing down' of educational standards. Notions of inherent 'ability', with levels of 'intelligence' distributed through society in the shape of a pyramid, and only the relatively small layer of those at the top deemed suited to a university education, is remarkably persistent. Yet the achievements of women poses a problem here – those who have traditionally been in the top segment of this pyramid have been privileged middle-class men. Women's success is therefore positioned as a result of a 'dumbing down' of standards (such as 'easier' assessment that is assumed to test diligence rather than intelligence). This parallels Cohen's (1998) analysis that when boys and men do well, it reflects their inherent ability (and when they do badly, it is a result of external factors such as a 'feminized' education system), whereas girls and women's achievements tend to be explained by factors external to themselves, rather than as a reflection of their ability.

The association of women's success in a particular field with a reduction in the status of that field is not, of course, confined to the field of education, nor is the assumed loss of status, or 'dumbing down' of HE only associated with the mass entry of women. It is the entry of any despised 'Others' into the academy that provokes anxiety on the part of the traditionally privileged, with Kingsley Amis's infamous comment on the development of new universities in the UK in the 1960s, 'More will mean worse' (cited by Silver, 2003: 179) emblematic of this. As Morley notes 'there is a powerful discourse of crisis, loss, damage, contamination, and decay in higher education' (Morley, 2003b: 5).

The feminization of higher education – a moral panic?

Public debates about the feminization of higher education have been accompanied, as has been seen, by somewhat dramatic newspaper headlines.

So is this simply a case of 'moral panic'? A decade ago, Epstein and colleagues suggested that popular debates about boys' underachievement could be seen 'as a kind of globalised moral panic' (Epstein et al., 1998b: 3), and here we consider whether this could also apply to the contemporary focus on higher education. Cohen, whose work on 'Folk devils and moral panics' about the 'mods and rockers' of the 1960s has been seen as a classic text on the notion of a 'moral panic' (Cohen, 1972), has more recently criticized some uses of this term (Cohen, 2002). Indeed, given its original usage in relation to a moral panic about 'folk devils' – that is, marginalized minority groups such as specific groups of working-class young men (mods and rockers, football hooligans, vandals and so on), its application to half the population, women, does require a rather different analysis. Far from being constructed as a 'deviant' group in society which provokes the moral concern and outrage of the mainstream, it is women's successful achievement in a high status arena that is the subject of this 'panic'. Cohen is, however, critical of the 'liberals, radicals and leftists' (2002: viii) he accuses of using the term 'moral panic' as a way of trivializing and denigrating the concerns and anxieties of the public, and hence it is worth considering the use of the term in relation to feminization debates.

Media attention to this issue does appear to fulfil many of the criteria of a moral panic identified by Cohen, including a concern about a perceived threat, hostility to those who 'embody the problem', some level of consensus that the problem exists, and 'disproportionality' or an exaggeration of the extent of the problem or level of threat.

There is clearly a concern about a perceived threat to men, masculinity and the 'natural' gender order in discourses of the feminization of HE. As Miller (1992: 1) noted in relation to debates about the feminization of schooling: 'A strange nostalgia for school-days when boys were boys and teachers were men regularly erupts'. Blackmore (1999: 40) argued that fear of feminization cannot be disconnected from the 'fear of making men effeminate', and such a fear, which is implicitly homophobic, does seem to underpin some contributions to debates about the 'feminization' of HE. Women are seen to be increasingly encroaching upon a space that was previously the preserve of men alone. Ahmed, in her analysis of fear of racial difference, discusses the ways in which spatial relations and in particular relationships of proximity, are implicated in the fear of the Other, and suggests that 'fear does not involve the defence of borders that already exist; rather, fear makes those borders, by establishing objects from which the subject, in fearing, can stand apart' (Ahmed, 2004: 128).

In this way, women in general and feminists in particular are constructed as opponents in a sex war of a masculine imaginary, through which the boundaries around traditional constructions of masculinity can be redefined and reasserted. Moreover, these fears work to 'align bodily and social space' (Ahmed, 2004: 63) in an attempt to keep women and others 'in their place'. A similar 'sex war' discourse is evident in media debates about boys' assumed 'underachievement' (Mahony, 1998). Hostility to women, and particularly to feminists, is also very evident in some of the more extreme accounts, including that of Gilder (2005) above, although this kind of misogyny is hardly new (see Dyhouse, 2006), or specific to debates about the feminization of HE.

There also appears to be some level of consensus that the 'problem' of feminization exists, expressed, as has been seen, in the popular and educational press. In the UK, this is also evident in the funding of widening participation activities and projects specifically directly at men,[4] and the emphasis on partnerships between universities and school to 'embed the careers and educational advice that is necessary to engage, inspire and inform young working-class men to make suitable life choices' (Denham, 2007). But to what extent is this 'problem' exaggerated? Does Cohen's test of 'disproportionality' in moral panics apply? As will be seen in Chapter 3, women now outnumber men as undergraduates in many (though not all) countries across the world. However, this is only part of the story, with significant levels of subject segregation and persisting disadvantages for women in the labour market.

A major problem of the feminization thesis is the homogenization of women and men that takes place within these debates. Some men continue to do extremely well academically, and some women do not participate at all. Indeed the massive increase in the participation of women in the UK, for example, is predominantly an increase in the numbers of middle-class women, with those from the lowest socio-economic group almost as unlikely to participate in HE as men from that group (discussed in Chapter 4). King, in a discussion of US data, argues that:

> while women do earn the majority of degrees awarded each year, the gender gap is dwarfed by the educational chasms related to race/ ethnicity and social class. Therein lies the 'crises'. Low-income and minority men have a particularly difficult time excelling academically, but their female counterparts continue to lag behind whites as well. (King, 2000: 17)

We also take issue with the cultural feminization thesis in relation to HE, and argue that despite the increase in undergraduate women students and the activities of feminist academics, the culture of HE remains predominantly masculinist. Indeed it can be argued that the new managerial, audit, individualistic and competitive aspects of academic culture are an example of a re-masculinization, reflecting Mahony et al.'s (2003) thesis in relation to new managerial trends in schools. But perhaps the best test of the level of exaggeration is to compare the concern now given to a greater participation by women with the relative lack of concern to the serious under-representation of women throughout much of the history of higher education across the

---

[4] See, for example, the 'Bright Boys' project at the University of Liverpool www.liv.ac.uk/newsroom/press_releases/2004/06/brightboys.htm (accessed 18 January, 2008).

world. In this context, the response to recent 'feminization' does seem rather disproportionate and exaggerated.

There is one further facet of a moral panic discussed by Cohen and that is 'volatility', or a rapid eruption and dissipation of the panic without warning. Given that concerns about the feminization of higher education are hardly new, this criteria is perhaps the one that is the least well-matched by the feminization debate. Women's entry into HE has long been assumed to threaten the status of higher education institutions, with, for example, resistance to co-educational medical schools in the first decades of the twentieth century in the UK based on a fear that a female presence would challenge the elite reputations of these institutions (Dyhouse, 2006). Brown suggests that in the USA in the late nineteenth and early twentieth centuries:

> coeducation at the college level carried implicit contingencies – that female students not threaten men's dominance in the classroom or on campus and that graduates use their college educations either to be better wives and mothers or to be moral, magnanimous spinsters in the social service occupations designated for women. (Brown, 1990: 1)

Brown also says that when this wasn't seen to be happening, there was a backlash based on a fear that not only were women feminizing colleges 'with their enthusiasm for classical and liberal arts courses', but also that college was masculinizing women and threatening marriage and fertility. It is interesting that in contemporary debates, the challenge to gender identity is framed less in terms of concerns that women are becoming masculinized (though such concerns have also been evident in the UK at different times and in various contexts), but rather about the feared emasculation of men. Yet the 'panic' does tend to erupt on the annual publication of university statistics in the UK (for example showing the gender gap in applications or degrees awarded), and then die down again until the next statistical release or research study which can be seen to legitimize the concern.

We do feel, therefore, that it is appropriate to talk about discourses of feminization in terms of a moral panic. In higher education, a particular focus of this is the feared 'dumbing down' of the academy as more women and other previously excluded groups participate. At the root of the feminization thesis, however – and this, we suggest, applies to discourses of feminization that have emerged at different times and in different places – is a cultural anxiety about changing gender identities and gendered power relations, something to which we now turn.

Feminization and constructions of gender

The feminization thesis both rests on and posits gender change. At the same time, essentialized constructions of gender as a fixed dichotomy of male/masculine and female/feminine underpin many of the discourses of feminization discussed above, and there is evidence of considerable resistance to any change in the traditional gender order from some constituencies in this debate. Indeed, it is precisely this resistance, along with fear of change in the gender order that is, we suggest, at the heart of the feminization thesis. The question of the relationship, therefore, of discourses of feminization to the construction of gender and gender inequalities is a pertinent one.

In a discussion of the feminization of the labour market, and in particular of the upper levels of the occupational hierarchy, Le Feuvre (1999) identifies four perspectives, each of which posits a different understanding of the implications for gender. In the first of these, feminization is assumed to make no difference to gender inequalities, as the areas that women enter are then devalued and hence the traditional gender order is preserved. This parallels the 'dumbing down' discourse in higher education. The second perspective is a form of cultural feminization where 'feminine' values (caring, empathy, sensitivity, etc.) are inserted into the field in question. This, suggests Le Feuvre, better reflects the needs of both women staff and clients, but still rests on a notion of a gender binary, with traditional constructions of masculinity and femininity preserved intact. Again this can be related to the feminization thesis in higher education, where an academic culture that is seen to prioritize the support and emotional wellbeing of students, and which emphasizes the development of personal and 'people' skills, is assumed to be better for women and to disadvantage men. The third perspective identified by Le Feuvre is one that acknowledges that relatively few women reach the upper echelons of the occupational hierarchy, and suggests that those that do have to become surrogate men. The jobs and culture in which they are located are constructed as masculine, so it is only by performing masculinity that these women are able to succeed. This again therefore suggests little change to the gender order; indeed it could be argued that the success of a few serves to legitimize the idea of a neutral meritocracy whilst effectively preserving the status quo. Gender inequalities are therefore maintained. Le Feuvre argues, however, that the fact that some women do reach these positions suggests a *potential* challenge to the masculine/feminine binary. In HE, there has been little focus in media debates about the feminization thesis on women entering top academic posts – presumably because relatively few still do, and this particular perspective therefore does not fit easily with discourses of the feminization of HE. The challenges presented, however, by a masculinist managerial culture to women academics at all levels has been well documented in feminist academic literature (see, for example, Spurling, 1997; Morley, 1999; Goode, 2000; Currie et al., 2002) and is discussed in Chapter 7. Finally, the fourth perspective discussed by Le Feuvre is one of gender transformation, where equal numbers of women and men challenge traditional gender constructions and assumptions. This is potentially the most radical perspective that Le Feuvre considers. It rests on a social constructionist approach through which there is potential change to both the field into which women enter and to the construction of gender. This perspective can be seen in some discourses of the feminization of higher education – where gender transformation is assumed to be happening or to have happened, and often feared. These assumptions and fears relate both to changes in the field of higher education – its constitution, culture and practices, and in the gender regime, or 'the state of play in gender relations' (Connell, 1987: 120) of universities.

The relationship between the feminization thesis and constructions of gender is, therefore a complex one – epitomized by the contradictions of positions which simultaneously posit both gender essentialism and assumptions/fears of a radical disruption of the traditional gender order.

But to what extent might such a gender transformation mean the end of gender, where gender ceases to have any significance? Adkins (2002), whose research also focuses on the labour market, considers the extent to which feminization may be indicative of a process of gender detraditionalization. She critically engages with theories of reflexive modernity which propose a declining influence of social structure (and hence of social categories such as gender and class) and a growing individualization (e.g. Beck and Beck-Gernsheim, 2002), to argue that rather than ceasing to be significant, gender is being reconfigured. There clearly is a greater mobility and fluidity of gender and gender identities, with, for example, both women and men able to perform qualities traditionally associated with femininity. Adkins, however, draws on the work of McDowell (1997) to argue that femininity is naturalized for women, so that whilst men can take on characteristics associated with femininity and be applauded and rewarded in the workplace for doing so, women's performance of the same characteristics is not recognized for reward. Such an analysis has implications for gendered constructions of the student and future graduate as subjects who able to use and perform the 'people skills' demanded by the labour market – something that is further discussed in Chapter 6. Adkins argues, therefore, that there is little evidence that gender has become irrelevant or that traditional gendered power relations have been usurped. Similarly, Le Feuvre (1999) concludes that whilst some women do contest and subvert both the gender binary and dominant constructions of femininity and masculinity, on the whole, the traditional gender order has shown signs of modification and adaption rather than of disappearing entirely.

In the following chapters, we consider in detail the extent to which discourses of the feminization of higher education can be considered to adequately describe and account for changes and continuities in the field of HE in the UK and globally. As part of this, we necessarily discuss the extent to which a gender transformation of higher education might be taking place. As will be seen, our analysis concurs with that of Adkins and Le Feuvre, that despite numerical changes in participation, there is little evidence that this has, as yet, resulted in a serious challenge to the traditional gender order.

Conclusions

In this chapter, we have shown how the term 'feminization' has been used to describe an increase in the number (or a majority) of female subjects in a particular field. This is frequently assumed to lead to a cultural transformation of that field, as 'feminine' values become dominant, which may also be associated with concerns about a 'feminization' of male bodies and/or masculine subjectivity. Discourses of the feminization of education in general, and of higher education in particular, can be seen to draw upon and encompass each of these referents. We have criticized the 'feminization of higher education' thesis on the basis that it homogenizes women and men and reasserts a binary divide, essentializes gender, and rests on traditional constructions of heterosexual femininity and masculinity.

Feminization is also often associated with a devaluing of the field in question, and this can been seen in the associated discourses of the 'dumbing down' of the academy. We have argued that debates about the feminization of higher education can be seen as an example of a 'moral panic', evidenced by the level of exaggeration in these debates, the hostility to women, and the assumption that feminization constitutes a threat to men and/or masculinity.

This reminded us of Dale Spender's research from the UK in the 1980s on the attention that girls and boys received from the teacher in the classroom (Spender, 1982). Spender discovered that boys objected as soon as girls received slightly more of the teacher's time than usual, even though boys were still receiving significantly more attention than girls (girls had, on this occasion, received 38 per cent of the teacher's attention). It does seem as if something similar is happening here; as soon as women approach some level of equality with men, albeit in a very specific context, there is a panic and resistance or backlash. As Mackinnon (1998: 11) noted:

> At the turn of the last century highly educated women with the potential to be economically and sexually independent caused extreme anxiety in western societies. Women were an enigma, represented by that archetypal symbol of the enigmatic – the sphinx. They were boundary crossers who threatened and destabilized the established categories of society. They challenged the relegation of women to the emotional, men to the rational. . . . The battery of weapons, ideological, 'scientific', cultural, linguistic which were brought to bear on these pioneers were formidable. Overall the counter attacks attempted to contain women by returning them to the confines of a binary discourse. . . . What was at risk? What caused such social unease? Underlying much of the hysteria was the threat to sexual boundaries – to the notion of heterosexuality, of monogamous marriage and the family.

Although there have been changes in the social acceptability of different sexual identities and constructions of the family in some contexts, Mackinnon's analysis is also instructive for a consideration of the level of fear and anxiety evident in the feminization of higher education thesis at the beginning of the twenty-first century. What continues to cause such unease is, we suggest, the perceived threat to the traditional (heterosexual) gender order. Bartky's (1988) recognition of the ways in which greater freedoms for women have often been accompanied by a more strongly reinforced femininity, assisted by the power of the media, is also relevant. Is it, for example, coincidental that at a time when women are clearly demonstrating their intellectual prowess, cosmetic surgery is normalized and young girls are increasingly sexualized in the western media – both of which reinforce traditional heterosexual femininity?

Of course, this is not to say that we do not also have concerns about the low levels of participation and achievement of (some, particularly working-class) men in higher education, just as we are concerned about the many women who also do not participate or succeed at university. Rather we want to challenge both the masculinist and misogynistic assumptions that underpin the feminization thesis, and the assertion that women are taking over the university – as will be seen, we are clearly not. Indeed, the continual assertions that universities are now feminized arenas may well serve to have the opposite of intended effects – i.e. rather than challenging the presumed 'dominance' of women, it might actually persuade more men that higher education is not a place for them.

3

The global context: gender, feminization and higher education

---

UNESCO World Declaration on Higher Education for the Twenty-first Century[1]

Article 4 – Enhancing participation and promoting the role of women

(a) Although significant progress has been achieved to enhance the **access of women** to higher education, various socio-economic, cultural and political obstacles continue in many places in the world to impede their full access and effective integration. To overcome them remains an urgent priority in the renewal process for ensuring an equitable and non-discriminatory system of higher education based on the principle of merit.

(b) Further efforts are required to eliminate all gender stereotyping in higher education, to consider gender aspects in different disciplines and to consolidate women's participation at all levels and in all disciplines, in which they are under-represented and, in particular, to enhance their active involvement in decision-making.

(c) Gender studies (women's studies) should be promoted as a field of knowledge, strategic for the transformation of higher education and society.

(d) Efforts should be made to eliminate political and social barriers whereby women are under-represented and in particular to enhance their active involvement at policy and decision-making levels within higher education and society.

---

[1] Adopted by the World Conference on Higher Education, 9 October, 1998. www.unesco.org/education/educprog/wche/declaration_eng.htm (accessed 15 April, 2008).

It is telling that this declaration needed to be made at the end of the twentieth century. Despite the arguments put forward in the feminization thesis that women are taking over the academy, there is still an urgent need to address the participation and role of women in higher education across the world.

As Delamont (2006: 179) remarked, 'Women are newcomers to higher education.' Modern universities date from the twelfth century, although Plato's Academy in ancient Greece has been called the 'first university' (Rowse, 1936), and many trace the origins of today's institutions back to earlier Middle-Eastern and Egyptian civilizations (Pederson, 2003). It was only in the nineteenth and twentieth centuries, however, that women began to access higher education as a direct result of the determination and persistence of women across the globe, and of active feminist campaigning (see, for example, Badran, 1995; Dyhouse, 2006).

Yet as Carol Dyhouse (1984: 52) notes in relation to the English context, the history of women's entry into the academy is not a simple linear story of progress from women 'storming the citadel' to a wonderful state of equal opportunities for all. It soon became apparent, as we looked at the evidence from different countries, that at different times and in different contexts, women's participation has declined as well as advanced. In France, for example, women constituted 2.3 per cent of the student body in 1899–1900 and this had risen to 40.1 per cent in 1939–40. A decade later, however, in 1949–50, women's participation had fallen to 35.4 per cent and a decade after that, in 1959–60, it was still only 39.8 per cent (Ourliac, 1988). In Nigeria, there have also been periods when the relative proportion of women students has declined significantly. In the period 1956–60, the proportion of women students enrolled increased from 10.1 to 17.1 per cent. It was halved in 1962, then increased steadily to 33.6 per cent in 1991 (Pereira, 2007), only to decrease again in the most recent period. As will be seen below, it is not only in Nigeria that there has been a recent decline in the proportion of women in the HE student population. So, as Dyhouse asked in 1984:

> Why, in spite of one-hundred-and-fifty-odd years of struggle at all social levels, in which the *rhetoric* of equality emerged triumphant, women's situation remains what it is. Why, if the gates of the universities are theoretically open to girls on the same terms as boys, have women not been able to *use* education to alter the basic features of their social position? Why are women *still* so massively under-represented, so conspicuously lacking in power and status in the more exclusive areas of higher education today? In other words, if there was indeed a 'revolution' in the higher education of women over the last century and a half, why did it achieve so little? (Dyhouse, 1984: 52, emphasis in original)

Sadly, her questions are still relevant in the early twenty-first century.

What have become apparent as we have conducted the research for this book are the ways in which different political and ideological systems, in different times and in different places, have played their part in the exclusion of women from higher education. Social, economic and cultural factors obviously impact strongly on the provision of higher education and on who is able to access it in different countries at different times. Wars and civil unrest, for example, have sometimes made it possible for women to enter universities as men left to go to war, but war also has devastating consequences for women, not least through increased incidence of rape and sexual violence (BBC, 2006). Colonialism and imperialism have both reinforced and produced racist and patriarchal ideologies and practices (Enloe, 1990). In some countries at different times, girls and women have been prevented from taking part in any formal education (for example, under Taliban rule in Afghanistan – see *www.rawa.org*). The ways in which ideological, social, political and economic factors impact on the participation of women in specific countries, however, needs to be analysed with attention not only to global developments, but also to local contexts.

Pereira (2007), for example, discusses Pittin's work on northern Nigeria, and notes that the Hausa tradition, traditional religious ideology, British colonialism and more recent Islamic interventions have all worked in different ways to disadvantage women and girls in relation to education. Pereira goes on to argue that in the post-colonial period as well, both military and civilian governments have been anti-democratic and hence have produced highly discriminatory societies. Jansen (2006), though, suggests that whilst the impact of a resurgence of Islamist groups in Jordan has been mixed for women, there have been some positive effects. For example, the increasing use of the headscarf and the support for private universities and segregated provision for women has made it possible for some women from conservative religious families to go to university. Similarly, Shavarini (2005: 336) suggests that increasing numbers of women studying at university in Iran may be connected to 'the Islamic "packaging" of higher education'. In Germany, although historically women had been more or less absent from academic life prior to the 1930s, the status of women academics declined even further under the Nazis who saw women only as wives and mothers, and it was after the Second World War before things slowly began to improve for women in HE (Zimmer et al., 2007). Similarly, in Poland, Siemienska (2000) suggests that after the Second World War, the education of women was prioritized in the newly established communist system as a way of meeting the needs of the labour force. However, Silova and Magno (2004: 417), in a discussion of women in HE in Central/Southeastern Europe and the former Soviet Union, argue that 'gender equity under the socialist regime was largely a myth'. They also add, though, that things have not necessarily improved with democratization, as this has been accompanied in some countries with a revival of nationalism, the increasing prominence of religion and a resurgence in patriarchal values that has increased disadvantage for women. In the 1990s, economic decline and increased poverty have also disproportionately affected women and has resulted in growing gender disparities in the labour market. Indeed the rise of neo-liberalism across the globe in the 1990s has been associated with increased inequalities, as Chanana (2004) notes in relation to India. In Australia as elsewhere, a new emphasis on efficiency and performativity has resulted in gender equity yet again being pushed off the agenda, so that it is seen as a luxury that can be ill-afforded (Blackmore and Sachs, 2003a). In central Asia and the Caucasus, neo-liberal 'reforms' have also reinvigorated the sex industry, resulting in more women being forced into prostitution (Silova and Magno, 2004), with obvious effects on higher education opportunities. Whilst neo-liberal policy developments in HE such as quality assurance and audit might appear to have potential benefits for women in opening up opportunities for promotion into newly created management posts, as Morley (2007) notes, the implications for women in the academy are mixed, with potential dangers for women collectively as well as possibilities for some women individually (see Chapter 7). And of course science has played its part, from the anatomists of Victorian England who argued that higher education was out of the question for women as the female brain was smaller and therefore inferior to the male brain (Burstyn, 1980), to the former President of Harvard University,[2] USA, who in 2005 said that the reason that fewer women succeed in careers in science and maths may be because they do not, he suggested, have the same innate abilities in these fields as men (Bombardieri, 2005).

Women students have, however, made significant inroads into higher education in many countries since the 1980s, as we now move on to discuss.

Women students' participation in higher education

Across the world, significantly more women than men participated in higher education in 2005. This is a relatively recent development – in 1999, men were more likely to participate, but the expansion of higher education over this period has largely benefited women. This is not the case everywhere, however. In the vast majority of 'developed' countries and those in transition, women are in the majority, though in sub-Saharan Africa, South and West Asia, and East Asia, men remain in the majority.

The regional pattern of women's participation across the world in 2005, derived from UNESCO data (UNESCO, 2008) can be seen from Figure 3.1.[3]

---

[2] Harvard University now has its first woman President.

[3] The data used here refers to those studying at ICSED level 5a. This is a descriptor for higher education study on largely theoretical degree programmes of at least 3 years' duration, intended to provide access to advanced research programmes or high skill professions. It excludes those studying for doctoral level research degrees (e.g. PhD), but may include Masters equivalent level qualifications (which in some countries are part of a standard 4 or 5 year degree course) as well as first degrees (such as BSc or BA in the UK).

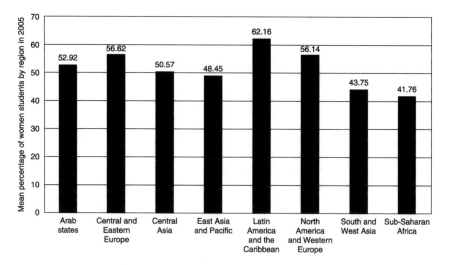

Figure 3.1 Women's participation in higher education across the world, 2005

Data derived from UNESCO (2008) Education for All Global Monitoring Report for the percentage of women at ISCED level 5A (higher education academic degree not including doctoral level). Only those countries for whom data was available for 2005 are included in the analysis for this chart.

However, the mean participation scores on which this figure is based disguise some notable differences between countries within regions (as grouped in the Annex to UNESCO, 2008). So, for example, within the Arab States, in Bahrain the proportion of women in higher education was 69 per cent, compared to Iraq where women made up 39 per cent and Mauritania 25 per cent of the total student population studying at this level. In Central and Eastern Europe, women were in the majority for all countries for which data was available for 2005, except for Turkey where women constituted 43 per cent of HE students. A similar pattern is evident in North America and Western Europe, where women comprised less than half of the student population only in Germany and Switzerland (48 per cent for both countries). In Central Asia, women's participation ranged from just over a quarter of all students in Tajikistan (26 per cent) to a high 62 per cent in Mongolia. In East Asia and the Pacific the proportion of women students extended from 32 per cent in Cambodia, 41 per cent in Japan and 55 per cent in Australia, to 69 per cent in Brunei Darussalam. In South and West Asia, only 35 per cent of the students studying at this level in Bangladesh were women, whilst in India the figure was 39 per cent and in Pakistan it was 46 per cent. In this region it was only in Iran that women made up more than half, where they constituted 55 per cent of the student population. The Caribbean had amongst the highest proportion of women students of any region, with women constituting 80 per cent of the higher education students in Saint Lucia, 75 per cent in the British Virgin Islands and 73 per cent in Aruba. In Peru, however, the proportion of women was only 45 per cent. In contrast, the lowest percentage of women was recorded in sub-Saharan Africa, where women constituted just 21 per cent of students in Niger in 2005, and only 19 per cent in the Gambia and 12 per cent in Eritrea in 2004. Whilst the overall picture globally is of increasing women's participation, in some countries the trend between 1999 and 2005 has been in the other direction, with fewer women participating over this time frame in Burundi, the Congo, Djibouti, the Gambia, Nigeria, Vietnam and to some extent Macao, China (UNESCO, 2008).

European data suggests that where a relatively higher proportion of the population are enrolled in higher education, the proportion of women in these countries also tends to be high, for example in the Baltic and Nordic countries. This is perhaps related to the association, in discourses of feminization, of massification with the 'dumbing down' or loss of value of the academy discussed in Chapter 2. Where relatively small numbers of the population go on to higher education, for example in Cyprus, Liechtenstein and Turkey, men tend to be in the majority (European Commission, 2007). Not surprisingly given the recent increase in the proportion of women studying in higher education, the number of younger women graduating with first degrees (level 5a) across Europe has increased faster than for men in recent years (European Commission, 2007).

Comparative achievement data related to gender and higher education is not easily accessible for many countries. As we discuss in Chapter 4, women students in the UK are achieving higher grades than men on average, but this is more to do with removing historic barriers for women rather than men increasingly 'underachieving', and girls have traditionally had higher rates of achievement in school. This is a pattern that seems to be replicated in many countries. In Turkey, although a lower proportion of women than men go to university, and they tend to have lower entry scores than men, they outperform their male counterparts once they have entered higher education (Dayioğlu and Türüt-Aşik, 2007). It is also important to consider drop-out and retention rates, although global data on this is also difficult to obtain. As will be seen in Chapter 4, in the UK, men are more likely to drop out than women, although class is a major consideration here, with poorer students far more likely to leave their courses early. In Nigeria, in contrast, Pereira reports that although there are difficulties with the data, it does appear that there are particularly high drop-out rates for women, often as high as a third and sometimes two thirds of women students in some universities and some courses. The highest drop-out rate for women was 87.2 per cent for those studying law in one university, in comparison to men for whom the highest was 67 per cent of men studying administration at the same institution, suggesting, says Pereira, that 'institutional factors are at play' (Pereira, 2007). Pereira also noted that additional factors are likely to be the prevalence of sexual harassment on campus and poor accommodation options which have implications for women's safety. In addition, students' awareness of prejudice and discrimination in the labour market which reduce women's chances of getting a job even with a degree may be a factor in women leaving their studies.

The reasons for these differences in participation and achievement are, therefore, complex, and need to be analysed in relation to specific local conditions. Silova and Magno (2004), for example, suggest that the reasons why women's participation has increased in most countries in Central/ Southeastern Europe and the former Soviet Union is likely to be related to a higher proportion of men studying in vocational schools in order to obtain jobs, higher levels of achievement for girls in school, and women's commitment to education as a way of compensating for, and increasing their opportunities in, a gender discriminatory labour market. This latter consideration parallels Mirza's (2005) analysis of black women's commitment to education in the UK. In discussing women's relatively poor participation rate in Nigeria, Pereira (2007) draws on the Longe Report on the position of girls and women in education that was produced in 1992. This report highlighted the low priority given to girls' education compared to boys when resources are low, gender stereotyping and assumptions that women are intellectually inferior, restricted mobility, women's role as child-bearers and incidences of early marriage that prevent women from accessing HE.

Women also often tend to have a shorter educational career path than men. Jansen (2006), for example, reported that in Jordan, 'too much' education is seen as unnecessary for women and the costs of postgraduate study are high. She noted that in 1999, across all universities, women constituted 46 per cent of first (Bachelor) degree students, but only 29 per cent of MA students and 22 per cent of PhD students. In Taiwan, in 1996–97, women achieved 48 per cent of bachelors degrees, 25 per cent of masters awards but only 16 per cent of doctoral degrees (Wang, 2001). Although the numbers of women doing advanced degrees in Jordan and Taiwan are particularly low, the pattern across the globe is of lower proportions of women in doctoral level study, with women constituting less than 40 per cent of students studying advanced research degrees such as PhDs (ICSED level 6) worldwide.[4] Again this average figure disguises some differences which in part reflect different levels of gender participation in lower level higher education degrees (ICSED 5a) in different regions. On average, however, Central Asia, Central and Eastern Europe, and North America and Western Europe do rather better than other regions in that the gap between average women's participation in ICSED level 5a and level 6 courses is less than 8 per cent. In contrast, in Latin America and the Caribbean, the gap is over 20 per cent, with a high 62 per cent of students on level 5a courses being women, but only 41 per cent on the more advanced level 6 programmes (although this still exceeds the average worldwide) (European Commission, 2007). In the Baltic states, Spain and Italy, women are in the majority at this level (European Commission, 2007).

---

[4] Based on an analysis of available country data for 2005 in the UNESCO (2008) Global Monitoring Report.

For many countries, data on the social class or ethnicity of women and men students is difficult to obtain, and data related to disabled students in higher education almost impossible to find, so it is not easy to identify *which* women and *which* men are participating and succeeding. The OECD (2007) presents social class data for ten countries, but based only on blue or white collar status of students' fathers, with no reference to mothers. In addition, the analysis presented by the OECD does not examine any possible differences between women and men students, so we are unable to determine the extent to which working-class women – and which working-class women by ethnic group, for example – may be more or less likely to attend university than their working-class male peers in the same country. From the data available, however, the OECD reports significant differences between countries in the extent to which students of blue-collar fathers enter higher education, with Ireland and Spain doing well in this regard and Austria, France, Germany and Portugal doing badly. In these last four countries, working-class students are only half as likely to be in higher education compared to the participation rate that would be expected given their proportion in the population. The data also indicated the importance of having a father who had accessed higher education. In Austria, France, Germany, Portugal and the UK, such students were twice as likely to be in higher education than students whose fathers did not go to university. In India, lower caste students have particularly poor participation rates (Chanana, 2004), and throughout India, Pakistan and Bangladesh, the expansion of higher education has largely benefited the middle class (Morley, 2005b). An affirmative action programme in Tanzania has had some success in increasing women's participation in science and engineering courses, but again these students were mostly from middle-class families, and there was less success in recruiting women from poorer backgrounds (Lihamba et al., 2006). In Russia, the cost of going to university is prohibitive for many students from poorer families and those students who do go are more likely to work on a regular basis (Vishnevskii and Shapko, 2002), something that has also been identified in the UK as strongly related to social class (Moreau and Leathwood, 2006a). Silova and Magno (2004) also report the educational disadvantages of children from lower socio-economic groups in Central/Southeastern Europe and the former Soviet Union, with poverty often a result of military conflicts. Because poverty affects girls more, and when resources are scarce, boys' education is prioritized, the growth in inequalities in this region is likely to have a disproportionate effect on girls and women. In Tajikistan, for example, the low proportion of women in HE is likely to be related to the costs and risks of study, including transport costs from rural areas to urban universities, as well as issues of safety and violence. Similarly in Nigeria, costs of study impact more strongly on the participation of women, with parents more likely to prioritize boys' education where resources are low (Pereira, 2007).

Ethnicity is also likely to be a factor in the opportunities students have to access higher education. In the European Union, for example, young people from minority ethnic groups are less likely to participate, with Roma and travellers being most at risk of educational discrimination across the EU (European Monitoring Centre on Racism and Xenophobia, 2006). This was something that Silova and Magno also noted in Central/Southeastern Europe and the former Soviet Union, with Roma girls more likely to be out of school than boys as a result of domestic responsibilities and/or marriage at early age (Silova and Magno, 2004). In Canada, only 8 per cent of Aboriginal people had a university degree in 2006, compared to 23 per cent of non-Aboriginal people (Statistics Canada, 2006), whilst in the USA, young black men are more likely to drop out of school and not to progress to higher education than either white men or black women (Hefner, 2004). Indeed, Hefner notes that black women are enrolling and graduating at almost twice the rate of black men: of all first degrees awarded to black students in 2000, women gained almost 70 per cent. Hefner suggests that a range of factors are impacting on this, including teacher expectations in school, social class, individual educational aspirations and the perception of the availability of well paid jobs that do not need a degree. Similarly Kaba (2005) points to a range of social factors including the impact of poverty and the propensity to imprison a high proportion of young black men. In the UK, as will be seen in the next chapter, social class is the biggest predictor of higher education participation, with working-class students (largely irrespective of gender or ethnicity although there are some differences between groups) seriously under-represented in higher education.

Women students and subject 'choice'

Despite women's increased participation in higher education in most countries across the world, gendered subject stratification remains entrenched, with women still representing less than a quarter of students on average in 'engineering, manufacturing and construction', and not much over a third in 'agriculture' and 'science' (UNESCO, 2008). In contrast, women constitute approximately two-thirds of students studying 'education' and 'health and welfare', and only slightly below this in 'humanities and arts'. It is only in the 'social sciences, business and law' where gender parity appears evident, with women constituting 51 per cent of students on average. However, there are likely to be considerable differences between subjects within these broad fields, as in evident in the UK data discussed in Chapter 4.

In all regions except sub-Saharan Africa and East Asia and the Pacific, 'education' is the subject field with the highest proportion of women (see Figure 3.2). In East Asia, it is the 'health and welfare' subject field which has the highest proportion of women, though only by a small margin (where they constitute 64 per cent of students, compared to 62 per cent in the 'education' area). In sub-Saharan Africa, the highest proportion of women students are in 'humanities and arts' (47 per cent), followed by 'health and welfare' (44 per cent), 'social science, business and law' (42 per cent) and

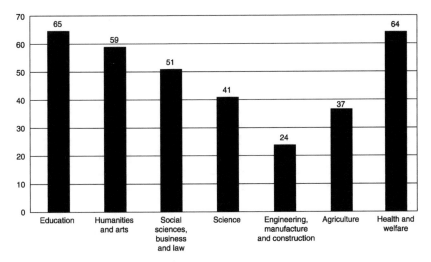

Figure 3.2 Proportion of women by subject area worldwide

Data derived from UNESCO 2008 Global Monitoring Report based on the mean score for those countries for which subject field data was available.

then 'education' (39 per cent). 'Engineering, manufacture and construction' is the subject field with the lowest proportion of women students in all world regions. There are, however, some countries where more than a third of the student population in this subject field are women, including Denmark (38 per cent), Mongolia (41 per cent), Pakistan (43 per cent) and Kuwait (50 per cent). By comparison, Australia manages only 21 per cent, the UK 19 per cent and the United States 16 per cent, all countries where women students constitute over 50 per cent of the student population overall. Across Europe, approximately two-thirds of students in 'science, mathematics and computing' are men, as are over three-quarters of students in 'construction' (European Commission, 2007). In the US, men were awarded 86.5 per cent of all computing BA degrees in 1971–72. A decade later, women had increased their share to 35 per cent, but in 1991–92 this had fallen back again to 28.7 per cent (Suriya, 2003). Despite a range of initiatives to encourage women into the field, its masculine ethos and the male dominated structure and culture of the IT industry is thought to deter women. Norway, however, introduced a quota system for women in computer science in 1997 which increased the proportion of women to over 30 per cent in the first two years, whilst in Romania, women outnumber men in 'science, maths and computing'. In Jordan too, women have made more inroads into these subjects, with 41 per cent of first year students at the Jordanian University of Science and Technology in 1998–99 being women. This may, suggests Jansen (2006), have something to do with students being allocated their field of study based on previous levels of attainment, rather than being able to choose their subject. Gender-segregated education in Jordan has also encouraged more women to take up subjects which tend to be seen as masculine such as 'pharmacy', 'business administration' and 'accountancy' (Jansen, 2006). Similarly, in the UK, girls in single-sex schools are more likely to choose 'masculine' subjects than their peers in mixed-gender schools (Francis and Skelton, 2005).

Although across Europe women outnumber men at first degree level (ICSED 5a) in the subject fields of 'education', 'health and welfare' and the 'humanities and arts', the proportion of women in these fields declines at advanced research degree level (ICSED level 6) by over 10 per cent across the 27 member states compared to the proportions of women studying for first degrees (European Commission, 2007). In some countries this decline is far more marked. For example in Belgium, Hungary, Iceland and Malta, the proportion of women falls by over 30 per cent at level 6 compared to level 5a.

Different subjects tend to have different levels of prestige, with those in which men predominate, often also referred to the 'hard' subjects, being more highly valued on the whole than the 'soft' subjects that higher proportions of women tend to study. This is not only related to gender, as Chanana (2004) notes that lower caste students in India are more likely to study lower status subjects. It might be expected that the more highly valued the subject, the harder it would be to gain access, but in Taiwan, this is not necessarily the case. As the social science and humanities tend to be popular, and the number of places are limited, the competition for places is very high – and these are subjects which more women tend to choose. In contrast, the science and technology subjects that men are more likely to choose are far less popular, meaning that competition for a place is relatively low (Wang, 2001).

In Chapter 9 we discuss the gendered constructions of knowledge and the differential valuing of disciplinary areas in relation to these patterns. We therefore offer, in that chapter, explanations for the persistent and widespread horizontal stratification that is evident from the data presented here.

Women students and institutional 'diversity'

In an increasingly competitive global higher education market, an increasing differentiation between institutions is evident, especially in economically advantaged countries (Arum et al., 2007). Some countries have always had an elite university sector (for example the Universities of Oxford and Cambridge in the UK), but others are rapidly developing one, including Germany (Chapman, 2004) and Italy (Bompard, 2004), with increasing differentiation also evident in the Australian university sector (Maslen, 2005). There is also an elite group of universities worldwide – the International Alliance of Research Universities (IARU) which describes itself as 'an alliance of ten of the world's leading research universities' (http://www.iaruni.org/). The members are The Australian National University,

ETH Zurich, the National University of Singapore, Peking University, the University of California Berkeley, the University of Cambridge, the University of Copenhagen, the University of Oxford, the University of Tokyo and Yale University. Increasing competition in the global market for higher education and the pressure to be judged 'world class' or 'excellent' is making its mark on the sector.

The growing importance of national and international rankings of universities is further driving this development. Examples of worldwide university league tables include the THES-QS World University Rankings (produced by the *Times Higher Education Supplement* in the UK) and the Academic Ranking of World Universities (produced by the Shanghai Jiao Tong University Institute of Higher Education). There are serious methodological problems with such rankings and they tend to 'measure' research and levels of prestige rather than teaching quality or performance, with a bias towards Western and English-speaking institutions (CHERI, 2008). Nevertheless, they are having a significant impact on the HE sector as universities compete for international students and global reputations (BBC, 2008).

In Chapter 4, we discuss how the university sector in the UK is stratified by social class, ethnicity and gender, with higher proportions of white middle-class men located in the elite universities, and working-class, minority ethnic and women students disproportionately positioned in universities at the lower end of the league tables. Our research for this chapter indicated that such a pattern is not confined to the UK. Arum et al. (2007), for example, in their study of 15 countries (from Western and Eastern Europe, Israel, the US and Australia), note that where higher education had previously consisted of a unified system of research intensive universities, rapid expansion was resulting in a second tier of institutions being developed for the new intake. 'Thus, at the same time that members of the working class found new opportunities to enroll in higher education, the system was being hierarchically differentiated so that these new opportunities may have had diminished value' (Arum et al., 2007: 1). Arum and colleagues argue, however, that despite this, because of expansion, the sector was increasingly inclusive, as it 'extends a valued good to a broader spectrum of the population' (p. 29). They acknowledge that some will argue that education is a positional good (i.e. that it can be exchanged for more financially rewarding and prestigious employment in the labour market), and therefore the value of a degree from a less prestigious institution is less, but they insist that students will gain human capital from their study, and do not, therefore, seem to regard this class-based stratification as a problem. In contrast, our view is that whilst higher education brings a range of benefits to the individual, their community and society as a whole that extend beyond the worth of a degree in the job market, it is nevertheless an important issue of social justice if some students, by virtue of their social class and/or ethnic background, or their gender, are restricted to less prestigious and less well-resourced institutions. Indeed this is one way in which higher education can reinforce existing social inequalities rather than challenge them, something that is evident in India where lower caste students are denied access to elite courses and institutions (Chanana, 2004).

Arum and colleagues' study did not explore gender or ethnicity in relation to institutional diversity. In contrast, Wang (2001) examined the proportion of women in universities and junior colleges in Taiwan. She noted that by 1998, women constituted just over half the higher education student population, but they were under-represented in universities (constituting 46.51 per cent in 1996–97) and over-represented in junior colleges (53.51 per cent), i.e. in non-university institutions. The latter have lower levels of prestige and this has implications for the value of the qualifications attained. In the USA, there was a shift in the type of institution in which students from specific minority ethnic groups enrolled between 1995–1996 and 2005–2006, with a decrease in enrolment in universities (non-doctoral and private 4-year institutions) and an increase in enrolment in 2-year colleges (GAO, 2007). In 2006–07, almost 60 per cent of Hispanic students and 50 per cent of Asian/Pacific Islander, Alaskan Native and Black students were in 2-year colleges, compared to just 43 per cent of White/non-Hispanic students. In Poland, although more women are studying in higher education than ever, they tend to constitute a far higher proportion of students in less expensive types of study such as evening, weekend and extramural courses, and shorter programmes (Siemienska, 2000). As Morley (2005a: 117) notes,

> we need to keep posing the question about social reproduction and/or transformation. Elite formation can function to produce multiple higher educations, with differential educational experiences and exchange rates for qualifications in the labour market for different social groups.

Women in Jordan, however, are more likely to be in the most competitive state university – the University of Jordan (Jansen, 2006). In 1998, 65.9 per cent of first year students were women, reflecting the higher achievements of girls in schools. Although historically, private universities in Jordan have been important in opening up opportunities to women, women students still constitute a lower proportion of the students (34.5 per cent compared to 50.7 per cent of state university students in 1999). Jansen suggests this may be related to financial considerations, as families are more likely to pay for boys' education, but class is also obviously an issue here.

One further aspect of increasing institutional diversity worldwide is the opportunities that are provided for student mobility between countries. Going to another country to do a degree can be particularly advantageous in terms of future career prospects as the mobile student acquires educational, cultural and social capital. However, opportunities to be mobile are likely to be restricted for poorer students. There is also evidence, however, that women are less mobile than men (presumably again because of financial considerations as well as family responsibilities and expectations), with men far more likely to study in another country (European Commission, 2007).

The benefits of higher education for women students

Women graduates of higher education in OECD countries have a significantly increased likelihood of being in employment than their less qualified peers, and the gender gap between the employment rates of women and men is narrowed for the more highly qualified (OECD, 2007). In terms of entry into the labour market, therefore, it is beneficial for women to go to university, although their employment rates on average are still ten percentage points behind those of their male peers with comparable qualifications. In Jordan in the 1990s, where only 15 per cent of women of working age were in the labour market, the unemployment rate for graduate women was 31 per cent, compared to 12 per cent for graduate men. The requirement that women have male approval, from their father or husband, in order to work is a factor here (Jansen, 2006). In Iran, only 20–25 per cent of women graduates enter the labour market. In contrast in Nigeria, Pereira (2007) reports that in 1998, the graduate unemployment rate was higher for men, with 12 per cent of graduate men unemployed compared to 5.2 per cent of graduate women.

Of course these figures do not tell us anything about the kinds of jobs that graduates enter, although several pieces of research in the UK indicate that the likelihood of graduates entering a 'graduate-level' as opposed to a 'non-graduate-level' post (that is, for which a higher education qualification is not necessary) is related to ethnicity, social class, gender, age, subject of degree and the university attended (Moreau and Leathwood, 2006b). Given the extent to which the labour market globally is gendered, classed and racialized, it seems highly likely that similar patterns would be observable elsewhere. Malveaux (2008), for example, writing about the US, notes that:

> while African-American women represent two-thirds of all African-American undergraduates, and the majority of graduate students, African-American women are less likely than African-American men to reach the pinnacle of their occupations, especially in corporate America. Indeed, while a handful of African-American men lead Fortune 500 corporations, as do a dozen or so White women, not a single African-American woman has ever led such a corporation.

Sims (1999), in a discussion of women's success in higher education in the Caribbean, also argues that this has not been translated into success in the labour market with women more likely to be unemployed, restricted to certain occupations and receiving lower rates of pay even where they have the same qualifications and length of service as men.

A gender pay gap for higher education graduates persists across the world. For all OECD countries for graduates (ICSED levels 5a and 6) aged between 33 and 44, women's salaries varied from an average of 59 per cent of men's annual earnings in Italy to 81 per cent in Turkey (OECD, 2007). The respective figures were 60 per cent for the USA, 61 per cent for Australia, 63 per cent for the UK and 65 per cent for Canada. For those graduates aged 55–64, women only earned 52 per cent of men's annual salary in Ireland, reaching a high of 84 per cent in Belgium. As Assié-Lumumba and Sutton (2004: 349) note, 'the educational edge in academic achievement of the female population has not yielded proportionate socioeconomic attainment for women'.

Differences in salary levels are often explained (away) in terms of the subjects students study and the careers they go into, with the careers in which women predominate (such as caring, health and education) being more lowly paid than the fields in which men predominate (such as the sciences, technology and engineering). This, of course, begs the question of why and on what basis caring, health and education are deemed to be of lower value than the science and technical fields. The only rationale that makes sense, we suggest, is that women's work, whether in the home, community or workplace, has always been undervalued and that caring is seen as a natural attribute of women and therefore not deemed worthy of monetary reward. Of course the same logic does not apply to management or leadership qualities, often assumed to be natural attributes of men, which tend to be highly rewarded. It is, we argue, both irrational and unjust to value caring work less than its technical counterparts, and hence also to provide different financial rewards for work in these respective fields.

The flawed rationale used to justify the gender pay gap also places responsibility for their lower earnings on to women themselves, as they could have chosen to study and work in more technical and highly paid areas. This kind of reasoning is very evident in neo-liberal educational policy discourse, where the responsibility, and hence the blame, is placed on to the individual and away from the state. This can be seen, for example, in the UK where the emphasis is on providing individual careers advice to girls and women to enable them to make 'informed choices' rather than on tackling inequalities in salary levels (Leathwood, 2007).

Other forms of rationale relate to women being more likely than men to be in part-time paid work, to take time out of work for child-rearing, or simply not to apply for senior posts. Of course, if men undertook an equal share of caring and domestic work, then paid working hours and patterns of employment could also be shared more equally. In terms of senior posts, the 'glass ceiling' which prevents women reaching higher levels is well recognized. The construction of management and leadership posts as masculine, as well as a masculinist culture that pervades many organizations, is also relevant here, and we discuss this in relation to academic staff in HE in Chapter 7.

Employment opportunities and increased salary levels are not the only outcomes of HE. Based on research with young women in HE in Iran, Shavarini concludes that:

> college or university studies represent for female students many things:
> a sphere of hope, a refuge, and a place to experience limited freedom

beyond restrictive family environments; an asset that can increase a woman's value in the marriage market; a right that may make possible financial independence; and a vehicle that can earn respect for women. On the whole, the desire for *higher education* illuminates the challenges facing women in Muslim nations and the ways in which Muslim women are using this institution to change their social status. (Shavarini, 2005: 329)

Quinn's (2003) research into women in higher education in England also identified university as a space of refuge and freedom for women, whilst Jansen notes that in Jordan, the cultural prestige associated with higher education is a key issue which reflects positively on the family, father and husband: 'it enhances her attractiveness and makes her worthy of a good partner' (Jansen, 2006: 485).

This raises a question about the ways in which higher education may both challenge and reinforce traditional gender relations. Many women across the world clearly see higher education participation as a way of changing their lives, providing new opportunities for the future for themselves and their children, and increasing their financial independence. In Uganda, for example, higher education for women is seen as an important route out of poverty whilst also providing women with an opportunity to be engaged in the development of their country (Kwesiga, 2002, cited by Pereira, 2007). Jansen notes that in Jordan, education has had 'the paradoxical effects of, on the one hand, teaching women an ideal of femininity based on domesticity, modesty and obedience while, on the other, encouraging them to take on a public role' (Jansen, 2006: 484). She concludes that although women have increased access to higher education, this has not, as yet, been translated into equality of status for women with men in the labour market, the family or society as a whole. The evidence suggests that such a conclusion is applicable worldwide.

Women in the academic labour market

We now turn our attention away from students to consider the position of academic staff in universities. Before we do so, however, it is important to note that the vast majority of women working in higher education worldwide are not, almost certainly, academics, but instead are largely employed as low paid and undervalued service personnel, doing the cleaning, catering and administrative support work without which universities would not be able to function at all. Data about such workers is particularly difficult to obtain, and in a neo-liberal global economy, they are increasingly employed by private companies rather than directly by the university or state authority. Where this has happened, for example in the UK, such workers saw their pay and conditions of service deteriorate significantly as their work was 'contracted out'. It is, perhaps, not coincidental that these workers are more likely to be women, working class, people from minority ethnic groups, and/or refugees. In comparison, academic staff, to whom we now turn, are in highly privileged positions:

> Women entered academia at a disadvantage, being appointed at lower ranks than men at the start of their careers as well as being more likely to start their careers in temporary posts. Subsequently, women's mobility within the system was slower than men's because of the gender division of labour that freed men from domestic work, whilst simultaneously casting it as 'women's work'. (Gaidzanwa, 1997, cited by Pereira, 2007: 13)

This account is a summary of research findings on women's academic careers at the University of Zimbabwe, although we suspect that many readers from other countries will recognize the pattern described here. Despite the gains made by women students in many parts of the world, women academics remain seriously under-represented, with vertical and horizontal stratification and lower pay seemingly ubiquitous.

Women constitute approximately one third of teaching staff in higher education (teaching on ICSED level 5a and 6 programmes) across the OECD countries (OECD, 2007). The OECD average for the proportion of women in 2005 was 35.9 per cent; the EU average was fractionally higher at 36.7 per cent. Japan had the lowest proportion of women teaching in HE at just 16 per cent, whilst New Zealand had the highest with 48.1 per cent.

Just as for students, women academics across the world tend to be clustered into specific subject fields (see, for example, Zimmer, 2003; Pereira, 2007), and into lower status higher education institutions, for example in Spain (Bosch, 2003), the UK (Vázquez-Cupeiro, 2003) and Germany (Zimmer et al., 2007), with implications for their future careers. As Lafferty and Fleming (2000) note in relation to Australia, in an increasingly competitive HE market marked by funding cutbacks, inequalities between universities have increased, something that has also been observed in the UK (Leathwood, 2004). There is also evidence from the USA that the higher the status of the university, the lower the proportion of women awarded full professorships. So in 2005–06, women comprised 19 per cent of professors at doctoral universities, compared to 29 per cent at baccalaureate institutions and 28 per cent at masters institutions (Banerji, 2006). There does seem to be an exception in Nigeria, where Pereira reported that the first generation, oldest, universities have the best record in appointing women at professorial level (Pereira, 2007).

In many countries, women have increasingly made inroads into lower level academic posts since the 1990s, although there have also been reversals. Siemienska, for example, argued that in Poland in the 1990s, the proportion of women in academic posts declined, with more employed in non-teaching posts and in the lower ranks of the academic hierarchy than in earlier periods. The relatively low proportion of women in senior academic posts has proved resistant to change almost everywhere. The higher the grade, the fewer the women – worldwide. In the University of Idadan, Nigeria, for example, in 2004–05 women represented 29 per cent of academic staff over-all: they constituted 30 per cent of senior lecturers/researchers, but only 14 per cent of professors or readers. The highest proportion of women was at the lowest grade of assistant lecturer or junior research fellow, with women 41 per cent of staff at this level (Odejidea, 2007). Morley (2005b) reports that in 2002, women constituted 8.4 per cent of professors in Nigeria but 42.1 per cent in Jamaica. In the same year across the European Union, women were 14 per cent of full professors on average (European Commission, 2004), ranging from 2 per cent in Malta to 20 per cent in Finland and 23 per cent in Latvia. Sweden, despite its positive reputation for gender equity, does no better than the average at 14 per cent, which is likely, suggests Husu (cited by Olson, 2006), to be a result of resistance in the academy.

The proportion of universities run by women worldwide is even lower – Munford and Rumball (2000) give a figure of 7 per cent in 2000, and using data from 2002, Morley reports that in Nigeria, women constituted 2.5 per cent of vice-chancellors compared to 24.4 per cent in Australia (Morley, 2005b). In China, of over 1000 universities and colleges, there were only approximately 20 women presidents or vice-presidents in the late 1990s – only two of whom were university presidents (Jianqi, 2000). Pereira (2007) reports that men also dominate educational policy and decision-making in Nigeria, and again this is likely to be replicated elsewhere.

Data is particularly difficult to obtain related to the ethnicity or social class backgrounds of senior women in academia, though research in seven European countries illustrated that professors, both women and men, are likely to be from 'well-educated families' (Zimmer, 2003: 12). In 2001, the first African-American woman president of an ivy-league university in the United States began her tenure, an event sufficiently unique to hit the newspaper headlines.

As in other professions and areas of work, women in academia tend to be paid significantly less than their male peers. In the US, for example, the gen-der pay gap for academic staff has hardly changed since the 1970s (Banerji, 2006), with the average women's salary 82.7 per cent of the average men's pay in 1972–73, dropping slightly to 81.5 per cent in 1999–2000 (Schuster and Finkelstein, 2006). In 2005–06 across all academic posts, women earned 81 per cent of men's salary on average, whilst for professorial posts, the corresponding figure was 88 per cent (Banerji, 2006). In the UK, the gender pay gap for academic staff as a whole was 14 per cent in 2003–04, with women earning on average 86 per cent of the average male salary, although this fell to 84 per cent for women managers in universities (AUT, 2005). More recent figures suggest that women academics in the UK receive 17.2 per cent less than that of their male colleagues in higher education (Lipsett, 2007a).

As with the gender pay gap for women graduates, the reason often given is that women are working in subject areas where staff salaries are lower, or that they are less experienced and/or produce fewer academic papers, although research from the UK in the subject area of economics shows that even within the same field, and where staff have equivalent levels of experience and productivity, women academics are still paid 9 per cent less than men on average (Booth et al., 2005). Similarly, the argument that women are not attaining more senior posts due to insufficient women being in the 'pipeline', that is, with appropriate qualifications, is refuted by research in the US in relation to women professors in the sciences and engineering (Committee on Maximizing the Potential of Women in Academic Science and Engineering, 2006). This research showed that since the 1980s women have constituted more than 30 per cent of social science doctorates and more than 20 per cent of life sciences doctorates. Therefore qualified and highly experienced women are available, yet only 15.4 per cent of full professors in the social and behavioural sciences, and 14.8 per cent in the life sciences at the top research institutions in the US are women. In other sciences, women constitute fewer than 10 per cent of professors, and minority ethnic women are more or less absent from leading science and engineering departments.

Just as women students are often held responsible for continued subject segregation, so women academics tend to be blamed for not applying for promotion, prioritizing family, and so on. As Pereira (2007) discusses, an equal opportunities discourse is used to claim that that there is no systematic discrimination, and that opportunities are open for all who want to apply. This ignores, however, the myriad structural and cultural barriers that women academics continue to face (Bagilhole, 2007) – something discussed in detail in Chapter 7.

The increasing casualization of academic staff has been noted across Europe, with suggestions that women may be particularly adversely affected (Zimmer, 2003). In the USA, women are less likely to be appointed to tenure-track positions, even in so called 'feminized' areas such as sociology (Kulis et al., 2002). In the UK, there is evidence that women and minority ethnic staff are more likely to be on fixed-term contracts (AUT, 2005), and to be on them for longer (Bryson, 2004), with women in particular experiencing the negative effects of the increased commodification of academic research and labour (Reay, 2000; Hey, 2001). Similarly, in Australia, the pattern is repeated, with women academics far less likely to have full-time and tenured posts, to lead research teams and to apply for and hold research grants (Asmar, 1999). In relation to this, Brouns (2000) found that in Holland, women applicants for research grants had slightly better publication scores than the male applicants, and that only well-qualified women tended to apply. Whilst there were some differences between disciplinary areas, the assumed correlation between an applicant's track record, peer review and success rate only appeared to apply for male applicants, and when average publication scores were equal, men were far more likely to be rated 'excellent' than women. Brouns (2000: 199) concludes:

> One of the power mechanisms used to reduce the access of women to areas in which they are already active in the lower levels is evaluation of their achievements and attribution of scientific competence. There is a subtle difference between rejecting women researchers because of their

sex and linking the idea of excellence to researchers who are men. The image and social status of the excellent researcher corresponds easily to that of a man, especially when in competition with women scientists.

Gaining positive appraisals from peers and being awarded research grants are important academic credentials, but there is evidence of a range of discriminatory practices that restrict women's progression. In Germany, for example, research with women and men professors indicated that men had been in a better position to gain promotion from the time they were doing their PhDs. For example, they were more likely to be employed by their university at the time, and more likely to receive mentoring (Zimmer et al., 2007). Interestingly, the majority (73 per cent) of male professors surveyed in this study perceived their women peers to be well integrated into the academic community and accepted in senior positions; in contrast only 37 per cent of women professors shared this view. In China, women have fewer opportunities to study abroad and to gain a PhD, which is important for promotion in a context where research is valued over teaching (Jianqi, 2000). Women academics in Poland also feel that they need to accumulate higher levels of educational capital than men to progress (Siemienska, 2000). Promotion that requires the invitation of senior academics raises particular difficulties for women. A study conducted in Kenya in 2000 by Onosongo (cited by Morley, 2005b) found that 92 per cent of men reported being encouraged to apply for promotion, compared to 69 per cent of women, whilst it is suggested that promotion by invitation is a major reason why so few women reach senior positions in Finland, despite many years of gender equity initiatives (Husu, 2000). Similarly, lack of developmental programmes and mentoring for women academic staff have been noted in Sri Lanka (Gunawardena et al., 2006) and South Africa (Mabolela and Mawila, 2004; Shackleton et al., 2006). In addition, the difficulties posed for women academics of systems of informal patronage have been reported in Singapore, where women have to be loyal to more senior colleagues (almost invariably men), work hard and show initiative, but to do so in a 'womanly' way (Luke, 2001b: 162). Similarly, in European universities, 'due to the very traditional male dominated patriarchal culture of universities', women have to be both 'tough' and 'charming' to succeed (Zimmer, 2003: 14), whilst there is evidence of gendered organizational cultures, curriculum, networks and organizational systems which disadvantage women in universities across the Commonwealth (Morley, 2005a). In some contexts, the overt blocking of applications from women for senior posts has been observed (Kwesiga and Ssendiwala, 2006). Again these issues are discussed further in Chapter 7. However, before we leave this account of the position of women as academic staff in universities across the world, we want to discuss the gendered pattern in academic staff in relation to a core component of the feminization thesis, the link between feminization and a 'dumbing down' of the academy.

Several researchers have argued that working conditions and academic salaries have declined since the 1990s relative to other professions, for example in Germany (Zimmer et al., 2007), Poland (Siemienska, 2000), Russia (Suspitsina, 2000) and China (Jianqi, 2000), resulting in men leaving the profession to find better paid opportunities elsewhere. In Poland, Siemienska reports that men have more opportunities in the labour market in general because employers prefer to appoint men. Therefore men have the option to leave academia, creating space for women to enter at a time when the funding for higher education has declined and there is less money, for example, for research. Siemienska argues that:

> This situation makes women in academe 'winners among losers'. The frequently observed model is once again repeated here: when a given profession loses its appeal, mainly material, men withdraw from it, and young people choose it less frequently, looking for more remunerative employment which, for this reason, is often associated with greater prestige. (Siemienska, 2000: 171)

Similarly, Zimmer et al. (2007: 29) argue that in Germany, 'While women are increasingly accepted as legitimate members of the scientific and university community, the very profession of a university teacher and thus the position of a professor are losing esteem and reputation.'

As has been seen, however, although more women have been employed in lower grade academic positions in most countries in recent years, this has not been translated into progression to higher grade posts. Are women, therefore, destined to remain the 'academic lackeys' (Hey, 2001) of the higher education sector?

We did find one piece of research that specifically investigates the evidence for a change in the gender balance of particular fields of study in relation to feminization thesis (England et al., 2007). This was a statistical analysis of women and men receiving doctoral awards between 1971 and 2002 in the US. The researchers note that although the proportion of women achieving doctorates increased from 14 per cent to 46 per cent over this time period, there was no evidence that men were deterred from entering fields with declining salary levels, but some evidence that 'above a certain percentage of women, men are deterred from entering fields by the fields' further feminization' (p. 23). The findings on the extent to which more women entering a field may have an effect on salary levels were, however, mixed.

Conclusions

The evidence presented in this chapter does not, we suggest, provide very much support for the feminization thesis, even solely in terms of the numbers of women. Although in many countries women are now in the majority at first degree level, they are not in all, and in some countries the proportion of women has declined since the 1990s – a pattern that has also occurred historically at different times in different places. Men still dominate at the level of advanced research degrees across most of the world, and the horizontal segregation across subject fields remains a largely consistent and highly persistent pattern. The data for academic staff also does not tell a very promising story, with discrimination against women and minority ethnic staff very evident. In the USA, a report into the position of women academics in science and engineering concluded that 'Women are paid less, are promoted more slowly, receive fewer honours, and hold fewer leadership positions than men' (Committee on Maximising the Potential of Women in Academic Science and Engineering, 2006: 2), a conclusion that could be applied globally to academic staff in all subject fields.

In later chapters, we pay attention to academic cultures and constructions of both the student and the academic to further consider the extent to which these could be regarded as feminized. In the next chapter, however, we focus on the UK, exploring in detail the numerical representation of women as students and staff in a country in which women students *are* in the majority as undergraduates, and in which the feminization thesis has been vociferously promulgated.

4

Gender, participation and higher education in the UK

For eight centuries, men totally dominated higher education in the UK; for just one decade, women have constituted a slightly higher proportion of the graduate population. This, in itself, puts the feminization thesis into context.

In this chapter we provide a gender analysis of higher education in the UK, examining patterns of access, participation and achievement for women and men students. The sector is a complex one, including universities, colleges of higher education and higher education provision within further education colleges. In addition, the range of courses it is possible to study has expanded from the traditional undergraduate or postgraduate degree to also now include access courses, foundation degrees, work-related short courses and specialist professional training. Because of this complexity, we have concentrated here mainly on undergraduate and postgraduate degrees (ICSED level 5a and 6) in universities. Consideration is given to gendered patterns of subject 'choice', institutional stratification and labour market outcomes as well as to gendered patterns of staffing in the sector.

The historical context

> Laying siege, storming citadels, bastions falling: the discursive narratives of both the history of women's entry into higher education in Britain since the mid nineteenth century, and indeed accounts of gender relations in universities in more recent history, are replete with the tropes of battlement. (Dyhouse, 2006: 121)

Women's historical exclusion from university education was increasingly challenged during the nineteenth century. In 1870 Emily Davies and Barbara Bodichon worked together to set up Girton College, Cambridge, which was the first university college for women, although it was not recognized by the university authorities. Newnham College, also at Cambridge, was established in 1880. From 1881 women could take University of Cambridge exams, but they were not awarded full degrees at Cambridge until 1948. The University of Oxford permitted women to take degrees in 1920. There was, however, considerable resistance to women's full entry into universities. In 1897 and again in 1920, for example, when the admission of women was debated at Cambridge, riots, ridicule and blatant misogyny were very much in evidence.

In 1901, only about 5 per cent of the male population went to university, and a far smaller proportion of women (Delamont, 2006), yet even before the end of the nineteenth century, some universities were claiming that they made 'no distinction of sex'. During the 1920s, the proportion of women increased to reach approximately 27 per cent in 1930 (Delamont, 2006), and then fell back again to about 25 per cent at the beginning of the Second World War, with figures for the late 1960s showing little improvement (Dyhouse, 2006). The 1960s were, however, a time of significant expansion, with a number of new universities created which proved particularly attractive to women (Dyhouse, 2006). Although the majority of women entering university historically were white middle-class women, working-class and black women were both present and active in the struggle for women's participation (Dyhouse, 2006; Mirza, 2006a: 139), despite what Mirza refers to as a 'collective amnesia' about their presence. What is also clear is that just as for many other countries, the story of women's entry into higher education in the UK is not a linear one of progressive inclusion, but one marked by periods of exciting new developments and improvements in women's access, followed by periods of decline or stagnation. It was only in 1996–97 that women constituted a higher proportion of the graduate population than men for the first time.

Gender and student participation in UK higher education today

In 2006–07, women constituted 57.2 per cent of the entire HE student population and 59.2 per cent of UK domiciled undergraduates (Higher Education Statistics Agency, 2008). If we consider undergraduate degree students only, women constituted 54.1 per cent of total applicants accepted on to undergraduate degree courses in the UK for the 2007–08 academic year.[1] Some students, in particular part-time and mature students, apply directly to universities rather than through the universities applications service (UCAS), and hence would not be recorded in these figures. The 2006–07 data from the Higher Education Statistics Agency[2] for UK domiciled students

---

[1] University and Colleges Admissions Service www.ucas.ac.uk/about_us/stat_services/stats_online/data_tables/abusgender/ (accessed 15 March, 2008).
[2] Higher Education Statistics Agency www.hesa.ac.uk/index.php?option=com_datatables&Itemid=121&task=show_category&catdex=3 (accessed 15 March, 2008).

shows that women constituted 54.93 per cent of full-time undergraduate students, but 63.57 per cent of part-time undergraduates. At postgraduate level, only 47.22 per cent of full-time research degree students were women, and 50.56 per cent of part-time research students. Of non-UK domiciled students, women constituted 51.87 per cent of all HE students (full and part-time and pre- and postgraduate) from the European Union and 45.70 per cent of students from other (non EU) countries – the latter make up just over 10 per cent of the total HE student population.

It is hard to understand the moral panic about women's supposed domination of the higher education sector from these figures. Although the proportion of women students has increased dramatically in the last few decades of the twentieth century, women still only constitute slightly over half of the total student population studying in UK universities. In addition, a major factor in the increase in numbers of women in universities in recent years has been the designation of the nursing, teaching and social work professions as graduate-only entry and hence requiring university study. This hardly provides evidence for the mass take-over assumed by some protagonists of the feminization thesis. It is also important, however, to ask *which* women are participating, *how*, and *where* in the academy they are located – something to which we now turn.

We start with one aspect of the *how*, and in particular the data which shows that women and mature students are more likely to study part-time than their male and younger counterparts. This is usually assumed to be a matter of 'choice', although as women still undertake the vast majority of unpaid domestic and caring labour in the UK, 'choice' may be rather a misnomer. Research by UCAS (the Universities and Colleges Applications Service which only caters for full-time courses) shows that older women and minority ethnic applicants are less likely to get places at university than other UCAS applicants, with women making up 66.2 per cent of the 'no offer' group. The study found that those not gaining places were more likely to be older, poorer and to have vocational or access qualifications rather than the more traditional 'A levels' (Lipsett, 2007b). The image of the typical student as an 18–21-year-old full-time undergraduate persists in the UK, but as Morley (1997a: 237) notes:

> Half of the new student intake in the UK is now outside the 18–21 age range, but the term 'non-traditional learner' is still used. This nomenclature adopted by universities to describe mature students insidiously reinforces normative constructions of students . . . the academy not only defines what knowledge is, but also defines and regulates what a student is.

It may therefore be that some of these applicants become part-time students instead. Studying part time, however, has disadvantages, with students receiving very little financial support from the state compared to their full-time peers. Before the election of the New Labour government in 1997, full-time students did not have to pay tuition fees and a means tested grant was available for living costs. Part-time students have always had to pay their own fees. Tuition fees for full-time degree students in England are now in place, set at a maximum of £3070 for 2007–08. These students are entitled to a low-interest student loan to cover the cost of tuition fees and to contribute to accommodation and other living expenses which does not have to be repaid until after they graduate and are earning above a threshold level (£15,000 p.a. in 2007–08). In addition, they may be entitled to a small means tested maintenance grant as well as a bursary from their chosen university. From 2008, however, students who are taking a qualification at an equivalent or lower level than one they already hold, will not be eligible for any public funding at all.[3] Different arrangements are in place for students living in Scotland (who, for example, pay no tuition fees), Wales and Northern Ireland. In contrast, part-time students have to pay their tuition fees up front, and there is no maximum limit to the part-time course fees set by universities. Part-time students are not eligible for student loans, although those on a very low income or state welfare benefits may be entitled to a means-tested fee and/or course grant to help towards the costs of study. In practice, many undergraduate students need to do paid work to survive financially – with students from working-class groups undertaking the most paid work during term time (Moreau and Leathwood, 2006a), something that has been shown to negatively impact upon final degree grades (Callender and Kemp, 2000).

This raises the issue of *which* students are participating in higher education. Examination of the data on socio-economic group indicates that the expansion of higher education student numbers has predominantly been due to the increasing participation of middle-class students. Despite government policy initiatives to widen participation to other groups, the proportion of students from working-class groups has hardly increased at all since the 1960s (see Ross, 2003). In a written answer in the House of Commons in 2007, it was reported that UK domiciled students from working-class groups constituted 30.8 per cent of full-time undergraduates at all higher education institutions in 2002/03 and 31.5 per cent in 2005–06.[4] However, if we look at applicant data for those from the lowest group (Group 7 – 'routine occupations'), they constituted only 4.36 per cent of all accepted degree applicants in 2007. Women were 55.87 per cent of this very small

---

[3] There are a few courses in high priority areas that are exempt and for which students will still be entitled to the same funding as other full-time students in England.

[4] House of Commons Hansard written answers for 13 March, 2007 (pt 0017) www.publications.parliament.uk/pa/cm200607/cmhansrd/cm070313/text/70313w 0017.htm (accessed 15 March, 2008). This data uses the Standard Occupational Classification 2000 which is a seven point classification from Group 1, 'higher managerial and professional occupations' to Group 7 'routine occupations'. Working-class groups are assumed to be groups 4–7 on this classificatory scale.

proportion.[5] The increase in participation of women students has therefore been predominantly of middle-class women, with their working-class peers still very much in a minority. Working-class students are also less likely to progress on to research degrees than their middle-class peers (Wakeling, 2005).

Representation of black and minority ethnic (BME) groups in higher education in the UK tends not to be seen as a problem. Indeed BME groups are often referred to as 'over-represented' in higher education (Tolley and Rundel, 2006). In 2006–07, minority ethnic students constituted 16.4 per cent of all first year UK domiciled higher education students of known ethnicity (Higher Education Statistics Agency, 2008). Within this, however, black Caribbean and Bangladeshi students have the lowest levels of participation, and black African and Indian the highest. Although women from BME groups are more likely to participate than men from these groups, again there are differences between groups, with Bangladeshi women students' participation rates being lower than white women's participation (Tolley and Rundel, 2006). Data from 2006–07 shows that amongst first degree full-time undergraduate students, there is a higher proportion of women than men in all ethnic groups except Asian or Asian British-Pakistani, Chinese and those from other Asian backgrounds (Higher Education Statistics Agency, 2008). BME students are more likely to study part time and to be mature students than their white peers (Modood, 2006), and black African-Caribbean applicants are significantly less likely to be accepted on to degree courses than their white and Asian counterparts (Tolley and Rundel, 2006). In addition, as is discussed below, BME students have lower levels of achievement and are more likely to be studying in universities with lower levels of overall prestige and funding.

The relationship between social class and ethnicity in this analysis also needs to be considered. Modood (2006) notes that whilst approximately two-thirds of white students are from middle-class family backgrounds, two-thirds of Pakistani and Bangladeshi students are from lower working-class backgrounds, with their parents either in manual work or unemployed. Education policy discourse in the UK tends to homogenize working-class groups and assume that a reason, indeed perhaps one of the main reasons, for low participation rates amongst the working classes is low aspiration. The situation, however, is far more complex, with a body of research drawing attention to the classed cultures, identities and actions that inhibit working-class participation (see, for example, Ball et al., 2000; Reay, 2001; Ball, 2003; Reay et al., 2005).

The proportion of students declaring a disability in higher education has increased in recent years, particularly for students with dyslexia (Riddell, 2006). Riddell shows how disabled students are more likely to be from a

---

[5] UCAS data 2007: www.ucas.ac.uk/about_us/stat_services/stats_online/annual_datasets_to_download/.

middle-class background than other students, and more likely to be male and white. There are also suggestions in this study that the ways in which disabled students are able to negotiate their identities in higher education, and their rights to access resources, reflect issues of social class and gender.

Student achievement

On undergraduate degree programmes, women are, on average, achieving higher results than men. In 2006–07, a higher proportion of women achieved upper second class honours (49 per cent of women compared to 43 per cent of men), whereas more men were awarded lower second (30 per cent of men, 27 per cent of women) or third class honours (7 per cent of men, 4 per cent of women) degrees. Overall, 63 per cent of women students (full and part-time) at UK higher education institutions achieved a first or upper second class degree, compared to 57 per cent of men. However, proportionately slightly more men received first class honours, with 11 per cent of women and 12 per cent of men being awarded first class honours degrees (Higher Education Statistics Agency, 2008).

There are also differential retention and achievement rates related to social class and ethnicity. As has already been noted, the need to work during term time negatively impacts on the achievements of working-class students, and issues of debt (levels of which are much higher for working-class students; Callender 2004), are one of the factors that may lead to a student dropping out of their course prior to completion. Black and minority ethnic students also tend to receive a lower class of degree than their white peers, with black African students most likely to achieve a third class degree (Tolley and Rundel, 2006). Of course social class also needs to be considered here, but these patterns of lower levels of achievement are evident when other factors, such as age, gender, deprivation, disability and prior attainment are controlled for (Broecke and Nicholls, n.d.). Broecke and Nicholls were not, however, able to control for parental income or student term-time working. Women minority ethnic students tend to do better than minority ethnic men, and the gap between the achievements of men and women is greater than for white students (Tolley and Rundel, 2006).

The ways in which these differences tend to be explained is illustrative. As we noted in Chapter 2, increases in achievement in the number of degrees awarded, and in particular the increasing proportion of higher grades, have been articulated in the context of a 'dumbing down' discourse – if more of the new insurgents into the academy (women, the lower classes, minority ethnic students) are doing well, then standards must have declined. In particular, women's achievements tend always to be seen as a result of hard work rather than intellect. As Walkerdine (1994: 58) noted, 'no matter how well girls were said to perform, their performance was always downgraded or dismissed in one way or another', reflecting Clarricoates' (1989) research in primary school classrooms in the 1970s. Jacobs and colleagues (2007), in a study of views about attainment related to gender and ethnicity in English higher education institutions, found that the main explanation given for gender differences in achievement related to factors in teaching, learning and assessment. Many noted what they felt were differences in 'learning style', with women perceived as more likely to work steadily and conscientiously, and men more likely to take risks, something that we discuss further in Chapter 8. As Burman (2005: 356) asked:

> what is 'over-performance' if not a discursive device to throw such achievement into question, to portray it as artefactual, a product of particular performance features rather than emanating from some stable, internalized notion of ability?

Interestingly, however, Jacobs and colleagues (2007: 36) found that some used a deficit model to explain the poorer performance of some men:

> With regard to gendered degree attainment, it is clear that use of a deficit model was widespread within this study. The 'deficit', however, was not seen to pertain to women, as in (older?) stereotypes of them as irrational beings. Rather, it was 'carried' by men, particularly young working-class men. This group, and its racialised sub-divisions, were seen to lack study skills and commitment to academic work and study. Additionally, [many] men were viewed as carrying a deficit from their lack of commitment to education at secondary level and poorer entry qualifications.

Some, however, also argued that whilst women's performance exceeded men's on the whole, this tended to be *despite* discriminatory attitudes about women, rather than because such attitudes were no longer evident. Respondents commented, for example, on the differential valuing of women's and men's work at an examination board – with men's work being more highly valued, and on the ways in which young working-class women are derided for their appearance in a way than men are not (Jacobs et al., 2007). In relation to ethnicity, although a deficit discourse was articulated by some respondents in this study, most argued that institutional and discriminatory factors went some way to explaining differences in attainment. In particular, issues of the culture, curriculum and unrepresentative staffing of higher education institutions – and discrimination in relation to these – were felt to be important.

We now move on to an analysis of *where* students are located, first in relation to subject of study and then by type of institution.

Gender and students' subject 'choices' in UK higher education

It perhaps comes as no surprise that, like elsewhere in the world, there are significant and persistent gender differences in subjects studied in the UK.

Figure 4.1 shows that women are in the majority in most subject areas, particularly in subjects allied to medicine, education, veterinary science and languages. Women are very much in a minority, however, in engineering and technology, computer science, architecture, building and planning, and also constitute less than 50 per cent of students in mathematical sciences, physical sciences and business and administrative studies.

There are also differences within these broad categories. Using the data for UK domiciled students, in subjects allied to medicine the vast majority of women are in nursing, whereas there are far more men in anatomy, physiology and pathology. In biological sciences, women are in the majority overall, but more men study sports science. In agriculture, although again there are more women overall in this broad subject grouping, more men study forestry and agricultural science. In social studies, significantly more men study economics and politics. In the physical sciences, where it looks as though women are at least making their presence known, they outnumber men in forensic and archaeological science, but they trail very badly in physics itself.

Minority ethnic students are more likely to study law, medicine, dentistry and engineering and less likely to study education, although there are also differences between minority ethnic groups with more Indian and Pakistani students studying medicine and related subjects and more black African and Black Caribbean students studying biological sciences, law and creative arts and design (Tolley and Rundel, 2006). Students declaring a disability are more highly represented in the creative arts and design (Riddell, 2006).

In terms of social class, there are some suggestions that students from working-class backgrounds are more likely to study vocationally-related courses and modules, and the type of institution attended may be one factor in this – something which is discussed below. It may also be as much about

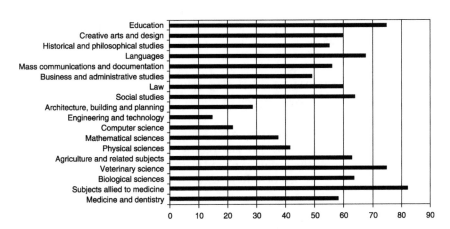

Figure 4.1 Percentage of women UK HE students by subject of study

Data extracted from HESA (2008) for 2006–07 for UK domiciled students.

the higher levels of risk associated with higher education participation for working-class students (Archer et al., 2002), as about 'choice' per se:

> We suggest, however, that the desire for work-related learning may not simply be a matter of preference, or a consequence of earlier educational experiences, but may also be a response to the underlying insecurity of many of these students: i.e. it is not simply an instrumentalism that stems from a desire to earn a lot of money or get a good job, but rather (or also) a defence against getting nowhere and having nothing. (Leathwood and O'Connell, 2003: 611)

Choice is also often used to explain gendered subject divisions. The overall pattern, as has been seen, is that women are still seriously under-represented in the higher status science, technology, engineering, maths and computing areas. We suggest that the reasons for these gendered (and racialized) patterns are multiple and relate to historical and social constructions of masculinity and femininity as well as to the constructions of subjects and bodies of knowledge – something that we discuss further in Chapter 9. Yet within dominant education policy discourse, a neo-liberal emphasis on individual choice and responsibility predominates. After all, there have been many attempts in the UK to persuade girls and women to choose science, engineering and technological subjects, and given that these subjects tend to lead to higher salaried careers, women can (yet again) be constructed as irrational when they fail to 'choose' these subjects (Leathwood, 2007). This draws on the classical economics conceptualization of choice which is discussed in some detail, and seriously problematized, in Chapter 6. And as Kenway et al. (1994: 194) found, many young women encouraged to take traditionally masculine subjects 'felt diminished or insulted because their different preferences for knowledge and work were implicitly downgraded'. A key issue must be the differential valuing (and salary levels) of different areas of work – in particular the lack of status and reward accorded to traditionally feminine subjects and areas of work, both paid and unpaid.

Student participation and the institutional 'diversity' of higher education in the UK

A key characteristic, and policy commitment, of the UK higher education sector is that of institutional diversity. Universities in the UK tend to be divided into the 'elite' (including the Universities of Oxford and Cambridge along with a small number of other research intensive institutions), 'pre-1992' universities (those in existence as universities prior to this date), and 'post-1992' institutions. The latter are those that were awarded university status as a result of the Higher and Further Education Act 1992 and were, mostly, polytechnics prior to that date. Although students attending polytechnics were able to study for degrees, the degrees were not awarded by the institution itself (unlike universities) but by a central body (the Council for National Academic Awards). Polytechnics tended to focus more on vocational courses and did not have the same academic research remit as the universities. The 1992 Act was heralded as removing the 'binary divide' between universities and polytechnics, but a hierarchy of differential institutional status and resource levels persists.

The government presents the diversity of higher education institutions as desirable in terms of meeting the diverse needs of higher education stakeholders and ensuring 'best fit' with those needs:

> A diverse higher education sector is one with the capacity to meet the varying needs and aspirations of those it serves: students, employers, purchasers of HE services, and the wider community. . . . It is a means of securing the best fit with the needs and wishes of stakeholders, both current and future. Diversity is valuable to the extent that it helps to improve that fit. (HEFCE, 2000: 4)

As Mirza (2006b) notes, this is not diversity framed in terms of equity. Instead, the main focus of higher education policy is on individual 'choice' – and a diverse range of institutions is presented as a better way of facilitating choice (although as noted in Chapter 6, 'choice' is also presented as increasing equity in this policy discourse). The 'best fit' aspect is key here, and is evident in policy discourses that construct less prestigious courses and institutions as the most appropriate place for the 'new' students of the academy (Leathwood and O'Connell, 2003).

The majority of working-class and minority ethnic students in higher education are in post-1992 universities, with the exception of Chinese students who are more likely to go to pre-1992 universities (Archer et al., 2003; Reay et al., 2005; Tolley and Rundel, 2006). What is less well recognized is that women are more likely to attend post-1992 universities as well (Leathwood, 2004). Indeed it was the old polytechnics that, following on from the 'new' universities that were established in the 1960s, initially welcomed women in greater numbers into the higher education sector.

The persistence of the binary divide is evident from university league tables. On the whole pre-1992 and elite universities dominate the top of these league tables, whilst the post-1992 institutions are clustered in the lower end. As we noted in Chapter 3, the methodologies used for producing league tables has been seriously problematized and the rankings, which rest on and promulgate the assumption that the higher up the league table, the 'better' the university, need to be questioned. Watson and Bowden (2002), for example, have demonstrated that position in the league table closely correlates with level of funding, with those nearer to the top of the league table being the richest institutions. Roper, Ross and Thompson (2000) suggested an alternative measure for ranking universities: the extent to which a university promotes social inclusion. This would have resulted in a dramatic reversal in the universities allocated top and bottom places in the rankings and hence was not likely to be welcomed by the elite universities. It has not been adopted, also reflecting the commitment to and pressure of the marketization of higher education in policy circles.[6]

The more mainstream university league tables continue to dominate, however, reflecting both the prestige and financial resourcing levels of different universities, and hence it is one of these, the *Good University Guide 2008*, that we have used in the following analysis to illustrate the extent of institutional stratification in the UK. In Table 4.1, we have examined student participation data related to gender, state or private school attendance and social class group for the ten universities at the top of this league table, and the ten universities at the bottom. As can be seen, although the mean score for the proportion of UK domiciled women undergraduates is above 50 per cent for universities at both ends of the league table, there is a significant difference between the 50.62 per cent of women at the top ten universities and the far higher 62.5 per cent of women at the bottom ten. Of course this partly reflects subject specialisms, with for example, Imperial College of Science, Technology and Medicine having only 35.86 per cent of UK women undergraduates. Southampton Solent University in the lower section of the table, however, also has a relatively low proportion of women students. The proportion of students from state schools is a signifier of social class – it is predominantly the middle classes who can afford to send their children to private fee-paying schools, and they often do so precisely to gain the positional advantage of a place at an elite university (Reay, 2001; Swift, 2003). The final column shows the proportion of students from working-class groups – again the majority are at universities lower in the league tables. We have not been able to include ethnicity data as, in contrast to data about gender and social class which is provided by the Higher Education Statistics Agency (HESA), data about the ethnicity of students is not publically available, perhaps because minority ethnic students are seen as 'over-represented'. A newspaper report in 2006, however, which examined data for 2003–04, reported that over 60 per cent of students at London Metropolitan University[7] were from minority ethnic groups, compared to less than 7 per cent of students at Bristol University (Curtis, 2006). According to this analysis, 53 universities had fewer than 5 per cent of students from minority ethnic groups, whilst about 20 have more than 40 per cent. Of course some of this is a geographical effect, reflecting the higher concentration of minority ethnic communities in some urban areas, but a gender, class and race divide within the higher education sector in the UK is clearly evident.

---

[6] There is also an alternative league table in the US that ranks colleges and universities according to how welcoming they are to LGBT students – see Stewart (2007) – no doubt precisely because some institutions have recognized the monetary value of such students.

[7] London Metropolitan University used to occupy a position towards the lower end of the league tables, but in recent years has refused permission for its data to be used. It is a post-1992 institution.

Table 4.1 Institutional diversity: league table ranking, gender and social class

League table position[1]	University	% women UK undergrads[2]	Mean % UK women undergrads	% state schools[3]	Mean % state school	% from socio-economic groups 4, 5, 6, 7	Mean % groups 4–7
1	The University of Cambridge	56.91		56.8[4]		12.4	
2	The University of Oxford	50.88		53.7		11.4	
3	Imperial College of Science, Technology and Medicine	35.86		61.3		17.3	
4	The London School of Economics and Political Science	46.19		59.4		17.5	
5	The University of St Andrews	56.49		60.9		15.2	
6	University College London	51.16	50.62	62.4	63.33	17.5	16.15
7	The University of Bristol	55.68		65.1		16.4	
8	The University of Warwick	57.05		76.0		18.7	
9	The University of Bath	43.86		75.9		18.7	
10	The University of Durham	52.10		61.8		16.4	
103	Thames Valley University	65.40		96.2		36.7	
104	Anglia Ruskin University	69.06		98.1		34.5	
106	Southampton Solent University	43.97		96.0		35.5	
107	Middlesex University	60.68		98.2		44.6	
107	The University of Wolverhampton	60.74		99.0		50.0	
109	The University of Lincoln	55.33	62.52	96.9	97.54	35.6	40.44
110	Liverpool Hope University	73.36		97.8		40.0	
110	Edge Hill University	77.59		98.0		38.5	
111	London South Bank University	60.77		98.0		41.9	
112	The University of Greenwich	58.27		97.2		47.1	

Notes

1 For this analysis we have omitted the University of Cumbria, which is ranked at position 105 in the *Good University Guide* 2008, and was formed on 1 August, 2007. As such, student data for 2006/07 is not available. This university was therefore replaced in this analysis by Thames Valley University ranked 103.

2 UK women undergraduate students as a percentage of all UK undergraduate students 2006/07 (HESA 2008).

3 Data on percentage figures of students from state schools and socio-economic groups taken from HESA data, T1a Participation of under-represented groups in higher education: young full-time first degree entrants 2005–06. www.hesa.ac.uk/index.php/content/view/409/141/.

4 University of Cambridge data for percentage state schools and socio-economic group was not available for 2005–06. The figures included here are therefore taken from the equivalent 2004–05 data.

As is discussed below, the status of the university attended impacts on the career opportunities open to students post-graduation, but there is also likely to be an impact on the student experience during their time at university.

Table 4.2 uses data from *The Good University Guide 2008* to illustrate the resourcing differences between universities at the opposite ends of the league tables. Of course, a lower student–staff ratio does not necessarily mean that students see members of staff more often – indeed there are suggestions that students at elite universities are more likely to be taught by post-graduate research students whilst the academic staff and particularly the

Table 4.2 Resource indicators[4] for universities by league table ranking

League table ranking: The Good University Guide 2008	University	Student–staff ratio[1]	Spending per student on academic services[2]	Spending per student on facilities[3]
1	The University of Cambridge	12.2	1,576	574
2	The University of Oxford	13.0	2,220	370
3	Imperial College of Science, Technology and Medicine	9.7	2,551	479
4	The London School of Economics and Political Science	13.2	1,210	211
5	The University of St Andrews	15.4	818	208
6	University College London	9.4	1,435	179
7	The University of Bristol	14.9	1,199	279
8	The University of Warwick	17.1	1,472	233
9	The University of Bath	16.7	804	411
10	The University of Durham	20.3	892	331
103	Thames Valley University	19.4	467	109
104	Anglia Ruskin University	19.9	432	154
106	Southampton Solent University	21.6	612	324
107	Middlesex University	29.6	1,068	358
107	The University of Wolverhampton	21.2	610	354
109	The University of Lincoln	26.3	637	162
110	Liverpool Hope University	24.3	828	140
110	Edge Hill University	22.8	708	123
111	London South Bank University	23.1	669	110
112	The University of Greenwich	24.0	705	144

Notes
1 Based on HESA data 2004–05.
2 This includes library and computing facilities using HESA data 2004–05.
3 This includes sports, health, advice, counselling and careers services from HESA data 2002–03, 2003–04, 2004–05.
4 All taken from the *Good University Guide* 2008.

professors are doing their own research. Nevertheless, students at Oxford and Cambridge are far more likely to receive frequent and regular individual and/or small group tutorials than their peers in post-1992 institutions. The figures above also point to differences in the resourcing of libraries and other student services and facilities which are not negligible. For example, the mean spend per student on academic services such as library and computing resources is £1418 for the universities ranked 1–10, and only £673.60 for those ranked 103–12. For spending on 'facilities', which includes sports, health, advice and counselling, the respective difference is £327.50 for the top ten, and £197.80 for the bottom ten. These inequalities in funding have been noted by Brown (2004), who pointed out that in 2001–2002, Imperial College had eight times the income per full-time equivalent student than Thames Valley University.

The distinction between elite universities and post-1992 institutions is not only maintained but further reinforced through government discourses and practices of 'diversity', research selectivity, and 'excellence'. Government ministers and spokespersons regularly talk about 'good' universities – and this phrase is also continually repeated in the press. This is a euphemism for elite and perhaps some pre-1992 research intensive universities, and certainly not, as Reay and colleagues (2001) note, a university attended by significant numbers of black and working-class students. As David Starkey, a writer and historian at the University of Cambridge was reported as stating:

> The problem is ... we pretend that all universities and all degrees are the same. We have got ourselves into a situation where we're pretending that a degree from the London Metropolitan University is the same quality as a degree from Cambridge. It's not. There are Mickey Mouse students for whom Mickey Mouse degrees are quite appropriate. (Brockes, 2003: 2)

The UK government is committed to further increasing university 'diversity' and competition in the higher education market. Although universities at present have the right to charge variable fees for undergraduate courses, there is currently a cap on these fees and most universities have set their fees at this capped rate. However, there is growing pressure from elite universities for the government to remove the cap. If it is removed, it is likely to lead to far higher fees at elite universities (albeit with some bursaries for poorer students), whereas many post-1992 universities with a poorer student intake will be unable to increase their fees significantly. The differential resourcing of universities is likely, therefore, to increase, further segmenting the stratification, indeed segregation, of the present system. Naidoo (2003) also notes how the imperatives of commodification work differently on different universities in different countries, and there are implications here for post-1992 universities in the UK who are under greater government pressure to develop courses directly linked to labour market needs (with, as discussed in Chapter 9, implications for the curriculum offered to different groups of students).

The analysis we have conducted here does not take into account students studying higher education courses outside the university system. A growing number of students, predominantly working-class students, are now taking degrees, including 'foundation degrees' (broadly equivalent to the first 2 years of a 3-year honours degree), in further education colleges where the unit of resource per student is significantly lower. These colleges also have far lower levels of prestige than universities.

The reasons for this institutional stratification of student participation are complex, but include differences in qualifications attained, with the elite universities only taking students with very high entry qualifications. The obstacles to attaining high grades at school for many students from working-class backgrounds are significant, with research indicating that the main predictor of school attainment is social class (Skelton et al., 2007). As such, working-class students irrespective of gender or ethnicity are likely to be at a disadvantage. However, this is not the only factor involved. Modood (2006) reported that white students were more likely to be offered a place at a pre-1992 university: a white student had a 75 per cent chance of receiving an offer, compared to a Pakistani student with the same level of qualification, who had a 57 per cent chance. In addition, many students choose to study at a university with a diverse student population and where they are more likely to find students like themselves (Archer et al., 2003; Read et al., 2003; Reay et al., 2005) and/or select a university close to home because that is the only way they can afford to study. 'Choice' of university is not a free choice for many students (Reay et al., 2005), yet the focus of government policy is simply on facilitating student choice through the provision of information such as that provided in university league tables. But the discourse of 'choice' operates as a moral technology to legitimize the inequalities of a strongly hierarchical and segregated higher education system. The policy commitment to institutional diversity also utilizes a discourse of 'ability' whereby the 'bright' students, including, of course, 'bright' students from working-class groups, should go to a 'good' university. This rests on notions of meritocracy through which students go to the institution best suited to their needs and 'abilites'. Meritocracy as a concept has been seriously problematized (Goldthorpe, 1997; Leathwood, 2004; Leathwood, 2005a), not least by the person who originally coined the term in a dystopic novel, *The Rise of the Meritocracy*, brilliantly illustrating the dangers of constructing a society based on meritocratic principles (Young, 1971 [1958]; Young, 2001). Gillborn and Youdell (2000) argue that there is evidence of a new 'IQism' in educational policy discourses in the UK, whereby assumptions of inherited 'intelligence' underpin both policy and practice, and this can be seen in higher education policy which reifies choice and institutional diversity.

Students and the differential benefits of higher education

The status of the university attended impacts on graduate prospects. Data from the *Good University Guide* (2008) shows that for the ten universities at the top of the league table discussed above, the mean score for graduate prospects is 79.2, whereas for the ten universities at the bottom, the score is 55.8. 'Graduate prospects' refers to the proportion of students taking up graduate employment (that is, excluding non-graduate level jobs) or further study from all those with a known destination, with an adjustment made for subject mix.

There are particular advantages to having studied at the universities of Oxford and Cambridge (colloquially referred to as 'Oxbridge'). These graduates earn approximately 8 per cent more than graduates from other old universities, and between 11 per cent and 16 per cent more than those from post-1992 institutions (Conlon and Chevalier, 2002a). Ryle and colleagues (2000) reported that graduates from Oxbridge constituted 36 per cent of fast-track appointments to the Civil Service, 70 per cent of bishops, 73 per cent of newly appointed judges, and 37 per cent of hereditary peers. In 2004, analysis of the educational backgrounds of members of the UK government showed that approximately a third of the members of the Cabinet were from Oxbridge, and this proportion appeared to be replicated across the House of Commons as a whole (Leathwood, 2004). Not surprisingly, earnings also differ:

> For the 1985 and 1990 cohorts, Oxbridge graduates achieved a 7.9 per cent earnings premium over graduates from 'old' universities, while those attending polytechnics suffered a 3.8 per cent wage penalty compared to those attending 'old' universities. For the 1995 cohort, degree holders from former polytechnics suffered a 7.7 per cent earnings penalty compared to degree holders from 'old' universities. Even after controlling for the type of institution attended, returns continue to vary across socio-economic background. (Conlon and Chevalier, 2002b: 2)

From their study of elite recruitment of graduates, in particular through the use of company assessment centres, Brown and Hesketh report data from one of their case study employers, noting that graduates of Oxford University had a one in eight chance of success, compared to a one in 235 ratio for those from new universities. Most of the employers in their study did not collect socio-economic data, but Brown and Hesketh (2004: 7) note that:

> Widening access to higher education and the increased importance attached to 'personal capital' . . . has done little to increase the chances of working class candidates entering elite jobs. As the recruitment process is designed to expose the 'personal' qualities of individuals, the social, cultural and economic backgrounds of candidates have been increasingly exposed. It is very difficult for those from disadvantaged

backgrounds to gain elite credentials, let alone the 'social' education that is a crucial feature of elite employability.

They reported little evidence of gender discrimination, arguing that 'the stereotype of Oxbridge Man is no longer the gold standard in a number of organisations. The "gentlemen" are losing out to female and male "players" who combine elite credential with other aspects of personal capital' (Brown and Hesketh, 2004: 7). Yet they did note that where recruiters commented on applicants' dress, all but one of those applicants were women which, we suggest, indicates that gender expectations and regulation were a part of the recruitment process.

A slightly higher proportion of men whose destinations are known are likely to unemployed 6 months after graduation (6 per cent of men compared to 4 per cent of women in 2005/06; HESA, 2007b), as are students from black and minority ethnic groups (Connor et al., 2004) and disabled graduates (Disabilities Task Group, 2007). Mature graduates also face disadvantages in the graduate labour market, with age being a particular factor for older mature graduates (Purcell et al., 2003). Minority ethnic graduates were also less likely to get through each stage of the recruitment process for large organizations than their white counterparts (Purcell et al., 2003), and Brown and Hesketh (2003) reported a small number of examples of explicit discrimination against minority ethnic applicants in their study of elite recruitment. Chinese and Pakistani men are twice as likely as the average to be unemployed, whilst Pakistani women are very unlikely to experience high levels of economic returns on their degrees (Tolley and Rundel, 2006). There is research indicating that some employers may be reluctant to offer posts to Muslim women because of racist and sexist expectations and the assumption that they will leave to get married or have children (Tyrer and Ahmad, 2006). As Mirza (2006b: 102) notes, despite black women's 'desire for education as social transformation', their participation in HE and their qualifications, they continue to be 'underrepresented and underemployed in a racially divided and gendered segmented labour market'. Black and minority ethnic graduates are also more likely to undertake further study (Connor et al., 2004), as are women in comparison to men (Moreau and Leathwood, 2006b). Of those graduates who are employed women are more likely to be in non-graduate levels jobs than men, and also are more likely to be on temporary contracts (Moreau and Leathwood, 2006b). Graduates with disabilities are also more likely to be in part-time or voluntary work (Disabilities Task Group, 2007).

Women are certainly disadvantaged in the graduate labour market. Data from the Higher Education Statistics Agency shows that 3 years after graduation, male graduates on average are earning £1000 more a year than women graduates, whilst 40 per cent of men are earning more than £25,000 a year, compared to just 26 per cent of women (Osborne, 2007). The gender pay gap for company directors is even greater, with research showing that this increased to 22 per cent in 2007, from 19 per cent the previous year. In the voluntary and service sectors, women directors earned 26 per cent less than their male colleagues on average (Osborne, 2007). It is no surprise, therefore, that the government have estimated that it will take a woman graduate 16 years on average to pay off their student loan, compared to just 11 years for a man (Curtis, 2008). Younger graduates also tend to earn much higher salaries than their older peers (Purcell et al., 2003).

Gender and the academic labour force

If the statistics for the participation of women students in the academy fail to make a straightforwardly convincing case for the feminization thesis, the statistics for women staff provide even less support. Writing in 1980, Rendell (cited in Brooks, 1997: 11) noted:

> In Britain a woman was first appointed to an academic post in 1893 and to a chair in 1894. The proportion of women academics now is virtually the same as in the 1920s and the proportion holding senior posts virtually the same as in the 1930s ... individual women have learnt it is not enough to be better than men ... they are not perceived as scholars.

Things have improved somewhat since 1980. In 2006–07 (HESA, 2008) women constituted 42.3 per cent of all academic staff, and 62.6 per cent of non-academic staff. There has also been a steady increase in the proportions of staff from a non-white ethnic background since 1997–98 (Fenton et al., 2000: 2). Black minority ethnic staff constituted 10.65 per cent of all academic staff with known ethnicity in 2005–06 (HESA, 2007a). However, when only those of UK nationality are considered, the corresponding figure is only 5.92 per cent. As Fenton et al. (2000) note, the representation of non-British academics within the academic profession 'is not a representation of the British-born or the long-term settled non-whites or of the latter's social mobility within the UK; it is an index of the globalisation of the academic marketplace'. Of all staff for whom disability status is known, 2.4 per cent declared a disability in 2005–06 (HEFCE, 2006b). It is estimated that 20 per cent of the UK workforce has a disability, suggesting that this is a serious under-representation.

If we break these figures down, the persistent inequalities become very apparent. Of the academic staff women were:

- 17.5 per cent of professors;
- 36.8 per cent of senior lecturers/researchers;
- 45.8 per cent of researchers;
- 47.4 per cent of lecturers.

HESA data 2005–06 (HESA, 2007a) also shows that amongst non-academic staff, women constituted:

- 60.1 per cent of cleaners, catering assistants, security officers, porters and maintenance workers;
- 93.5 per cent of secretaries, typists, receptionists and telephonists.

Similarly, the higher the post, the lower proportion of minority ethnic staff (Bunting, 2004). In 2004, there were only nine black women professors in the UK, and five of those were in nursing (Mirza, 2006b: 106).

Despite these considerable gender disparities, the Higher Education Funding Council for England demonstrates that there has been a progressive improvement in the proportion of women permanent academic staff at all grades over the last decade (HEFCE, 2007). What does not seemed to have changed noticeably, however, is the appallingly low representation of women at senior and particularly professorial level. The assumption that often accompanies discussion of these figures in the educational press is that as more women are, undoubtedly, entering the profession as more junior researchers and lecturers, it is simply a matter of time until they work their way through the system – i.e. the 'pipeline' theory discussed in Chapter 3. An article in the *Times Higher Education* in March 2008 reported that 'at researcher and lecturer levels, women are poised to take over' (Oxford, 2008a: 31) and that women are predicted to be in the majority of all academics by about 2020, although the same projections show that women will not outnumber men at professorial level until 2070. There are suggestions, however, that men are leaving the profession for higher paid jobs elsewhere: between 1995–96 and 2005–06, the proportion of women lecturers increased from 34 per cent to 46 per cent whilst actual numbers of men declined from about 22,000 to fewer than 18,000 over the same period (HEFCE, 2006a). The discourse of academia as feminized and therefore also 'dumbed down', discussed in Chapter 2, is also articulated in this context, for example with newspaper headlines such as 'Men leave low status academy to women' (Hill, 2004).

The assumptions, therefore, are that the progress of women is unstoppable, and that it is simply a matter of time until there are enough women with the right levels of qualifications and experience. A study of women scientists, however, found that women were less likely to be promoted to professorial positions, and whilst some of this may be to do with them being younger or less experienced, 'between a quarter and a third is unexplained, which leads us to conclude that there is strong evidence that women do experience different treatment and disadvantage in terms of career progression' (Gilbert, 2008). And things can go backwards, with a recent study of women in boardrooms showing that numbers of women had gone into decline (Stewart, 2008).

Bryson (2004) found that men were more likely to get an academic post straight from being a student, obtain posts through non-competitive entry, and gain more secure forms of fixed term contracts. Overall women are more likely to be on fixed-term contracts, with an analysis of HESA data for 2003–04 conducted by the university lecturers union (AUT) noting that 50.8

per cent of women were on fixed-term contracts, compared to 40.5 per cent of men (AUT, 2005). Carter et al. (1999) also note that minority British staff were more likely than white staff to be on fixed-term contracts, as were women of all ethnic groups in comparison to men. In addition, Bryson discovered that men enter contract research staff positions at higher levels than women, are more likely to transfer from contract research to permanent posts and if they are lecturers, are more likely to be promoted. Casualization may affect the sector as a whole, but it impacts disproportionately on women (Hey, 2001).

There are also persistent salary differentials, with data for 2006–07 showing that at all academic grades, women in the UK are, on average, paid less than their male counterparts, with a gender pay gap of almost 16 per cent. In an analysis of HESA data for 2003–04, the AUT reported an ethnicity pay gap of 13 per cent on average in favour of white academics in the UK as a whole, and a gender and ethnicity pay gap for academic managers and for non-academic professional staff (AUT, 2005). At professorial level, the average gap was over £5000 a year in 2006–07.[8] Some of this is likely to be due to the different salary levels, especially at professorial level, between different subjects. Just as with their student counterparts, the highest proportion of women staff are in subjects allied to medicine (62 per cent) and education (58 per cent; HEFCE 2007), yet even in these female dominated areas, men dominate at senior levels. Staff in traditionally 'feminine' and therefore less valued subject areas are also likely to earn less, especially as the marketization of the sector is leading to an increased use of 'market supplements' to match equivalent salary levels in the private sector. At some institutions, men are five times as likely to receive additional discretionary pay as women (AUT, 2005). Although concern about the gender gap in academic salaries has been expressed nationally in the UK, including within government circles, this subject variability is largely accepted without question. Yet what is continually perpetuated is the serious undervaluing and lack of recognition for women's work – across the whole of the UK economy, not simply in academia. Differential salary levels between subjects are likely to increase as the marketization of the sector further develops.

There are also significant salary differences between institutions, with the elite universities paying significantly more, on average, than post-1992 institutions. The mean score for the proportion of full-time women academic staff at the top ten universities in Tables 4.1 and 4.2 is 31.90, compared to 43.71 at the ten universities at the bottom of the table (calculated using data from HESA, 2007a). Just like women, minority ethnic and working-class students, therefore, full-time women academic staff are more likely to be in institutions with lower levels of resources and paying lower salaries.

<hr />

[8] Higher Education Statistics Agency staff data 2006–07. www.timeshighereducation. co.uk/story.asp?sectioncode=26&storycode=401025 (accessed 13 March, 2008).

Interestingly, for part-time academics, there is little difference between the proportions of women in the two groups of institutions – with a mean score for part-time academic women of 54.36 for the ten universities at the top of the tables, and 53.78 for those at the bottom. The gender pay gap also tends to be larger at the elite universities, with an average 18.6 per cent gap, compared to 6.2 per cent at post-1992 institutions (Attwood, 2007). Furthermore, there is also evidence that women are less likely to be promoted to professorial posts in the elite university sector. Morley reported data from 2004 showing that just 8.8 per cent of professors at the University of Cambridge were women, and 9.5 per cent of those at the University of Oxford, compared to an average of 13 per cent for universities as a whole (Morley, 2007). Figures for 2006–07, however, show an average professorial salary in elite universities of £70,097, compared to just £55,419 in the post-1992 institutions. Many women, therefore, are likely to be doubly disadvantaged in terms of salary – paid less for being in a less well-resourced institution and, often, paid less again for being in a lower valued subject area. Salary differentials between institutions are also likely to be exacerbated if the predicted removal of the cap on tuition fees takes place, which will further increase resourcing disparities between institutions.

Gender differences are also very evident in research. For the 2008 Research Assessment Exercise (RAE)[9] – 73 per cent of the members of the assessment panels who make the judgements about the quality of research outputs were men and only 27 per cent were women (RAE, 2008). Only one black minority group exceeded 1 per cent of the total membership, and this was the Asian/Asian British/Indian group who comprised 1.5 per cent (HEFCE, 2006b).

Universities decide which staff to submit for assessment. These staff are deemed to be 'research active' – a classification that is likely to impact on future career opportunities. Data is not yet available on the gender breakdown of staff submitted for the 2008 exercise, but for the last one in 2001, men were 1.6 times more likely to be rated as research active than women (Court, 2004). Black and minority ethnic staff were also less likely to be submitted. An analysis of submissions in relation to gender conducted by the Higher Education Funding Agency for England reported that: 'Though not conclusive, these results were consistent with an explanation of the lower selection rate of women being due to a lower proportion of women having a research record that leads them to be selected, rather than bias in the selection process' (HEFCE 2006b: 3–4). The assumption here, therefore, is that fewer women are entered because they have a poorer research record. Accruing research credentials is obviously more difficult for those with significant levels of domestic and caring work – and this is more likely to be women. Yet a study from Sweden suggests more direct discrimination. An analysis of grant applications for post-doctoral

---

[9] The Research Assessment Exercise is an audit process used to allocate research funding to institutions and subject groupings.

fellowships to the Swedish Medical Research Council led the researchers to conclude that 'peer reviewers cannot judge scientific merit independent of gender' (Wenneras and Wold, 1997: 341) and either overestimated men's achievements and/or underestimated those of women. Women scored lowest on scientific competence, but also lower than men on quality of methodology and relevance of the proposal. The researchers also then examined applicants' scientific productivity, and found that women with equivalent productivity (for example in terms of journal articles), were still scored lower. Indeed it was only the most productive group of women who scored as high as men, but even these women were only rated equivalent to the least productive men. The analysis demonstrated that 'a female applicant had to be 2.5 times more productive than the average male applicant to receive the same competence score as he' (p. 342), or the equivalent of about 10 more years of work (Greenfield 2000, cited by Morrison et al., 2005)! Those who were personally known to the reviewers also scored more highly. The authors also cite other studies which indicate that men and women rate men's work more highly than women's when the person's gender is known, but not when it is unknown. They conclude:

> If gender discrimination of the magnitude we have observed is operative in the peer-review systems of other research councils and grant-awarding organizations, and in countries other than Sweden, this could entirely account for the lower success rate of female as compared with male researchers in attaining high academic rank. (Wenneras and Wold, 1997: 343)

The assessment of research outputs for the 2008 RAE is largely conducted by a process of peer review, and hence subject to the kinds of gender discrimination found by Wenneras and Wold. For the next RAE, there are plans to move to a 'metrics' system in which citation scores form the main component. Not only would this potentially penalize research in specialist minority areas as fewer academics are working in those areas and hence are less likely to cite research, it is also likely to have a detrimental effect on women and feminist research, with some evidence that male academics may be less likely to cite work by women (Shepherd, 2006).

Conclusions

The data presented in this chapter clearly shows that women are now in a majority at undergraduate level in UK higher education, but, as has been seen, this is only part of the story. It is predominantly middle-class women who are present in significant numbers, and they are segregated into typically 'feminine' subject areas that are less well valued than the subjects in which men predominate. Women, and particularly working-class and minority ethnic women, are also more likely to be in lower status universities, with implications for both their experiences at university and their future careers in the graduate labour market. Their salaries, on graduation, are likely to be significantly lower than their male counterparts.

For women academics, the picture is even more bleak. Women constitute slightly over 40 per cent of all academic staff, and are overwhelmingly located in the lowest grades and with the poorest conditions of service. They are also, like women students, unevenly represented across disciplinary areas, more likely to be in lower status and less well resourced institutions, and less likely to be recognized for their research expertise.

The data we have presented for both students and staff raise serious questions about the extent to which the UK academy can be regarded as a feminized space. What these figures do not do, however, is give any sense of the actual experiences of women studying and working in universities. In Chapter 6, we discuss the ways in which dominant constructions of the student are gendered, classed and racialized, and draw on a range of research to show how this creates particular difficulties for women students in taking on a student identity. In Chapter 7, we move on to explore the experiences of women academics and discuss the ways in which academic culture is perceived as a hostile and masculinist environment by many staff.

5
Institutional identities and representations of the university

So we talked standing at the window and looking, as so many thousands look every night, down on the domes and towers of the famous city beneath us. It was very beautiful, very mysterious in the autumn moonlight. The old stone looked very white and venerable. One thought of all the books that were assembled down there; of the pictures of old prelates and worthies hanging in the panelled rooms; of the painted windows that would be throwing strange globes and crescents on the pavement; of the tablets and memorials and inscriptions; of the fountains and the grass; of the quiet rooms looking across the quiet quadrangles. And (pardon me the thought) I thought, too, of the admirable smoke and drink and the deep armchairs and the pleasant carpets: of the urbanity, the geniality, the dignity which are the offspring of luxury and privacy and space. (Woolf 1992: 29–30)

In this passage of her famous 1929 essay 'A Room of One's Own', Virginia Woolf describes a view of the colleges of 'Oxbridge' University that can be seen to be part of a popular public repertoire of images that symbolize 'the university', even in the twenty-first century – the 'dreaming spires' of college buildings, built in stone the colour of pale gold – or ivory; dusty libraries of scholarly books in ancient, crumbling bindings, lovingly guarded by serious, twitchy, librarians; deep, comfortable antique armchairs in wood-panelled drawing rooms where pipe-smoking, white-haired professors ruminate and debate about Shakespeare, Hume or Einstein.

Of course Woolf (or at least the semi-fictional narrator of her essay) was gazing and imagining these colleges literally as an outsider – earlier that day she had been cautioned against walking on the grass lawn outside one particular college, and had been barred from entering its library: both of which were the privilege only of the all-male College Fellows. As we have discussed in the preceding chapters, women have made some gains in terms of participation and inclusion in higher education in many areas of the world since the time of Woolf's essay, although such gains have been uneven and by no means universal. However, the conception that universities have been, or are in the process of being, 'feminized' is a common contemporary refrain. As well as relating to a perceived numerical dominance, it is often implicitly or explicitly stated in this discourse that the very 'culture' of the academy itself has become feminized. In the remaining chapters of this book we will be critically exploring the contention that the 'culture' – or more validly, 'cultures' – of the academy are, or are becoming, 'feminized'. In coming chapters we will be looking in depth at constructions of the student and students' own identities; at the practices and identities of academic staff; at academic language and assessment; and at the curriculum and the forms of 'knowledge' valued in the academy.

This chapter however focuses on the discourses that infuse cultural representations of the 'university' in universities' own promotional material – in particular, universities' internet websites. The 'corporatization' of Higher Education Institutions (HEIs) in the 'west', and a shift to a more aggressive, market-driven competition between HEIs to recruit the 'best' and/or highest numbers of students has been well documented (see, for example, Becher and Trowler, 2001; Morley, 2003a; Osman, 2008). Before market pressures and government initiatives encouraged moves to widen access to universities across the west for previously under-represented groups, HEIs devoted little time or resources to overt marketing initiatives, instead relying on 'passive' forms of recruitment through national centralized bodies (Naude and Ivy, 1999). Fairclough, Osman and others have charted how universities have increasingly drawn on marketing strategies common in the commercial sector, 're-branding' their institutions utilizing corporate language styles and visual images in their promotional materials in order to attract the 'target market' of the potential student, herself 're-branded' as a customer/consumer (see, for example, Fairclough, 1993; Waters, 1995; Osman, 2008). We will be exploring the implications of the repositioning of the student as 'consumer' further in the next chapter. In this chapter, we will be focusing specifically on the ways in which photographic images in the universities' promotional websites on the World Wide Web draw on and are infused with particular culturally dominant gendered discourses, and the extent to which these images construct the university as a gendered (classed and racialized) space. How are such gendered constructions legitimized and given authority? And how far does such an analysis support the conception that university culture is 'feminized'?

Gendered images in advertising

As many social theorists have discussed, advertising 'is not just a business undertaken in the hope of moving some merchandising off the store shelves, but is rather an integral and important part of modern culture' (Warlaumont, 1993: 26) – a culture that is deeply gendered (see, for example, Kaplan, 1983). Since the 1920s, advertising in the West has increasingly relied on images as well as accompanying written text, with a move away from solely 'literal' textual explanations of images towards, from the 1960s onwards, including text that act as 'cryptic keys' to the intended interpretation of the metaphorical accompanying visuals (Leiss et al., 1990). More recently, advertising increasingly utilizes ambiguity (Rutledge Shields, 1990), irony and humour in visual images and texts – especially those aimed at a male audience (Cronin, 2000).

Early feminist work in this area tended to concentrate on the sexist stereotyping of women and men in advertisements (Cronin, 2000). However, later work critiqued such approaches for implicitly or explicitly essentializing gender, and presenting women (both as representations in images and as viewers) as passive and powerless, as well as perceiving advertising as encouraging 'fake' needs over ostensibly 'true', 'authentic' needs. Similar challenges have been placed towards some feminist studies of the construction of images according to the 'male gaze', originating with the work of Laura Mulvey (1975) in relation to film and used extensively in film theory and the interpretation of art (see Parker and Pollock, 1987; Kaplan, 2000; McCabe, 2004). Originating in feminist appropriation of Lacanian psychoanalysis, such analyses focus on the ways in which images of women are constructed through 'male eyes' – an interpretation of 'woman' that articulates the simultaneous masculine 'desire' and 'fear' of the feminine (Mulvey, 1975; Kaplan, 1983; Warlaumont, 1993). Men have the power of 'seeing': women need to 'make themselves worthy of being seen' (Warlaumont, 1993). Coward relates how women are only allowed to 'gaze' in contemporary culture through gazing at images themselves, a form of 'permissible looking' that does not involve the disruption of male dominance in structures of looking (Coward, 1985, cited in Warlaumont, 1993).

The sociologist Goffman (1979) also studied how structures of 'male dominance' and 'female subordination' are presented in display advertisements through particular symbolic constructions. These include women being presented as: smaller in size to men in images, and in spatially lower positions such as sitting or lying on beds or floors; 'passive' in comparison to men, who were more often the active 'doers' of tasks; performing 'submissive' or 'appeasement' gestures such as bending their heads, necks or knees (a 'bashful knee-bend'), smiling or acting less seriously; and looking away from the camera, 'tuning out' of the scene (see also Bell and Milic, 2002). Interestingly Wex, in an extensive study of gender representations in media and 'naturalistic' settings, found that women are just as likely to take on and 'perform' such submissive gestures in 'naturalistic' photographs as they do in more 'consciously posed' media images (Wex, 1979, cited in Bell and Milic, 2002). Recent feminist and pro-feminist work has found that many of Goffman's findings can still be seen in contemporary advertising (see, for example, Kang, 1997; Bell and Milic, 2002), although, for example, Bell and Milic found that women are more often seen looking directly at the camera rather than 'tuning out' in a 'licensed withdrawal' from the scene.

Many of these earlier studies concentrated on images of white women, and the complex relations between matrixes of power centred around gender, ethnicity and class were largely overlooked (Hill Collins, 1990). Such exclusions have increasingly been critiqued and challenged by BME and/or women of working-class origin, for example Patricia Hills Collins in the context of African-American women:

> From the mammies, Jezebels, and breeder women of slavery to the smiling Aunt Jemimas on pancake mix boxes, ubiquitous Black prostitutes, and ever-present welfare mothers of contemporary popular culture, the nexus of stereotypical images applied to African-American women has been fundamental to Black women's oppression. (Hill Collins, 1990: 7)

More recently the emphasis on women as the 'passive receivers' of the male gaze has come under challenge. Feminists such as Waldman (1989) and Rutledge Shields (1990) argue that more attention should be paid to the ways in which women can 'read against the grain' of hegemonically constructed images, exploring 'the dynamic ways of looking and reading which are both critical of, and responsive to, the particular representation or cultural form being investigated' (Rutledge Shields, 1990: 36). Some have argued that the increasing 'normalization' of men's concern with their own personal 'image', associated with a rise in male use of beauty products and cosmetic surgery, has led to men increasingly 'performing the aesthetics of the feminine through stylised presentations of self' and therefore 'may now be experiencing the traditional cultural traps of femininity ... becoming the subjects of an objectifying gaze' (Adkins, 2002: 63, discussing Gillette, 1994). Adkins notes that theories of 'looking' are moving away from the conception of a normative male gaze, and indeed, Ahmed (1999) and others have argued that much theorizing on the 'male gaze' is based on a misreading of Lacan, who conceived of the gaze as a fluid rather than fixed process: 'the spectator [is] a subject-in-process, not fixed by the text to a predetermined gender identification, but emerging through a complex interlocking of desires and identifications' (Ahmed, 1990: 173).

Although we might be seeing an increase in 'the representation of masculinity in terms traditionally associated with the representation of femininity' (Adkins, 2002: 63) and that ultimately neither the 'subject' nor the text can be fixed, nevertheless discourses that construct and legitimate masculine superiority/feminine inferiority are still often culturally dominant in societies worldwide and thus have more influence than minority discourses to influence a viewer's interpretation of an image. Foucault saw power not as monolithically imposed, but diffuse throughout the myriad discourses that come into play at any particular time and place (Foucault, 1977). He nevertheless described the ways in which some discourses have more power and dominance than others, due to greater capacities to legitimize themselves through particular 'regimes of truth' (Foucault, 1977; see Rose, 2001). Warlaumont (1993) and others have used the term 'visual grammars' to note 'conventions, or accepted ways of thinking about visual images and composition, which have been sanctioned by general custom and repeated use'

(Warlaumont, 1993: 34). Rutledge Shields (1990) talks more generally of cultural 'ways of seeing', 'culturally imbued codes which are consistent across not only advertising but other visual images as well such as oil painting or portraiture . . . [that help] define what is "natural" to be seen and enjoyed' (p.26). We can see these 'ways of seeing', these 'visual grammars', as particular discourses that are socially and culturally dominant at any one time. This does not preclude the possibility of alternative discourses, nor does it preclude the possibility of alternative interpretations or 'receptions' of texts that are constructed through such dominant discourses. However, it does acknowledge the dominance of particular discourses legitimized through particular 'regimes of truth' such as the conception of photographs as 'real', and the cultural authority of institutions such as the university to sanction and give weight to particular constructions of 'reality'.

The construction and reception of visual texts

In conducting our analysis of these websites, we are therefore conceiving them as 'texts' containing both visual and verbal signifiers, constructed through discourse. As Rose notes, 'discourses are articulated through all sorts of visual and verbal images and texts, specialized or not, and also through the practices that those languages permit' (Rose, 2001: 136).

Taking a post-structuralist view, we argue that the meaning of such texts are not 'fixed' in the texts themselves, but are contextually given meaning by the reader/viewer at the point of interpretation (Barthes, 1977). How, then, can we analyse the gendered construction of texts, if meaning lies with the reader rather than the author? In answer, we would agree with theorists such as Gadamer (1975), Hirsch (1982) and McGann (1983) that while meaning is not fixed until the point of interpretation, nevertheless the 'author/s' of texts can in some ways influence the possibilities in which the text can be read. The meaning constructed by the reader is not purely arbitrary, but is constrained in a number of different ways. First, the reader's interpretation of a text is influenced by her or his own culturally specific way of understanding the world (Gadamer, 1975). This way of understanding is constrained by culturally constructed webs of discourses that are historically and socially specific and which are continually in a process of change (see Foucault, 1981). Moreover, such understanding is not only culturally specific but is deeply influenced by the reader's social positioning and identities within this culture, including their gender. Hence structural aspects continue to impact on the reader/assessor's construction of a text (McGann, 1983; Francis, 2002a). Secondly, interpretation is also constrained to a certain extent by the words or visual images utilized in the text (Iser, 1974), the author's choice of words and technique retaining some impact on the interpretation of the reader (Hirsch, 1982). Thirdly, the construction of meaning is constrained by the socio-cultural discourses that influenced the construction of the texts themselves. Just as the reader's social positioning affects their understanding of the text, the author's social positioning and the wider political and social context surrounding the initial construction of the text impacts on the text's construction (McGann, 1983; Rutledge Shields, 1990; Bal and Bryson, 1991; Francis, 2002a). Thus, the interpretation of a text can never be 'objective' or 'true', but can merely be one of a plurality of interpretations, 'constrained' to a certain extent by the discursive and material positioning of both the author and current reader. As Gadamer (1975) states in relation to reading historical materials from the past, meaning lies in the 'fusion of horizons' between the two (p. 273).

This chapter is concerned with the 'horizon of meaning' constructed by the university – in particular the ways in which the images in university websites aim to influence students' interpretations and constructed meanings as to the life and 'culture' of institutions, and the gendered cultural discourses that infuse these constructions.

Methods

We chose fifteen different university websites to be the focus of this study of visual texts. It was decided to focus on universities in countries where English was the first language, as this is our first language, and we wanted to be able to comprehend any contextualizing textual information alongside the images we were analysing. Also, whilst many universities worldwide offer English translations of some or all of their websites we decided not to include such sites in our analysis, due to our inability to ascertain whether we would be analysing material that would be identical/very similar to that which would simultaneously be on offer to students in the country's first language. For this reason the universities selected are all from the 'West', therefore inevitably constraining our analysis.

The fifteen institutions were purposively selected to include HEIs from different English-speaking countries, and those of varying degrees of 'status', for instance liberal arts colleges (e.g. Alverno College) as well as Ivy League universities (e.g. Harvard, Berkeley) in the US, and pre-1992 universities (e.g. Oxford, University College London, Leicester, Glasgow) as well as post-1992 universities (e.g. Manchester Metropolitan, Middlesex, University of the West of Scotland) in the UK. We also included universities from Ireland, Australia and New Zealand.

The universities chosen are: Alverno College, USA; Glasgow University, UK; Harvard University, USA; Manchester Metropolitan University, UK; Middlesex University, UK; Oxford University, UK; University College Dublin, Ireland; University College London, UK; University of California, Berkeley, USA; University of Canberra, Australia; University of Canterbury, New Zealand; University of Glasgow, UK; University of Leicester, UK; University of Limerick, Ireland; University of Sydney, Australia; University of the West of Scotland, UK.

In analysing such images we have combined a form of discourse analysis (see, for example, Gee, 1999; Cronin, 2000) with a form of content analysis (Weber, 1985; Silverman, 1993; Bell and Milic, 2002).

In conducting a discourse analysis of website images, we have been concerned to look at ways in which particular views of 'reality' are infused in the construction of particular images, and the ways in which these are legitimized as 'true' accounts of 'reality' – particularly in relation to 'masculinity', 'femininity', the construction of the 'student', and the construction of the 'university' itself. As Rose, citing Gill (1996) states: ' "all discourse is organised to make itself persuasive", and discourse analysis focuses on those strategies of persuasion' (Rose, 2001: 140). In doing so we paid attention to several different dimensions of representation, or 'metafunctions', as discussed by Kress and Van Leeuwen (1996) and utilized in a study of gender and advertising by Bell and Milic (2002), although we have explicitly conceptualized them as discursive constructions. This includes taking account of 'representational' aspects such as the narrative processes or ('goings on') and conceptual 'ideas' presented in a particular images; the interaction between the 'viewer' and people presented in the image itself – the 'participants' (for example, issues of 'gaze' and the distance of the 'participant' to the perceived viewer); and the relation with the viewer established through the image (for example, relations of 'social affinity', appeasement or subordination through the averted gaze or through smiling at the viewer) (Bell and Milic, 2002).

In order to gain an understanding of the prevalence of different discursive forms we have also counted the prevalence of certain 'themes' in images – for example, number of men and/or women in images; number of people we have interpreted as 'students' or 'academics' and their gender, visible ethnicity, etc.; and whether such people are presented as smiling, looking directly or away from the camera, etc. However this was designed as a guide to the prevalence of discursive constructions rather than a quantitative analysis – for example we did not quantify or regulate the amount or 'type' of pages on each website to be included. Instead we concentrated on web pages that provided 'general' information for prospective or current students, including home pages, pages outlining general information about the university's history, current facilities, how to apply, etc. We did not include pages that were specifically intended for staff or business 'visitors', or that were subject, discipline, department or college specific. We did not include content of sites constructed by particular individual, or groups of, students or academics. Finally, we also restricted the analysis to still visual images rather than multimedia content.

University web pages: gender and webs of power

Although varying greatly in the overall aesthetic use of colour and font style, and the degree to which they utilized photographic or other visual images, the university websites we visited followed a similar overall setup and navigational format. The home page would give the title of the university in large letters, a logo and/or slogan, generally some links to 'headline' news stories of relevance to the institution, and a list of links to other pages giving information about/virtually 'representing' particular departments, services or subject areas. Some HEIs (especially the 'newer' institutions) specifically catered to the perceived differing 'needs' of different 'types' of visitor, and offered a specific 'way in' or viewing selection for those who were prospective students, current students, members of staff/faculty, or general visitors.

What was immediately striking in the website images was the way in which images of people were utilized. We will first be looking at the ways in which dominant discourses of femininity are articulated through images of white and (sometimes) BME women students – both as a welcoming 'friendly face' to the visitor and as the archetypical 'good student'. We will then go on to contrast these constructions with the ways in which male students are represented in the websites. Next, we will look at the gendered discourses infused in the websites' constructions of the academic, before finishing with a discussion of the 'others' absent and excluded from the 'scene'.

Images of students: the friendly, feminized undergraduate

Dyhouse (2006) describes how universities established in the 1960s in the UK were particularly attractive to women, and women featured heavily in their promotional literature:

> The cover of Warwick University's first students' handbook, in 1966, featured a wistful-looking blonde in a mini-skirt leaning against a sign-post in a rural setting, the signpost marked simply 'university'. . . . A series of articles on new universities in the newspaper Student Life included a piece on East Anglia (March 1968) illustrated with a photo-graph of three long-haired girls with high boots and even higher hemlines descending steps near the library. . . . The 'dollybird' was effectively part of the branding image of the new university. (p. 100)

Fashions may have changed, and representations may have become more multicultural than in the 1960s. However, as we shall see, in other respects, the marketing campaigns of 'new' universities in the brochures and news-papers of the 1960s seem very similar to the promotional materials on the internet today, in institutions old and new, and in different areas of the world. At first glance, the university as depicted in the websites we studied seems very much a feminized space. Women students are everywhere in the images presented on HEI webpages – sitting chatting with friends on campus lawns; working studiously in libraries; sitting in lectures or conducting alarming-looking experiments in laboratories that require sanitized plastic gloves, white coats and safety goggles. And although the majority are white women, there are also some pictures of women of different ethnicities happily interacting with each other at 'work' and at 'play' (more prevalent in some institutional sites than others, as will be discussed further below). Men students are also featured, but somehow the eye is drawn to the smiling women in the pictures – young, happy, conventionally attractive women that are not only smiling at other people in the photographs, or smiling dreamily into the distance or at others off-camera, but are also often smiling directly at us – the visiting viewer.

These patterns in the gendered representations of students can be seen simply in a comparison of the home pages of the websites we looked at. The majority of the university websites contained one or more pictures of men or women intended to represent students at their institution – either in prominent poses in large, central photographs (e.g. Paisley, Glasgow, Canberra, Middlesex); in large images that rotate with others when the viewer refreshes the page (e.g. Leicester, UCD) or in smaller 'box' photographs or illustrations of news items (e.g. Sydney, Harvard, Canterbury, Berkeley, Limerick, Manchester Metropolitan, Alverno). University College London and Oxford were the only universities not to feature representations of people on their home pages.

Most of the front pages that included pictures of people showed images of both men and women (sometimes together, sometimes separate) – the exceptions being Harvard, Canberra University and Alverno College. The latter, an all-women college, used a bank of refreshing artworks of women of a variety of different ethnicities. Harvard University has pictures of staff (illustrating news items) rather than students. Canberra University focuses on a single photograph of a white woman with long blonde hair, in graduation dress, raising her arms and clenching her fists in a triumphant gesture and smiling widely with happiness. A slogan accompanying the picture says simply 'Ready Steady Go'.

In this and many other sites women, and to a lesser degree, men, are prominently represented in the home pages as frontispiece representations of (what they would like to present as) the institution's 'typical' student. In doing so the institutions are not only aiming to present an idealized image that prospective students would like to emulate – they are also aiming to present, through these figurative images, a signifier of the university itself as an institution. And at first glance this signifier seems very much a feminized one.

For example, let's look at the images presented on the home page of University College Dublin (Figure 5.1). Five different images are presented in rotation every time the viewer refreshes or returns to the page:

1 A white man is talking to a white woman over a table, with what looks to be an x-ray in the background. He is talking (shown by his gesticulating hand gesture), she is listening. He is a bit older, in shirt and tie. She is young, with a brown bob, wearing glasses, and is smiling at him. From the age difference and the structure of listening it is reasonable to imply this is meant to be represent a man lecturer and a woman student.

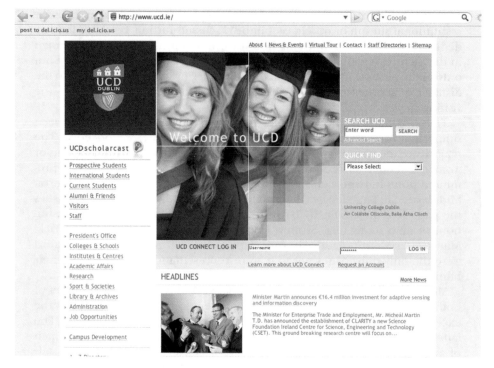

Figure 5.1 University College Dublin, 'Welcome to UCD, Ireland's education capital'
(The insert image features 2007 graduates from the Honours Degree of
Bachelor of Veterinary Science, University College Dublin, Ireland)

Source: Provided with the permission of University College Dublin © University College Dublin

2   A group of four young white women, all very pretty, all with long hair, two
    blonde, two brunette, in academic gowns for graduation, but also very
    clearly in 'feminine' party clothes. All are smiling widely.
3   Another picture of young women graduates in graduation robes – again
    they are all white, long haired, pretty, smiling.
4   A very modern white building with black glass windows, shot in the
    sunshine.
5   A young white man playing rugby with other players behind him. He is
    holding the ball and is running athletically with a very determined look
    on his face. Behind him one player from the other team is falling to the
    ground, presumably having failed to tackle him, and another player has
    come to a standstill looking at him in dismay. (University College Dublin,
    'Welcome to UCD, Ireland's Education Capital', 29 Apr. 2008, http://
    www.ucd.ie/).

As we can see from the descriptions above, women are prominently
featured in the rotational images as representations of the 'typical' student
and as representations of the university itself. The two groups of women in

graduation gowns represent students who have successfully accomplished what the institution has asked of them, and the institution has given them its 'seal of approval', symbolized (both in the picture and of course in the graduation ceremony itself) by the hats and gowns that all the women are wearing. The work they have done to accomplish this is symbolized by the first picture, where another smiling woman student listens to a man lecturer talking, and indicates her accommodation and lack of challenge by her smile and the body language that shows she is listening. In all cases, the women students are representing smiling acquiescence and accommodation to the institution itself as knowledge giver and prize awarder. As we shall see further in the next chapter, such aspects of the institution and its hegemonic position in relation to the student are not feminized or even neutral, but are actually *masculinized* in a variety of ways. The men students in the final picture lie outside this power dynamic, playing a game in which the central man in the photograph is represented as holding power through physical activity that gains him award/recognition without acquiescence (except, presumably, through acquiescing to the rules of the game itself). We will be looking at such representations of masculinity in more detail later in this chapter.

The women students, then, arguably represent a 'student body' that is disciplined and rewarded, rather than the power of the institution as knowledge giver. However, the woman student also signifies the institution in another way – by representing the institution's friendly and welcoming 'character'. As Rasmussen (2001), Tyler and Taylor (2001) and many others have discussed, culturally dominant discourses concerning the 'naturally' greater ability of women to 'care' for and 'empathize' with customers and clients have led to commercial and public institutions disproportionately hiring women in frontline service positions catering to the general public. Gustavsson and Czarniawska (2004) note the increasing trend for companies and institutions to utilize 'virtual' simulations of customer service people to help guide 'visitors' around their websites: by far the majority of these 'avatar' people are constructed as young, conventionally attractive women, who possess knowledge that will be of use to the visitor, whilst also acting as 'unthreatening' and subordinate to them. It could be argued that in some ways the representation of the female 'student' in the university websites we looked at occupy a similar role – they 'embody' the 'friendly' 'welcoming' qualities that the university wishes to portray about its institution, and imply that they (or others just like them) will guide and help the prospective student to fit in and feel comfortable and happy in a new and strange environment, in a way that does not 'emasculate', threaten or subordinate the (male or female) viewer.

Women represent these qualities in the websites we looked at through their overwhelming presentation as young and conventionally attractive. The women students shown are nearly always slim, pretty, with long hair and make-up – characteristics associated with culturally prevalent conceptions of femininity as passive, unthreatening and constructed for the heterosexual male gaze. This accommodation to the viewer is also signified through the smiles that the majority of the women wear in these photographs – a feature noted by Goffman (1979). Similarly, White (2006) found that women were often presented in photographs as smiling in websites marketing computer technologies.

The prevalence of such images is detailed below, in a content analysis that looked at: the number of photographs of men and women students in the home pages of our sample institutions; whether they are presented singly or in groups; and whether the men and women are smiling (either to others or towards the camera). We did not include Alverno College in this piece of analysis as it is a women-only college and could unduly skew the findings. We also did not include people we identified as lecturers, visitors or other members of the non-student body, crowds, and other pictures of people viewed from a distance where their features are not distinguishable.

We found that whilst men and women students are both commonly presented, women students are far more numerous, and are much more likely to be smiling or laughing.

Overall on the home pages of the institutions in our study, the majority of the 54 students are white – 39 of 54 students, with minority groups more likely to be represented by South or East Asian students rather than those of African heritage. They are also much more likely to be women – 33 to 21. Moreover, 23 out of 33 women are seen to be smiling, compared to only 8 out of the 21 men. Both men and women students were mainly presented in group photos, although those presented on their own are more often women – six women compared to three men (with one of these pictures being a small news item, and another the back of an anonymous man in graduation robes).

Many of the women students in these pictures can arguably be seen to act as friendly welcoming 'guides' to the viewer in a number of different ways. First, although slightly over half of the pictures of both men and women are looking directly at the viewer (thus supporting Bell and Milic's 2002 finding), the women are smiling at the viewer in nearly all of these 'direct gaze' pictures, compared to only half of the 'direct gaze' pictures of men.

Moreover, in some of these photographs the students are presented more directly as guides. Some websites present unnamed figures presented as students who could theoretically 'answer' the viewer's questions. For example the University of the West of Scotland presents 8 students in a banner photo. There are equal numbers of men and women, whilst six of the eight are white. Three out of the four of the women are smiling. None of the men are, although the barest whisper of a smile can be detected in one of the men's faces. All of them are looking directly at the camera, and a piece of text runs over the picture stating 'An inspired choice. Ask our students'. On another site, Middlesex, the main photograph is a striking image of a young minority ethnic man looking determinedly in the distance, with the accompanying text 'Fast Track Your Career. Postgraduate Open Evenings. Book Now' (Figure 5.2). As we go on to outline in Chapter 6, students are increasingly

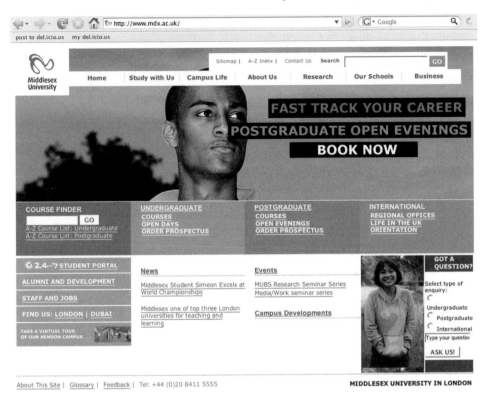

Figure 5.2 Middlesex University, "Middlesex University – Homepage," 29 Apr. 2008, <http://www.mdx.ac.uk/>

Source: Provided with the permission of Middlesex University. © Middlesex University

expected to acquire the 'skills' deemed necessary for the workplace, and these skills are complexly gendered. The man in the image can be seen to represent the culturally masculinized skills of drive and determination that the ideal prospective student is encouraged to emulate by booking a place on one of their courses. However, unlike many images of women in the sites, his unsmiling features and the direction of his gaze suggests he is not acting as a welcoming guide for the viewer. This role is explicitly taken by another image. Below the banner photo is a smaller boxed photograph of a smiling young East Asian woman who is wearing a sweatshirt with a question mark drawn on it. Next to the photograph is a piece of text stating 'Got a question?' and a dialogue box for the visitor to type their enquiry into, once they have clicked the cheery 'Ask us!' button. Other websites have profiled specific named students on particular web pages who explicitly act as guides by giving the viewer information about particular aspects of the student experience. The University of Canterbury for example presents an image of a Maori woman student on the home page. She too is looking directly at the camera and smiling (albeit a small smile in this instance).

Again, in these photographs of explicit 'guides', the gender differences in smiling at the viewer are striking – women are smiling in nearly all of the images (5 out of 6) whereas none of the men are (0 of 4 images). Similarly, the multi-ethnic character of these 'avatar' women students helps both to present the university as diverse and multicultural in a 'safe', unthreatening and depoliticized way to the (white) viewer, a trait Stuart Hall and others have discussed as common in contemporary visual representations of blackness (Hill Collins, 1990; Hall, 1996; see also Lazar, 2006 for the depoliticized appropriation of feminist discourses in advertising). As Mirza (2006b: 103) notes, 'diversity' in university advertising is 'skin-deep':

> We find that people of different ethnicities are celebrated in colourful brochures with smiling 'brown' faces – like a box of chocolates. There is often one from every continent and one of every colour: Chinese, African, Indian. Black women often find themselves appropriated, their bodies objectified and commodified for the 'desiring machine' of capital.

The construction of women students as 'guides' to the viewer thus presents a complex gendering of the image at the moment of construction, which then works to 'constrain' the possible ways in which such images are interpreted. The viewer may often not be (or even explicitly intended to be) male, nevertheless it is possible to see the ways in which culturally dominant discourses of the 'passive', 'submissive', 'friendly' feminine infuse such representations of the woman student as 'guide', in an unequal power relation between 'viewer' and 'viewed' that is highly gendered. The continued construction of the feminine in relation to the (more authoritative) masculine can also be seen in images of the 'good' woman student, in relation to the masculinized construction of the 'university' itself.

Images of students: the 'good' feminized student and the masculinized 'tradition' of the university

The preponderance of women students (especially smiling women students) is replicated in the other pages of the websites we studied – in nearly every website we noted more pictures of women students than men students, either singly or in groups. Moreover, there were also more women than men students pictured diligently working, undergoing activities seen as 'typical' to the apprentice academic – sitting on a bench or lying on the lawn reading a book; working at a desk or in the library, with reams of papers scattered around; listening intently in one of the tiered rows of a lecture hall.

As we shall see, such images often combine the 'modern/ inexperienced/ feminized' (the young 'feminine' woman student, wearing make-up and/or bright or fashionable clothes) with a symbol of 'tradition/ experience' that symbolizes the 'university' in the popular cultural imagination, and which hark back to an age when academia was far more masculinized in terms of its student body.

For example Harvard, Oxford, Berkeley, Glasgow and many other 'older' universities in the sample utilize many images of the architecture of the buildings on their campuses in order to present an image of themselves as a prestigious academic institution and the gatekeeper and producer of cultural knowledge. This includes many shots of neoclassical columns, pale white or golden sandstone stately buildings, gleaming spires, turrets and bell towers, neogothic or neoclassical cloisters and archways. Students are often depicted in juxtaposition to the architecture – as little points of colour on a wide shot of a lawn or a square; sitting on steps talking animatedly and smiling with other students; striding purposefully past with papers in their hands towards a lecture hall. Such architecture symbolizes wealth, prestige, and knowledge – indeed, many older universities utilized neoclassical architecture in order to explicitly link themselves with the power and learning of classical Greece – itself the starting point for modern western 'Enlightenment' thought (see, for example, Costello 2001). As we have already discussed in Chapter 2, the binarism of this epistemology often equates rationality and knowledge with the masculine; and in the case of the university, as we have outlined, the neoclassical buildings literally only housed men academics and students within its walls until the nineteenth and twentieth centuries. Such patriarchal dominance is not only indirectly represented by historical architecture but also figuratively or lexically represented by portrait paintings, archival collections, dedicated wings and colleges, and statues to previous male historical benefactors and alumni.

However, as we have noted, women are very much physically present and visible as students in the institutions of the twenty-first century – and often representations of women combine elements of the 'old' and the 'new', the 'masculine' and the 'feminine' in one single image.

For example, on Harvard's 'Visiting Undergraduate Student' page, a white or possibly East Asian woman can be seen, slightly out of focus, sitting at the top of some white stone steps. She is wearing a casual black top and jeans, and looks like she has her dark hair tied back in a pony tail. She is reading what looks to be some papers which rest on her lap. Directly behind her is a single white neoclassical column, and juxtaposed with the column is a beautiful tree behind the building in autumn reds and yellows. No one else is pictured and it looks like the student has successfully found a solitary place to study. Thus several binaries are in play in this image at once – the young (feminized) student and the ageless (masculinized) architecture; apprentice (knowledge-receiver) and institution (knowledge giver); past and present; life and colour (the tree) and death and sobriety (the stone).

Such juxtapositions are also sometimes explicitly used when representing images of minority ethnic students. For example, in a section that asks 'What kind of student goes to Oxford?' a young pretty African-Caribbean woman with a white top and pink cardigan is pictured sitting in a library, smiling widely, with an old hardback book open in front of her. She has a pen in her hand and it looks like we have arrived while she is making notes. A pile of similar hardback books teeter in the foreground, slightly obscuring the student; behind her lie rows and rows of what look like old bound hardback journals in large old wooden stack bookcases. Thus again we have a juxtaposition of the discourses of old and 'traditional' in the form of the aged bound books in old wooden bookcases with the young and 'non-traditional' to the university in the form of the minority ethnic woman student. The student's 'otherness' in terms of both gender and ethnicity is made unthreatening by her 'emphasised femininity' (Connell, 1987) in terms of dress and 'conventional' attractiveness, and by her smile – similar to Hill Collins's de-politicized smiling 'Aunt Jemimas' described above.

Another common juxtaposition in the websites, especially in universities whose architecture does not lend itself to the 'dreaming spires' archetypal image of the university, is to juxtapose the (more often female) student with high-tech, futuristic architecture or surroundings. Feminists in the fields of social geography and architecture have extensively explored the culturally dominant association of the architecture of urban 'public' buildings with the 'masculine', in contrast to the 'private', suburban, domestic sphere of the 'feminine' (Weisman, 1994; Rendell et al., 2003). Such 'futuristic' architectural images are also masculinized by the popular cultural association of science and technology with the masculine (Hekman, 1990; Harding, 1991).

Interestingly, Middlesex University also has pictures of students outside particular London landmarks such as the Millennium Bridge, and it also pictures an Asian man student outside the British Library – providing a signifier culturally associated with tradition, prestige and learning in a way that perhaps cannot as easily be constructed by images of the institution's 'newer' (yet not 'futuristic' enough?) architecture.

And what subjects are these students studying? In most cases it is hard to determine (although on one page on the Oxford website a smiling young woman student is pictured leaning on a windowsill of an old stone building or cloister, reading a book about Descartes, with other textbooks posed around her). However, students studying science and technology can be identified by the equipment they are using and their distinctive dress (lab coats, protective goggles, etc). As we shall be exploring further in Chapter 9, the sciences have been perceived as a particularly masculinized arena, and one where there are still far greater numbers of men than women students enrolling, especially in the 'hard' sciences such as physics and chemistry, and in disciplines such as engineering. However, this gender imbalance is not perceptible in the images of science students in the websites in our sample. Indeed, following the general pattern of the visibility of women students in the website images in our sample, there are almost three times as many images of women as men identifiably studying the sciences by their dress and/or the equipment they are utilizing (16 images of women compared to 6 images of men). There is also a distinct lack of African Caribbean students in the images. By far the majority of the students (16 of the 22) are white, and 6 of the students are South or

East Asian (all women). Only Harvard has an image of an African Caribbean student (a man) pictured with scientific equipment.

The images of the science students do in some ways challenge dominant cultural discourses about the 'masculinity' of science, and indeed often portray women in a less 'hyper-feminine' way – the women are rarely looking at the camera or smiling, and are much less likely to be wearing make-up or bright, fashionable clothes, as in many of the representations described in detail above. Leicester University stands out particularly in this regard. One of their student profiles is of an Indian woman research student, pictured in non-Western dress, who is studying Engineering, one of the most 'masculinized' of subjects in terms of recruitment (and 'culture') (see e.g. Powell et al., 2006). Also, one of Leicester's home page 'rotating' images (randomly appearing in rotation each time the viewer refreshes the page) shows a student who is possibly of European and/or Asian origin looking directly and purposefully at the camera, unsmiling. She has scraped back hair, no perceivable make-up and safety goggles, and is wearing a white coat (we also see she is wearing white pearl nail varnish, leather wristbands and a chunky ring). She is pictured sitting next to a piece of scientific equipment and is holding what looks to be a metal plate towards the camera. On another page this image is repeated, with the banner text 'Research That Changes the World'. Unlike the somewhat passive images of smiling, 'hyper-feminine' young women students who present the university as a friendly and accessible space, students such as this scientist are presented as actively 'producing' knowledge – indeed knowledge that can 'change the world'.

However such images are rare, and indeed in several of the images women science students are actually depicted as under the tutelage of men lecturers, as seen in an image on the University College Dublin site (one of the home page images described earlier), on the Berkeley site and two separate images on the Harvard site. Only in the Canterbury site do we see a woman student taught a science subject by a woman lecturer. And in none of the pictures of men science students do we see instruction by lecturing staff. These are obviously very small numbers and can do no more than indicate a possible gendered and racialized pattern in the construction and utilization of images of science students. However, the greater number of women students being taught by lecturers, and the greater number of men than women lecturers, is a small yet perceivable pattern that is replicated in general images of the lecturer/student dynamic on other pages, which we will go on to look at below.

Images of students: the 'active' man student

First of all though, we turn to the ways in which images of men students are constructed in these websites. Although women students are more numerous than men, a sizeable number of pictures of men students can be found on the websites. In many ways the depictions of men students are very similar to the depictions of women students – men are also depicted sitting reading books or walking around campus, conducting experiments or listening to lecturers in a lecture hall. As we have noted though, one of the ways in which depictions of men students arguably differ is the degree to which they are shown to be smiling, either to other students or towards the camera. As we have mentioned, they are much less likely to be positioned as a 'guide' figure.

They are, however, slightly more likely than women to be presented playing sports or other physical activities, which is quite striking when you consider that there are sizeably fewer representations of men students than women students in these website images. A large variety of sports are pictured: squash, martial arts, athletics, cycling, American Football, and the most popular sport (especially in the Irish, Australian and New Zealand universities), rugby. Interestingly, one of the most popular sports for men outside of the USA, football/soccer, does not feature at all in images. In terms of the images from the UK sites this exclusion could possibly relate to the way in which academic culture is classed, as football/soccer has associations with working-class culture in the UK in comparison to the association of rugby with the middle classes, although these associations are not held in most other countries. In Manchester Metropolitan's website, however, there is one picture of two white men dressed in what looks like football kit, sitting at a table and laughing with each other, emphasizing the social nature of such sports activities in these representations. Most of the sports activities played by men in these images are team sports. In the University of the West of Scotland's site there are also two separate images of men students gathered together playing pool.

Women are also regularly shown in a sports context, although in proportional terms they are much less likely to be shown playing sport than men. They are also more often presented in solo sports activities such as swimming or gym activities rather than competitive sports. A few exceptions are noticeable, however – Limerick in particular depicts women playing a wide range of sports including basketball, and features a woman throwing a javelin in an image on its home page. Also Berkeley and Alverno, (the only women's college in the study) also depict women playing numerous sports and women athletes proudly showing their medals.

However, in contrast to the dominance of images of women in the roles of 'guide' or 'industrious student', the association of men students with physical activity is interesting. Not only does it relate to dominant cultural associations of the masculine with activity, especially physical activity, it also shows men performing in an environment where they are acting as equals (competing only with themselves or other peer team mates) rather than subordinates. For women the roles of 'guide' or 'student' are both subordinate ones – the former to the wishes or needs of the 'visitor', the latter to the superior knowledge and authority of the lecturer and the institution itself. As we have already noted, many of the cultural archetypical images of the 'university' – the 'dreaming spires', the old buildings, books and monuments, are associated with the 'traditional' construction of knowledge as masculine.

As we shall see in the next section, this can also be seen in the depictions of academic *staff* in the sites.

Representations of the academic

Academic staff are pictured much less frequently on the 'general' pages of the websites designed for prospective or current students and visitors to the university. Where they do appear it is generally in one of three formats – as illustrations to featured news items; in specially drafted 'profiles' (in much the same way as the student profiles discussed earlier) and, most frequently, in generic anonymous images utilized in boxed photographs and banner/headers to pages illustrating academic life at the institution in question, particularly a tutorial with students or lecturing in a lecture hall.

Interestingly, in contrast to the numerical dominance of women students in the website images, there are twice as many men than women lecturers and researchers in the pages we analysed (33 pictures to 16). They featured predominantly in the 'older', more prestigious universities – some of the 'newer' universities, such as the University of the West of Scotland, Alverno College, Canberra and Limerick featured few or no academic staff (however, neither did University College London). The vast majority of the academics were also white. Moreover, especially in the prestigious Oxford and Harvard Universities, when a man lecturer is pictured with a student, the student was most often a woman. Eight men academics were depicted with women students (compared to two with men students, and one with a mixed group), including the following images:

> A young white woman who looks to be in an individual tutorial with a white male lecturer. She is sitting on a grey sofa talking to him, gesticulating. Behind her is a wall full of books. He is not looking at her but is looking at her work.
> University of Oxford, 'Studying at Oxford: An Introduction – University of Oxford', 29 April, 2008, (<www.ox.ac.uk/about_the_university/introducing_oxford/studying_at_oxford_an_introduction/index.html>, accessed 29 April, 2008)

> A young pretty white woman who is talking animatedly to a white man, in his 30s or 40s, who looks like he is listening to her, but is not looking at her. The image is cropped to show just their upper bodies, but it looks like he might be perching on a desk. She is holding the paper but somehow you know it is his office. The office is a typical 'old school' academic office with wooden furniture and lots of books on the bookcases behind them.
> (University of Oxford, "Interviews at Oxford – University of Oxford", 29 Apr. 2008, <http://www.ox.ac.uk/admissions/undergraduate_courses/how-to-apply/interviews/.)

Both these images present a particular activity that epitomizes the unequal power relation between lecturer and student, that of the lecturer judging or evaluating the student's work (or possibly, if the second image represents an interview, her entire suitability to enter higher education). The greater authority of the lecturer to assess the work of the student is implied by the interior space of the room: both spaces seem to be the lecturer's office, and both have bookcases full of books which work to legitimize a reading of the lecturer as holding greater social and cultural capital in terms of knowledge and prestige. Such constructions are obviously gendered through the embodiment of the lecturer as male and the student as female. Also, interestingly, in both cases the student is looking at the lecturer, whilst the lecturer (the figure with the most 'power') is looking away from the student. This stands in contrast to a relation more often discussed by 'gaze theorists', whereby a (male) authority figure articulates his authority by gazing directly at a (female) object. In these cases the gaze of the figures is reversed, yet the dynamic of the gendered power relation remains the same.

The repeated binary of the male lecturer and female student in these pages crystallzes and distils a general pattern in these pages of the prevalence of women in images of the (subordinate) student, and of men in images of the (authoritative) faculty. In contrast, when women academics featured, they were depicted with both men and women students equally. They were also more likely to be depicted in news items or specific profiles, such as the following from Harvard and Leicester, challenging the conception of science, and particularly Engineering, as an overwhelmingly masculinized space:

> Photograph of Joanna Aizenberg, Professor, long dark hair, smiling, in front of an old-style chalkboard full of scribbles. If you click on the link you find an article headed 'Finding ingenious design in nature: Joanna Aizenberg combs the beach for engineering marvels'.
> (<http://www.harvard.edu>, accessed 24 February, 2008)

> A profile of Prof Helen Atkinson, professor of Engineering, features her in a black and white photograph, in front of a bookcase, with hands gesticulating as if she is in the middle of an academic conversation.
> (<http://www.le.ac.uk>, accessed 19 March, 2008)

In both cases it is women academics, both scientists, who are presented in association with images of 'traditional' learning (the chalkboard, the familiar bookcase of books) that aim to legitimize their 'authority'. However, by far the majority of pictures of academics in these pages are generalized, generic images rather than specific profiles or news items, and it is these images that are even more polarized in terms of gender – 26 pictures of men academics as opposed to 9 pictures of women academics. Also, only 3 male academics and 1 woman academic were visibly from minority ethnic groups (three South Asian, one of African origin), although one university does show a mature white man and a mature African-Caribbean working with a medical dummy – either or both of whom could be lecturers). Thus the pictures work to (re)construct and legitimate a conception of the apprentice subordinate student as feminized, and the superior authoritative knowledge-giving faculty/institution as masculinized, and overwhelmingly white.

The 'negated' other

What is missing from these scenes? As well as lesser degrees of men students and women lecturers, there are others who are almost completely missing – like the (possible) African-Caribbean lecturer in the last section working on the dummy, we are not sure if we have seen them or not. As Cronin notes, just out of sight of the presented images of advertising lies those 'others' that flicker tantalizingly out of focus, at the border of the picture (Cronin, 2000). In these websites, as well as minority ethnic lecturers, there are many 'other' students that seem to be excluded from the 'picture' represented in these university websites.

First of all, despite some variation in terms of ethnicity (particularly in the Berkeley, Alverno, Leicester, Glasgow and Middlesex University sites) the majority of students presented in the pictures are white. African-Caribbean men are particularly marginalized in the pictures, with the exception of Middlesex University, an institution based in North London with a large proportion of BME students. Also virtually absent in the websites were visibly gay students; visibly disabled students; mature students; conventionally 'unattractive' students; physically 'larger' students; upset, angry or emotionally vulnerable students. As we have seen, by far the vast majority of students presented in the websites we visited were young, slim, conventionally attractive, with mid- or long-length hair if they are women, and short hair if they are men; able-bodied; wearing Western and 'gender-appropriate' dress.

We do catch an occasional glimpse of these 'others'. For example, Oxford has one photograph of a woman student reading a book who could be seen as 'overweight' by Western standards, however she is still young and attractive, wearing make-up and a hair accessory. One of the Leicester students who is profiled is 'larger' in size, as is one man student in a small photograph sitting with another man and a woman in a dormitory in Glasgow University. There are occasional pictures of people in their mid-20s or older who are probably students, looking at books in the library (Oxford), and on the 'Undergraduate Program' page at Harvard there is a picture of a more mature woman with short hair and glasses, laughing. Oxford and Glasgow have some profiles of mature students, and Glasgow also has a photo of some students in wheelchairs in a section about disabled students. It is also rare to see students in clothes other than Western dress (that are not part of a special ceremony or 'event'). As mentioned above, Leicester University profiles an Asian Engineering research student who is wearing a sari. Middlesex University also has a number of pictures of students helping out on open day activities, some of whom are wearing hijab.

Also hard to spot are identifiably gay students, although Berkeley does have a dedicated section on Lesbian, gay, bisexual and transgender (LGBT) student activities. Manchester Metropolitan University has a photograph of some men sitting on tables outside a bar on Canal Street. The text does not explicitly say that Canal Street is an area with numerous gay pubs and bars, although this is something that would be instantly known by many LGBT people worldwide, who are used to 'reading between the lines' of heterocentric information. Epstein and colleagues (2003) note how universities in cities with a strong queer culture or presence may be particularly attractive to queer students, although parents may well react differently and negatively to a university that explicitly markets itself as such.

Neither do we see many photographs of students taking part in political or 'alternative' social activities: Glasgow has one photograph of a student demonstration, and Canterbury and Berkeley have profiles on environmental groups and activities. The latter also includes photographs of past demonstrations in illustrating the institution's history. Alverno College also provides a contrast in that it is the only institution specifically targeting women students. Its promotional images include a variety of beautiful artworks painted by women artists, depicting women of a variety of different ethnicities (Figure 5.3). These are accompanied by text that seems to present a 'challenge' to the dominant cultural association of femininity with passivity – the women mostly look directly at the viewer with a strong, unsmiling gaze, and are accompanied by text comments such as 'Dream big', 'Never settle, 'Free. To become anything', and 'The world needs strong women'. However this site was the exception – most sites relied predominantly on photographic images, predominantly stylized 'generic' shots by professional marketing experts, with predominantly young, attractive men and (smiling) women.

Occasionally even within this format, there were some photographs that 'broke the mould'. An image that stands out is from the University of the West of Scotland's site. On the 'Apply' page for international students is a generic photograph that stands out because the students look like 'real' students in a candid shot, rather than handpicked students that have been professionally photographed. It is a group shot of four white students, all smiling at the camera. On the far left is a young man with short hair, glasses, thin with white shirt and beads round his neck. Next to him is a mature woman with dyed orangey-brown long hair. To the right of her is a smaller woman with long blonde hair, and finally a young man in a red top and short dark hair.

Such 'candid' shots are also more common on the websites of Limerick, Alverno and Canterbury universities, which also, not coincidentally, have a higher proportion of images of women that do not fit the predominant mould – some have shorter hair, little or no make-up, are older or larger, or are throwing javelins as well as smiling passively at the viewer.

It seems therefore that the less websites relied on stylized professional shots, the more diverse and challenging their images were. This is reinforced

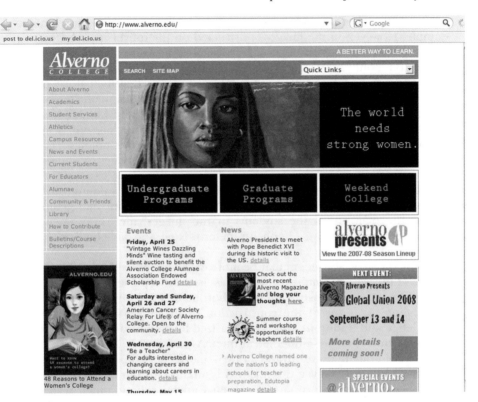

Figure 5.3 Alverno College, Wisconsin Women's Liberal Arts College

Source: Provided with the permission of Alverno College © Alverno College

by the finding that women academic staff were visible more in the 'news items' and specific profiles than they were in standard generic marketing shots. This highlights the problematics of utilizing seemingly apolitical website designers and marketing; such images are riddled with dominant cultural discourses of the accessible/friendly/feminine student and the traditional/powerful masculinized faculty.

Conclusion

This chapter has examined the gendered discourses that infuse cultural representations of the 'university' in institutional websites. We have focused particularly on the representations of women and men students and academics in order to explore the ways in which such sites construct an image of the university as both 'feminized' in terms of its student body, and 'masculinized' in terms of both the academic body and the culture of the academy itself.

As we have outlined in Chapter 3, women students *are* slightly in the majority in terms of undergraduate numbers in the countries we have used in our sample. However, in the images constructed on the university websites, this slight numerical majority is exaggerated, so that women students are far more commonly represented than men. This could be interpreted as an indication of the feminization of the 'ideal' student – that the culture of the academy is increasingly feminized, and that conceptions of the successful student are now typically embodied in the image of the woman student. However, as we have seen, women students are often represented in the position of (passive, subordinate) learner in relation to the 'timeless', masculinized construction of the university itself. Moreover, images of women students are often constructed in a passive, 'unthreatening' way to act as friendly welcoming 'guides' to the prospective (male or female) student. Students that do not fit the 'mould' of the 'ideal' or 'good' student are marginalized – by far the majority of the students in the images, men or women, are white, young, 'attractive', implicitly heterosexual and able-bodied, happy and smiling.

While the 'typical' student may be more often embodied in the (idealized) image of the woman student, nevertheless in these representations 'femininity' continues to be constructed in a subordinate, passive relationship to the 'masculine' in terms of the construction of the university and academic knowledge and tradition. This is emphasized by the prevalence of images of the 'academic' that are embodied as men. As we have already described, the majority of academics worldwide *are* men, particularly those in more secure, senior positions. However, this majority is inflated further in the representations by the far higher proportion of men academics than women academics in the images. Moreover, men academics are also often juxtaposed with women students, emphasizing the gendered dichotomy of 'learner' and 'learned', of the apprentice entrant to academia and the culture of the academy itself.

As we have outlined above, we see the construction and reception of such images as a complex process with the 'meaning' of images not fixed either completely at the moment of production or at the moment of 'viewing', but a 'fusion of horizons' between the two. Whilst this allows for the disruption and subversion of intended meanings, nevertheless it is possible to 'unpick' the ways in which culturally dominant discourses of gender and academic knowledge work to influence interpretations of the images by the viewer, and in doing so work to reinforce and reproduce the construction of the university *itself* as a masculinized space. Women can now enter; they will not be barred by beadles like Woolf's character in 1929. Indeed they may be seen in some ways as the archetypical 'good' student. Yet, the culture and traditions of the academy remain culturally constructed as masculine.

6

Student identities, femininities and masculinities

In this chapter we explore changing constructions of the university student in the context of the reconfiguration of both higher education and gender relations, with a particular focus on how these constructions are gendered. It is, of course, no surprise that the university student has traditionally been seen as a masculine subject, given the total dominance of men, as both students and academic staff, for most of the history of higher education across the world. But given the rapid increase in the proportion of women students at undergraduate level in many countries, we consider whether such traditional notions of the student retain any relevance in the contemporary field of higher education, and ask whether the university student might now more fittingly be considered as a feminized, and feminine, subject.

Constructing the university student

Traditional constructions of the university student in the West are rooted in longstanding conceptualizations of the individual in Western philosophy. As Pateman demonstrated, in the work of social contract theorists (Locke, Rousseau and others) on the founding of the liberal state, only men were deemed to be individuals: 'Only masculine beings are endowed with the attributes and capacities necessary to enter into contracts, the most important of which is ownership of property in the person; only men, that is to say, are "individuals"' (Pateman, 1988: 5–6). Such individuals were assumed to be free and equal – and to inhabit the realm of reason, an arena from which women were excluded. Lloyd (1984) has shown how throughout the history of Western philosophy from the Ancient Greeks onwards, men have been associated with reason, and women with nature: 'our ideals of Reason have historically incorporated an exclusion of the feminine, and . . . femininity itself has been partly constituted through such processes of exclusion' (Lloyd, 1984: x). Within this philosophical tradition, reason is achieved by transcending, leaving behind and/or controlling nature and it is concerned, argues Lloyd, not only with the production of 'truth', but also with what constitutes 'a good person' (p. ix). The male/reason/superior and female/nature/inferior binary has a long lineage, and is also classed and racialized.

Women were, therefore, excluded from the realm of academia, and traditional constructions of the university student were male – both materially and conceptually. Mazon (2003: 1, original emphasis) notes that 'In nineteenth-century Germany the idea of a female university student, or *Studentin*, was so improbable as to be a source of amusement', with plays, cartoons and so on illustrating how ludicrous and humorous such a notion was through the depiction of women taking part in the boisterous male student lifestyle. Mazon's summary of the main arguments against women's entry to university in Germany could be translated to many other countries: that women do not have the intellectual ability; that the entry of women would lead to a fall in standards; that a university degree would be wasted on women who subsequently marry; and a fear that women graduates would compete with men in the graduate labour market. Indeed some of these concerns are also evident, as has been seen in Chapter 2, in contemporary discourses of feminization.

A further aspect relates to the notion of 'academic citizenship' which, although specific to the German context, also has some parallels elsewhere. Drawing on her analysis of three nineteenth-century student handbooks, Mazon discusses five aspects of academic citizenship and the ways in which these are gendered. First, she discusses the achievement of maturity – of the boy becoming a man through independence from his family, something that was, at the time, unthinkable for a woman. For women, maturity meant the moving from one family into another through marriage and child-bearing. Secondly, and related to the first, is the notion of academic freedom, which referred to the right of professors to teach what they wanted, and the right of students to attend whatever classes they chose. But associated with this was also freedom from family constraints and sexual mores relating to the young man's growing independence, often displayed through boisterous and rowdy student behaviour – again this was unthinkable for women. Mazon cites Paulson who asserted that 'The university years are the test of whether inside the young person there is a man' and argued that the university was a 'school of self-reliance' where the student had to learn 'the difficult art of ruling himself' (Paulsen, 1899, cited by Mazon, 2003: 19). The third aspect of academic citizenship discussed by Mazon is that of student honour, which was regarded as a key value determined by 'courage, independence and truthfulness' (Paulsen, 1899, cited by Mazon, 2003: 35). Duels were fought to defend honour, and Mazon argues that it 'was highly masculine because of its origins in male physical prowess; both readiness to defend oneself and then taking action were crucial' (Mazon, 2003: 35). In contrast, honour for women was about chastity and fidelity. The task of studying and undertaking intellectual work is the fourth element of academic citizenship Mazon discusses. Citing Erdmann she explained '"true devotion to the subject of

intellectual love" consisted of "mastering it and winning power over it"'
(Erdmann, cited by Mazon, 2003: 38), and only men were thought to be
capable of this. Finally, Mazon notes that 'the greatest reward of academic
citizenship was *Bildung*, the development of the student into an "independent personality"' (p. 40). This was related to individuality and self-reliance
and required academic freedom in order to be attained – all of which were
seen as barred to women. Mazon concludes that 'historically, "woman" and
"student" were two mutually exclusive categories in Germany' (p. 20).

Unfortunately, such a view of the intellectual and academic capabilities of
women was not restricted to Germany, nor to the nineteenth century. Grant
(1997: 102, 105), for example, argues that academia presents 'a particular
construction of studenthood which for some students is almost impossible
to become ... it is often easiest for the young, white, middle-class male
to be constituted as the "good" student because the characteristics of this
position sit most snugly with his other subject positions.'

Constructions of the student, however, are inevitably being reconfigured
as more students, and in particular, a higher proportion of women, enter
the higher education arena. In addition, wider social and economic changes,
including the growth of neo-liberalism and an imperative to prepare
students for a changing labour market in the context of an increasingly
competitive global economy, mean that new student identities are being
produced. In the rest of this chapter, we examine four aspects of 'the higher
education student' in some detail: the independent learner; the 'needy'
student: academic support and the place of emotion; the student as consumer; and the future graduate equipped for the labour market.

The independent learner

Learner independence has long been both a goal (and at higher education
levels a requirement) of educational participation in the West, and the
student as an independent learner has both historical and contemporary
resonances. Historically, as has been seen, this was rooted in notions of
the individual as an autonomous subject in western philosophical traditions.
Radical pedagogical traditions, drawing on Freire's (1972) work on education
as 'the practice of freedom' have also emphasized learner independence
through, for example, a focus on 'self-directed learning' in adult education
(Brookfield, 1999). In the contemporary context, these historical roots continue to have resonance, but have also been joined by a new emphasis on the
independent and self-reliant individual of neo-liberalism – the new choice-
making subject who is required to continually 'invest' in their own up-skilling
to compete in the flexible labour market. The development of a 'mass' system of higher education with greater reliance on resource-based, online and
distance learning, necessitating greater levels of independent study, and the
neo-liberal imperative which increasingly places responsibility onto the individual rather than the state, are important aspects of this contemporary

context. In the UK, independent learning is a powerful pedagogical discourse in higher education, and the importance of independent learners was spelt out in a Government White Paper 'The Future of Higher Education':

> Today's generation of students will need to return to learning – full-time or part-time – on more than one occasion across their lifetime in order to refresh their knowledge, upgrade their skills and sustain their employability. Such independent learners investing in the continuous improvement of their skills will underpin innovation and enterprise in the economy and society. (DfES, 2003)

'Independence', however, is not a gender-free concept, as can be seen from Mazon's analysis discussed above. Indeed, the dependence/independence dichotomy is gendered, classed and racialized, with only white middle-class men traditionally having the status of an independent individual. Fraser and Gordon's genealogy of the term 'independence' is illustrative. They demonstrate how, with the rise of industrial capitalism, 'certain dependencies became shameful while others were deemed natural and proper' (Fraser and Gordon, 1997: 126), and these were gendered and racialized: 'those who aspired to full membership in society would have to distinguish themselves from the pauper, the native, the slave, and the housewife in order to construct their independence' (p. 130). Working men were regarded as independent, despite their dependence on contributions from their wives (and often their children too). Griffiths also notes that in a traditional family, it is women and children who are regarded as the dependents even though most men are dependent on women for domestic and emotional support (Griffiths, 1995). Whilst femininity has been constructed in relation to nurturing and support in the domestic sphere, masculinity is constructed as its opposite, with men as the breadwinner, the strong and independent provider.

Similarly, the ideal independent learner, unencumbered by domestic and family responsibilities, is a masculine construct, and is also middle class, white and able bodied (Ruddick, 1996). This is the 'turbo student' in Kirkup's (1996) words – able to complete in the shortest possible time and with the least demand on staff and other resources. Research one of the authors conducted[1] in an English inner-city university with a diverse student body also supported this analysis (Leathwood, 2006). Students in this study

---

[1] The Longitudinal Study of Students Learning and Experiences 1999–2005 was funded by the University of London/London Metropolitan University. It was directed by Carole Leathwood. The course team also included Paul O'Connell in the earlier year of the project, and Marie-Pierre Moreau. Undergraduate students (n = 310) from courses in four different disciplinary areas were tracked through their degree studies and post-graduation using questionnaires, focus groups and annual in-depth interviews with 18 case study students.

were very aware of the requirement to be independent learners on entry to university, and many of them welcomed this independence. Moreover, it was clear that independence meant different things to different students – and this reflected gender, age, physical ability and cultural background. Young men in the study, for example, tended to see the independence offered by university life in terms of a sense of freedom, for example from the dictates of parents and school teachers. They could do what they wanted, for example, choose to attend lectures or not, hence university life was seen as liberating. This is not dissimilar to the academic freedom of Mazon's (2003: 19) nineteenth-century German university students, where the student motto 'Frei ist der Bursch (The student is free)' has, argues Mazon, strong masculine overtones. In Leathwood's (2006) analysis, however, there was a downside to freedom, with many of the young men in the study reporting that they found the responsibility of being independent difficult, and they missed having someone to remind them of assessment deadlines. Indeed some felt that their grades would have been higher if someone had continually pushed them to do the work.

In contrast, young women students did not report any difficulty with taking responsibility for themselves, reflecting other research, discussed in Chapter 8, suggesting that women are more likely to commit themselves to studying. Instead, the difficulties they experienced with the idea of learner independence was the feeling that it meant learning alone, without the help and support of others. Some men were also concerned about this, and the students all felt that being an independent learner should not mean that they did not need, or should not receive, help and support. Dependency, however, and needing help or support, is pathologized in this dependence–independence dichotomy and through the imperative to be self-reliant in neo-liberal discourse. Therefore, asking for help was something that most of these students, in different ways, found difficult, something that is discussed further below.

The study highlighted the extent to which the model of the ideal independent learner was inappropriate for many students who did not fit the norm:

> This included women with children, working class students, those working long hours to survive financially, those from a different culture or country, students with an illness or disability, students new to the subject, and those who were shy or not very confident. Indeed, most students could be seen to fit into one or more of these categories.
> (Leathwood, 2006: 622)

Many of the first year students in the study argued that they initially needed help and support as they were facing new challenges, but that as they became familiar with the requirements, they would become more independent. This reflects the strong developmental discourse associated with independence and with notions of independent learning, with assumptions of a linear path from dependence (associated with childhood) to independence (or adulthood). As has been seen, however, this 'adulthood' is actually constructed as 'manhood', with Kolberg's (1981) influential theory of moral development a prime example of this. On Kolberg's scale, women were less likely to attain the final stage of development, that of rational, abstract, objective independent thought and judgement, again reflecting Lloyd's (1984) 'Man of Reason'. The normative standard is white, Western, middle class and male, with everyone else labelled as deficient in comparison (Bing and Reid, 1996). Gilligan's (1977) work on different forms of reasoning provided a valuable critique of this masculinist ideal.

In order to explore the extent to which a developmental process might be applicable for the undergraduate students in this study, repeat interviews were conducted with those in their later years of study. Although many of the younger students, both women and men, felt they had become more independent, the young men in the study were still struggling with taking responsibility for themselves. Moreover, the majority of students still felt that they needed help and advice with the new tasks they were presented with – at a time when academic staff were assuming that, as final year students, they ought to be able to work independently. And as with the first year students, those with a disability or illness challenged the notion of the ideal independent and self-reliant learner who can/ought to sail through their studies without the encumbrance of specific embodied needs. Yet all the students both claimed and demonstrated independence in many aspects of their lives – as workers, parents, carers, and so on. Their difficulty was with a construction of independence that denied the interdependency which marks all our lives.

Despite, therefore, its ubiquitous presence in the discourses and practices of higher education pedagogies, the dominant construction of the 'independent learner' is one which excludes the majority of students and continues to reify the white, middle-class male scholar as the standard against which all others are judged.

The 'needy' student: emotion and academic support

The construction of the ideal independent/autonomous student is reliant upon the production of its opposite – the dependent or 'needy' learner. As has already been noted, this dichotomy is highly gendered (as well as classed and racialized) and parallels the reason/nature binary discussed above, placing dependence and the need for support as firmly outside the traditional category of 'student'. However, the development of a mass higher education system and the participation of new groups of students in the academy has led to a new construction of the student – one that is, however, reserved solely for these 'new' HE students. These new students are frequently denigrated in UK policy discourse as 'lacking' in the necessary skills and attributes (Leathwood and O'Connell, 2003), and a new 'support culture' has been developed, particularly in those universities which take a higher proportion of 'non-traditional students. For instance, there has been an increased emphasis on building students' confidence and self-esteem as well as their academic skills, and on the provision of new student services and tutorial provision. Of course in the old elite universities such as Oxford and Cambridge, plentiful one-to-one individual tutor support has always been available, but this is constructed as academic support, geared to challenging students intellectually and so promoting their independence of thought and academic development. In contrast, the current emphasis on supporting 'non-traditional' students in educational policy and practice tends to position those students as in deficit and 'needy'.

The latter signifies an emphasis on emotional support as opposed to the rational development of the intellect, and is a key aspect of the critique by Hayes (2005) on the new culture of 'emotionalism' in higher education discussed in Chapter 2. Hayes argues that such an approach treats adults not as 'autonomous learners' but as 'dependent pupils'. The gendered independent/rational/hard/masculine and dependent/emotional/soft/feminine binary is both drawn upon and re-enacted here, with academic freedom firmly located on the masculine side – again reflecting Mazon's analysis of nineteenth-century Germany.

Students who need support are therefore feminized and pathologized in this construction. In the study discussed above (Leathwood, 2006), most of the students felt that they needed and wanted help and support at various times during their degree level study, and they resisted the idea that this should compromise their identity as independent learners. Despite this, however, asking for help proved problematic for many students, with some feeling that their request for help would be interpreted as a lack of ability. One young Chinese woman final year student, for example, discussed going to ask her tutor for help and said:

> I knew that he would help me if I was stuck. So he did but yes, every time I went into his office and I kept thinking oh no he's going to think they're really thick because I keep coming up to him and asking him about this assignment.

This student talked in the interviews about feeling that her work was never good enough, even though she consistently achieved high marks and graduated with a very good honours degree. Although asking her tutor for help was difficult for her, this did not seriously conflict with either her own identity construction as not being very good, nor enduring constructions of femininity as being needy and requiring the support and reassurance of a man – in this case her male tutor. She was able, therefore to continue to ask him for help, although the anxiety it caused was indicative of 'the intensification of the struggle girls face and indeed are willing to face (at times) in respect of the contradictions between messages of autonomy and the demands of compliance to notions of traditional femininity' (Hey, 2002: 235). The strong resistance, however, from other women in the study, to the pathologization and infantilization of identities constructed as needy and dependent was evident from their repeated insistence that wanting or requiring help and support with new tasks in new contexts was not in conflict with being independent. Yet in their final year of study some repeatedly felt that academic staff attempted to position them in this way, with, for example, one young woman reporting that tutors said things like 'we're not going to spoon-feed you'. When another student explained that she felt lost and alone when she arrived at university from another country and had 'no one to take my hand', another young woman immediately retorted 'I don't want anyone to hold my hand', thereby both challenging being constituted as a needy child whilst also asserting her own independence and maturity. In a study of young working-class and middle-class girls growing up, Walkerdine et al. (2001: 239) report that the educationally successful working-class girls in their research presented themselves as 'strong and independent', a narrative that, they argue, is linked to their parents' struggle and the girls' desire for 'escape'. Similar narratives were present in the accounts of working-class women students in this study. In addition, a strong determination to succeed 'against the odds' was evident amongst students, both women and men, who were the first in their family to go to university and who were determined to avoid the histories of struggle, in the context of racism and economic hardship, that their parents had faced (Leathwood and O'Connell, 2003).

The relationship between asking for help and dominant constructions of classed and racialized masculinity and femininity could also be seen in the words of a young Black Caribbean man – also a final year student. He explained that he had never actually been to see his tutor because 'I haven't felt there's a need for it. I haven't had any problem that was big enough to consult him.' Yet in the interview he had just explained that he was struggling to understand the content of a module on his course – surely a difficulty that would justify approaching a tutor. He went on to explain:

> I could have gone to other students but that's a big ask of someone because it was very complicated. I wouldn't ask another student to help me with that because it was very, very complicated. It would have taken them a long time to help me to do that. I don't really like burdening people because they've got their work to do and I've got my work to do.

This student's fear of being too needy and demanding illustrates how the need for help, advice or support, of being 'dependent', is feminized and at odds with the 'always able to cope' constructions of masculinity which underpin his words. The result was that he continued to struggle alone. As Seidler notes: 'in traditional masculinity terms we can only strive for independence through releasing ourselves from all the forms of dependency. This makes it difficult for men to acknowledge their emotions and needs without feeling that their masculinity is somehow brought into question' (Seidler, 1988, cited by Mac an Ghaill, 1994: 38). This student's account is also indicative of an academic culture that valorizes competitive individualisms and a context in which 'negative statements concerning the problems of particular groups of students and the "excessive" investment of time and staff they need, presented as necessary to achieve social justice, then become part of the discourse of derision used to justify exclusion' (Williams, 1997: 44).

One white British student did, however, manage to construct his need for help in a way which did not conflict with his masculine identity:

> It's a sort of place where if you expect somebody to do it for you and help you and come up to you and put their arms around you, I don't think they're going to do that but if you've got a problem and need to sort it out, you go to see the right person and you'll get that problem sorted out. Generally the lecturers I get on very well with and they've all been extremely helpful to me so I've not had any negative sort of situations with any of the lecturers at all.

This student presents getting help in totally rational terms: it is about technical problem-solving rather than emotional support, and hence masculinized rather than feminized.

This separation of (emotional) 'support' from 'rational' academic activity was also observed in discourses of new managerialism in research[2] conducted by one of the authors in the further education sector in the UK (Leathwood, 1999, 2000). In that context, new managerialist discourse and a belief in the positive potential of new learning technologies produced new constructions of learning in which support for learning (and the emotional aspects) were separated from the cerebral and thoroughly rational activity of learning itself. This was not a separation that was articulated by the teaching staff, who instead saw support for learning as an integral part of learning per se – the two were not conceptualized as separate or indeed separable. In contrast, within the new managerial discourse, support for learning was constructed as an add-on extra for those who needed it, and provided by support or tutorial staff rather than lecturers. This had likely consequences not only for students and student identities but also for staff, with women potentially positioned as the caring and supportive tutors – a responsibility of which men were more likely to be relieved – and men predominating in the core, higher status and more secure positions as lecturers.

So far we have discussed two different constructions of the university student, that of the independent learner – the white, middle-class, autonomous, able-bodied man; and the 'needy' 'new' student – an interloper into the academy who arrives without the required academic, financial, social or cultural capital to succeed independently at university, and whose physical embodiment positions them in terms of emotional need rather than intellectual autonomy. We now move on to consider another construction of the higher education student – that of the student as consumer.

---

[2] The research took place in two further education colleges in the late 1990s using a combination of in-depth interviews/focus groups of (over 70) managers, lecturers and academic support staff, observation of meetings and documentary analysis.

The student as consumer

Hilton (2003: 1) describes consumerism as 'a mobilising force at the heart of twentieth-century social and political history'. In the higher education sector of the early twenty-first century, *student* consumerism has been firmly established as a key aspect of the global market for higher education products and services.

The dominance of neo-liberal ideology has ensured that market principles are firmly established not only within the commercial sectors of the economy, but also in public and welfare services, most notably in the USA and the UK as well as in the policy discourses of global players including the OECD, the World Bank and the European Commission. The values of the market – of competition, scarcity, choice, self-interest and efficiency – are now well embedded in the global field of higher education, with cost effectiveness, quality and standards assumed to be ensured and continually increased through the informed and 'rational' choices of student consumers. Quality audits, league tables, student satisfaction surveys and the marketing activities of individual institutions are all aimed at providing students with the information they need to choose between competing universities. Increasingly too, the cost of higher education is being transferred from the State (through general taxation) to the individual student, with, for example, student loans and tuition fees being introduced in the UK by the New Labour Government in the late 1990s in place of the previous 'free' tuition and maintenance grants. Students thereby become paying customers, with, it is assumed, a greater incentive to make sure that they get what they are paying for. As Marginson argues:

> The logic of markets requires people to take on the characteristics imagined by neo-classical economists: the drive to maximise individual utility, the separation of the interests of one individual from those of another, and competitive behaviours. If subjectivity is always more complex than *homo economicus* would suggest, markets nevertheless leave their mark, calling up hard headed consumers, and efficient and entrepreneurial producers. (Marginson, 1994: 6)

Ferber and Nelson (2003: 7) note that 'feminist economists have questioned such fundamental neoclassical assumptions in economics as the "separative self", the ubiquity of self-interest, the primacy of competition over cooperation, and the primacy of efficiency concerns over concerns for equity', but it is precisely these assumptions from neoclassical economics that underpin higher education policy at the present time. Altruism has no place in such a construction, and value is constructed primarily in terms of exchange value rather than use value, resulting in the commodification of knowledge, the primacy of instrumental motivations for learning, and the introduction, in the UK, of variable tuition fees, justified on the basis of the differential returns that accrue from different degree courses from different universities.

The subjectivity discussed by Marginson above is also gendered. The market is based on economistic notions of free choice and the rational, autonomous 'economic man'; a 'detached cogito' (Nelson, 1993: 26) making perfectly rational and objective choices unburdened by material and social influences. O'Neill (1996: 404, original emphasis) argues that the 'operation of the market *and* the rational being who makes choices within it, are based on the endorsement of male attributes, capacities and models of activity', whilst Strassman notes that the construction of a free and autonomous rational chooser may be a realistic prospect for white, middle-class men, but is unlikely to reflect 'economic reality for many others' (Strassmann, 1993: 61). Indeed, Hatcher (1998) suggests that the idea that people make purely rational self-interested decisions based on a cost-benefit analysis (the axiom of rational action theory), often does seem to work in studies of middle-class educational choices. There is also, however, plenty of evidence to suggest that students' 'choices' of higher education institution are influenced by a range of material, social and cultural considerations, including the necessity to study near home for economic reasons or because of childcare requirements, and the desire to study in a place where there are 'people like me' (Ball et al., 2002; Archer et al., 2003; Read et al., 2003; Reay et al., 2005). As Reay, David and Ball (2001: 8.1) note in their research into 'choice' of higher education institution in the UK, 'there is little of the calculative, individualistic consumer rationalism that predominates in official texts', and instead, evidence of a process of 'class-matching' (Reay et al., 2005: 92). As Skeggs (2004: 152) notes, 'the disposition of entitlement is one of the most obvious ways that class is written on the body, as it can be read as rights, privilege, access to resources, cultural capital, self-authorization and propriety'.

So *homo academicus*, the 'free-thinking' independent scholar of traditional constructions of the university student, has been replaced by *homo economicus*, whose freedom to choose is paramount. However, both rest on gendered, classed and ethnocentric constructions of the individual subject, as discussed above. There are also contradictions between these different constructions of the student, not least popular assumptions of consumption as a feminine activity and as a democratizing, empowering and equalizing force. Choice in the higher education market is an essential aspect of this construction. James Purnell, a UK Labour Member of Parliament argued:

> The truth is that we do believe in using choice, both for pragmatic and ideological reasons. Our pragmatic reason is that our experience in government has convinced us that choice and contestability improve quality, and can reduce inequality, if the policy is designed correctly. But our commitment to choice is also based on values: we believe in autonomy and, other things being equal, choice gives individuals power. (Purnell, 2006: 1)

We are committed to choice because we believe it gives users power. In other words, it's not just about distributing power better between groups of users. It's also about redistributing power from providers to users.

Today, we can't afford to ignore autonomy, because we live in an autonomous society. . . . People want to do, they don't want to be done to. (Purnell, 2006: 2)

Choice in this discursive framing is always 'a good thing'. It works as what Edelman called a 'condensation symbol' (Edelman, 1977, 1985) – eliciting emotional responses and commitment with its signification of freedom, autonomy, individual rights and empowerment. As we have noted previously (Read et al., 2003), the consumer rights discourse can be perceived as empowering by students themselves and hence adopted as a form of resistance within the academy, with one student stating 'I'm paying for this, I want my money's worth', and another arguing:

> You pay lots of money for it and these people get paid and I'm buying a service. If I don't like the service then I need to complain . . . there was one lecturer who didn't let me in [to the lecture] because I was late . . . and I told him that he can't do this, I'm paying for this service.

The empowerment, however, is one of consumer power in the market, not political power, for example, to influence government decisions. As Apple notes, 'democracy is turned into consumption practices . . . rather than democracy being a *political* concept, it is transformed into a wholly *economic* concept' (Apple, 2005b: 215). 'In the case of neoliberal policies, democracy is now redefined as guaranteeing choice in an unfettered market' (p. 219). Appadurai, in a discussion of what he calls the 'fetishism of the consumer', also argues that the idea that consumer rights are about power and agency is an illusion, with the real agency resting with the producer rather than the consumer: 'These images of agency are increasingly distortions of a world of merchandising so subtle that the consumer is consistently helped to believe that he or she is an actor, where in fact he or she is at best a chooser' (Appadurai, 2006: 187).

Evans also notes the irony in this construction of students as empowered and agentic consumers when, she argues, they 'are now being subjected to a greater degree of surveillance than at any other time in the history of universities' (Evans, 2005: 118). In place of the active independent learner of traditional notions of the university student, students are in danger of becoming passive recipients, or purchasers, of pre-packaged, bite-sized knowledge, demanding their consumer rights to a high quality service – including the provision of course hand-outs and high grades (Morley, 2002). This is far removed from notions of active learners engaged in the challenging, critical and sometimes uncomfortable process of gaining, rethinking and constructing new knowledges and perspectives on oneself and the world.

This construction of a student consumer, as *homo economicus*, is a masculine subject, yet as noted above, the paradigmatic consumer par excellence of popular representations is a woman. Baudrillard distinguishes between a masculine and a feminine model of consumption. The masculine model, he argues, is:

> *particular* or *demanding* . . . a 'select' individual . . . There is no question of letting himself go or indulging himself; his aim is to achieve distinction. Knowing how to choose and not to let one's standards slip are equivalent to the military and puritan virtues: intransigence, decisiveness, valour. (Baudrillard, 1998: 96)

In the feminine model, in contrast:

> women are . . . enjoined to take pleasure themselves. It is not, in this case, selectivity and particularity, but self-indulgence and narcissistic concern for one's own welfare which are indispensible. At bottom, men are still being invited to play soldiers, and women to play dolls with themselves. (p. 97)

In this way, women's patterns of consumption are derided as frivolous in contrast to men's assumed rational choices. The student consumer/chooser is, however, predominantly based on a masculine model, but women cannot, it seems, escape the feminine one. Quinn (2004: 180) noted that in her research with women students, 'the recurring theme was femininity and the efforts taken to produce and maintain the culturally ascribed feminine body. Interspersed with days of study were days of body regulation: an equally time-consuming process to gaining a degree.' She argues that the women students' consumption of the body industry was more of a constraint than a choice, albeit sometimes pleasurable, and she concludes that 'becoming the right kind of student and female body cannot be separated' (p. 183).

Finally, we move on to consider the construction of the higher education student as the future graduate who is prepared, whilst at university, for their role in the labour market.

The future graduate

As higher education has come to be ever more closely tied to the needs of the economy, and with the OECD, European Commission and national governments all stressing the importance of raising skill levels in the context of an increasingly competitive global market, so universities have been tasked with producing the 'employable' workers the labour market is deemed to need. Universities in the UK, for example, have been encouraged to develop a range of employability initiatives and programmes designed to ensure that the new graduates gain the skills and dispositions that employers demand. At the same time, students are extolled to take every opportunity to make themselves more 'employable'.

These are the new graduates of neo-liberalism: self-sufficient, independent, competitive, flexible and taking full responsibility for continually updating their portfolio of skills, qualifications and aptitudes to enable them to succeed in a rapidly changing world. The discourse of 'employability' transfers responsibility for employment away from the State and on to the individual, with the new worker of neo-liberalism expected to be an 'entrepreneur of the self' (du Gay, 1996). Individuals are urged to remake themselves as the autonomous, flexible and enterprising subjects deemed essential for success in the context of international competitiveness in the global economy. They must become 'the right kind of employable subject' (see Walkerdine et al., 2001; Walkerdine, 2003), marketing themselves to prospective employers in the labour market. At the same time, as we noted in Chapter 2, they are expected to have the 'people skills' required by a growing service economy: to be emotionally literate, able to work effectively in teams, to communicate well and to be empathetic.

This new worker is not that dissimilar to the construction of the higher education student as an independent learner, nor to that of the student consumer – each assumes an independent, free and autonomous individual, and each is a product of liberalism. But whereas we argued that the independent learner is a masculine subject, there are suggestions that the new worker of neo-liberalism may assume a feminine subjectivity. Walkerdine, Lucey and Melody (2001: 8), note that 'the self-invention demanded of workers in the new flexible economy should include the adop-tion of characteristics predominantly constituted as "feminine".' This is the transposition of a feminine habitus into the economy presupposed by the cultural feminization thesis (see Adkins, 2002), and reflected in the emphasis on 'personal' and 'people' skills in the higher education curric-ulum. The self-inventing subject itself is also, agues Walkerdine (2003: 242), based on models of middle-class femininity:

> I would argue further that it is the qualities ascribed to femininity which are understood as the central carriers of the new middle-class individu-ality, building upon the long-established incitement to women to become producers of themselves as objects of the gaze. They are to look the part, sound the part and, moreover, they can make themselves and their homes over to conform to this middle-class aesthetic. The concept of the 'makeover' has been a staple of women's magazines for many years.

If this is the case, then perhaps the feminization thesis does have validity in relation to higher education. That is, if the new construction of the higher education student, that of the future graduate or new worker of neo-liberalism, is a feminine subject, then surely this is an example of the femi-nization of the sector, with women students far more likely to fit in and succeed than their men counterparts for whom the demands of femininity are more difficult to meet. Indeed, this could give further support to the fears discussed in Chapter 2 that boys and men are increasingly required to become feminized by the education system, and it could be argued that it is precisely this demand that men take on feminine characteristics and participate in a feminized culture that is deterring them from taking part in higher education.

In order to consider this, we will first discuss the ways in which the new graduate worker of neoliberalism, the 'entrepreneur of the self' in du Gay's (1996) terms, might be considered as a feminine or masculine subject, and then move on to discuss the emphasis on 'people skills' in higher education and the labour market and the extent to which women might be seen to be advantaged in this context.

Walkerdine argues that:

> The neo-liberal subject is the autonomous liberal subject made in the image of the middle class. . . . It is the flexible and autonomous subject who negotiates, chooses, succeeds in the array of education and retraining forms that form the new 'lifelong learning' and the 'multiple career trajectories' that have replaced the linear hierarchies of the education system of the past and the jobs for life of the old economy. . . . It is argued that these times demand a subject who is capable of constant self-invention. (Walkerdine, 2003: 239–40)

This subject can, therefore, be seen as embodying aspects traditionally associated with both masculinity and femininity – the autonomous liberal subject is, we have argued, a masculine subject, yet as Walkerdine notes above, the demand for constant self-invention is associated with femininity. Both aspects rest on a middle-class subjectivity:

> Theories of the enterprising self are premised upon models, ideals and the experiences of the middle–class and as a model of exploitation, labour relations or exchange, mainly redundant for the working-class, who do not have access to the same starting point, the same approach to accrual, access to the knowledge of how to accrues effectively and access to the sites for optimizing the cultural capital that they have acquired. (Skeggs, 2004: 75)

Both aspects are also, we suggest, racialized as well as classed and gendered.

Entrepreneurship embodies qualities associated with White Western constructions of masculinity – assertiveness, autonomy, confidence, making oneself distinct and competitive individualism. It is about 'winning deals, aggressive marketing and competitiveness' (Blackmore and Sachs, 2003b: 717). Britton and Baxter also suggest that the self-reflexivity and self-transformation required of this new subject is based on a masculine individualism and self-centredness. From their longitudinal study of mature students, they noted four different narratives of the self: 'struggling against the odds' and 'credentialism', which they identified as feminine, 'unfulfilled potential' which was common to both women and men, and 'self-transformation' which was identified as masculine: 'This idea of the actor actively transforming himself appears from our data to be a masculine narrative which is also linked to class processes' (Britton and Baxter, 1999: 189).

The research conducted by one of the authors discussed above (see Leathwood, 2006) also supports this. The self-transformation required appears to be about becoming a go-getting entrepreneurial subject who is willing to market themselves and grab the opportunities on offer, and men in the study appeared more at ease with this than women. Will, for example, a white British mature student, had no trouble with the idea of selling himself in the market when he explained:

> At the end of the day a lot of that comes down to yourself because you get the interview or the job and you have to sell yourself and I think that is what people are interested in.

Will described his accent as 'common' and says that 'the judgement is that I am a bit thick', but felt he could turn this to his advantage:

> If I get into the industry, and hopefully I will do, it might have a positive effect because I may come across as a bit different, and have a different outlook on things, which is better than the usual crap which I am sure they get.

Here Will constructs his difference as a marketable commodity which he is able to use as a mark of distinction to distinguish himself from others. In contrast, the women students and graduates interviewed did not use a discourse of distinction in this way and were less comfortable with the idea that they had to sell themselves. For example, Paula, a white European mature student, discusses the efforts she has made to find suitable employment and she explains that she has not written '*cold-calling*' type letters (to send her curriculum vitae on spec to a range of companies) because 'it's like if I don't do it, I don't fail, subconsciously, and I don't feel that confident . . . I feel I'm faking it'.

'Faking it' suggests a performance – presumably as a (potentially) successful graduate, which is an identity that Paula does not appear to feel is hers of right as a working-class woman. To write such letters is to risk failure and being found out as fraudulent, something that others have written about in relation to working-class women (see, for example, Mahony and Zmroczek, 1997; Plummer, 2000). And whilst risk-taking is congruent with dominant constructions of masculinity, it is at odds with femininity. Fear of failure was also preventing another woman in the study from applying for graduate jobs. Alice, an African-Caribbean mature student, had already graduated when she said:

> I've not applied for any jobs yet. I've left university and I've got the degree under my belt. . . . The only problem is now I am so frightened of going out there and doing it now because I think am I going to fail, am I going to meet the criteria? . . . I mean I've been working obviously but not in that field, not in a professional manner and this is what is so frightening.

This is not to suggest that only women fear failure (although it was mostly women who articulated such a fear), but that the sense of self required to market oneself in the graduate labour market is more closely associated with productions of a masculine rather than a feminine identity. Britton and Baxter's (1999) analysis of data from their study of mature HE students is also relevant here. They suggested that the masculine self-transforming subject rests on the production of an active self, whereas women's narratives were more about a 'latent, subordinated or unrecognized' self. Both Paula and Alice are from working-class backgrounds, and both struggle to perform the confident, entrepreneurial self of the neo-liberal subject. Yet this should not be seen, we suggest, as a matter of individual (or women's) psychology. Instead, following Sandra Bartky (1990), we suggest that 'confidence' is produced within systems of oppression and that 'rather than seeing emotions as psychological dispositions, we need to consider how they work, in concrete and particular ways, to mediate the relationship between the psychic and the social, and between the individual and the collective' (Ahmed, 2004: 119).

Women students did, however, construct graduate identities that were more comfortable for them. For example, Alice provides an example of her negotiation of gendered, classed and racialized identities in a discussion of her desire to be a manager in human resources:

> I want to be the boss. Albeit a nice boss but I want to be the boss. I want to make the decisions and so on like that. I don't want to be making the tea, although I could be a boss and make the tea but it's not the point. I just want to be there.

She also says that she wants to work in human resources and describes herself as '*a people person*', but:

> well the image I see when I talk to those from human resources they are very bubbly and very lovely, into that marketing thing. I don't know if I'm going to be accepted there because I'm just a matter of fact person. I've not got that bubbly sound to my voice, I've not got that oomph that they have. They sound like they've just stepped out of a series on TV, like home shopping or something. I do it in a more believable way, a non-patronizing way. . . . I'll get the job done and that is that and I don't try and tread on toes while I'm doing it. I'll help others, inspire others, motivate others and that's I think what will help me get on that higher ladder of management. I'm a very sort of motherly type of person. I'll take people on board and help them out.

Alice constructs a desired identity that combines being 'a boss' with a feminine identity. She wants to be a 'nice boss', and resists the stereotypical female role of making the tea – though she is happy to do this if she is the boss, and implies that bosses certainly could (and perhaps should?) make the tea. Manager identities also signify a middle-class identity, and Alice's construction of a manager who can also make the tea and who does not appropriate the work of others (e.g. by treading on their toes) could also be seen as a form of resistance to a construction of identity which is decidedly middle class and which eschews manual, menial or domestic tasks. She also resists the feminine identity of a '*bubbly*' person, with its connotations of youthful and 'fluffy' (Holland, 2004) heterosexual femininity, with its connotations of frailty and childishness, in favour of a more serious identity as a '*matter of fact person*'. She does, however, define herself as motherly, a more acceptable feminine identity for a mature woman than the bubbly persona she resists, and one which can be translated into the workplace as a caring manager.

There are clearly costs for women in trying to take up and perform a masculine subject position (Walkerdine et al., 2001), but there are also limitations in the extent to which mobility across gender identities is possible – at least for women. Adkins and Lury (2000: 159) for example, argue that while men's feminized performances at work tend to be seen 'as a product of reflexivity and are mobilized as workplace resources, women's "masculinized" performances tend not to be recognised as reflexive at all. On the contrary, they are demeaned and trivialized, defined as inappropriate, unexchangable performances.' They conclude: 'it is difficult for women workers to achieve such reflexive identities because their labour of identity may be naturalised as part of their selves' (p. 163). Yet if a cultural feminization of the workplace is taking place and skills and attributes associated with femininity are in demand, surely this means that women will be at an advantage in the workplace? Adkins (2002), in a review of McDowell's work, concludes that this is not necessarily so. It appears that whilst men can perform femininity and be rewarded for it, women's performances of similar skills or attributes tend to be seen as 'natural' advantages, that is as part of what is expected for a woman, and therefore not recognized or rewarded. Skeggs's (2004) analysis of how some bodies are mobile and others become fixed in place is relevant here: whatever women's skills and achievements, it appears that women cannot escape their bodies. White middle-class men are not tied to their bodies in the same way – they still, it seems, inhabit the realm of reason whilst women are located with nature and bodies. Walkerdine et al. (1999: 59) suggest that changes in recent years, not least the impact of feminism, have 'created the possibility of making the feminine rational or the rational feminine', thereby allowing middle-class girls to enter the professions as rational subjects. This point, we suggest, needs some qualification. Walkerdine and colleagues acknowledge that this comes at a price for young women. In our own research, some women graduates talked about their experiences of going for job interviews in ways that suggest that it was their embodied presence that raised questions about their suitability for the post. For example, Sharon, a young Caribbean British woman, said 'I'm not quite what they're looking for . . . You have to look a certain way and come from a certain area, speak a certain way.' She described how she was different, in terms of ethnicity and dress, from other staff she saw at the company. For Alice, it was her age that she felt went against her: 'They're looking for someone young they can mould'. Skeggs's (2004) analysis of the ways in which capitals become embodied, and hence how different bodies are differently valued, is relevant here. As Tretheway (1999: 425) notes, 'our notions of professionalism are . . . intimately and inextricably connected to a particular type of embodied and constructed femininity'. This highlights the difficulties of some post-structuralist/queer notions of free-floating gender identities which anyone can choose to perform, and highlights the importance of an analysis that recognizes embodiment. These women cannot escape their bodies – bodies that are marked by gender, class, ethnicity and age – in their performance of gender identities.

Yet the 'people skills' and emotional literacy demanded by employers are assumed to benefit women – irrespective of whether or not they are seen as essentialized characteristics of womanhood. As Illouz (1997: 43) notes: 'in commanding that we exert our mental and emotional skills to identify with others' point of view, the communicative ethos orients the manager's self to the model of traditional female selfhood.' She argues, however, that this idea of selfhood is different from traditional femininity as it relies on expert knowledge rather than nurturing self-sacrifice; that despite the attention to emotions, the underlying assumption is of an independent and self-reliant subject, not a dependent one; and that whilst empathy is demanded, this 'never cancels out one's self-interest or even mild forms of manipulation of others; the feminine art of sympathy, on the other hand, aims at bonding with another, even at the cost of self-effacement' (p.43). Illouz goes on to note:

> By an ironic twist of cultural history, the self-interested *homo economicus* of Adam Smith has been recast by psychologists as a *homo communicans* who reflexively monitors his words and emotions, controls his self-image and plays tribute to the other's point of view. This overarching model of communication cloaks social domination with an ideology of harmony and efficiency of the workplace. (p. 45)

A similar analysis is made by Evans in relation to the requirement for such skills in higher education. She argues that feminizing the universities:

> has involved the socialization of undergraduates into those skills traditionally associated with women, and women employees. Those skills are skills about being reliable, cooperative and able to recognize different points of view. These 'feminine' skills are not far away from the skills which students are now expected to acquire at the same time as a knowledge of a particular curriculum: skills of meeting deadlines, producing presentations with other students (the much validated 'group work' of many teaching manuals) and the accurate precis of hand-outs of distributed material. The ideal undergraduate is today the student who attends all required teaching and hands in essays on time, the person who behaves as the perfect functionary of a bureaucratic world. For women, the paradox of the twenty-first century university is that it appears to offer entry into a space once reserved for men. Yet once women occupy that space, we are required to behave as the 'good girls'

who obeyed every social rule and implicitly accepted the authority of a male order. (Evans, 2005: 67–8)

This analysis mirrors Ferguson's conclusion that:

> Feminization involves the extension of the depoliticizing, privatizing aspects of women's traditional role to the sectors of the population who are the victims of bureaucratic organizations, both the administrators and the clientele. Both groups of individuals are placed in institutional situations in which they must function as subordinates, and they must learn the skills necessary to cope with that subordinate status, the skills that women have always leaned as part of their 'femininity'. (Ferguson, 1984: 93)

This suggests that this form of 'feminization' has serious consequences for both women and men. Yet by associating these developments in the field of higher education with feminization and, by implication, with women, it is women who are held responsible for contaminating or polluting the ivory tower.

The university student – multiple possibilities?

We have presented four constructions of the student in this chapter: the independent learner, the 'needy' student, the student consumer and the future graduate, and all can be identified in the contemporary academy. Does this mean, therefore that there are now multiple possible student identities ensuring, perhaps, that there is 'something for everyone'? Are there now many different ways of being a student, thereby increasing the accessibility of a student identity, and hence the academy, far beyond that which Mazon (2003) identified in nineteenth-century Germany?

The fact that there *are* more women in universities than ever before in many places does make higher education more of a possibility, at least for middle-class women. As we have seen, however, the four student identities discussed above are gendered, classed and racialized and cannot be straightforwardly taken up at will. Men, particularly white middle-class men, are likely to find it easier to take on these identities as all draw on, and are consonant with, dominant constructions of masculinity. The complex negotiations, suppressions and self-regulation that all Others must undertake to find a place and a student identity that is comfortable is not without cost. Social identities are embodied and differently in or out of place in the academy. Mirza, in her discussion of the in/visibility of black women in higher education in the UK, draws on Puwar's analysis:

> Social spaces are not blank and open for anybody to occupy. Over time, through processes of historical sedimentation, certain types of bodies are designated as being the 'natural' occupants of specific spaces. . . . Some bodies have the right to belong in certain locations, while others

are marked out as trespassers who are in accordance with how both spaces and bodies are imagined, politically, historically and conceptually circumscribed as being 'out of place'. (Pewar, cited by Mirza, 2006a: 147)

A key concern for many working-class and minority ethnic students in the UK is to find a university in which there are more likely to feel they belong – a place where there are other people like themselves – not too 'posh' and/or with an ethnically diverse student population (Archer et al., 2003; Reay et al., 2005), that is a space in which they might feel less 'out of place'. However, taking on a student identity is still risky for many (Archer and Hutchings, 2000). Research conducted by Archer and colleagues (2003) indicated that 45 per cent of working-class people responding to a national representative survey reported that 'the student image is not for me', with students being perceived as predominantly middle class, white, and immature. Universities were seen as alien middle-class places by most of the non-participants in focus groups, but there were also gendered and racialized dimensions to this, with a student identity perceived to be at odds with different constructions of masculinity for working-class white, Asian and African-Caribbean men, for example as not 'manly, 'cool' or conducive to providing for a family. Despite assumptions of the feminization of higher education, white working-class women in the study also faced particular conflicts with constructions of femininity which assume they will stay close to home, find a good man, get married and have children, and certainly not get ideas 'above their station' by going to university. In contrast, the African-Caribbean women saw higher education as an opportunity to secure their, and their children's, futures, echoing Mirza's (1997) account of the importance of a discourse of meritocracy and a commitment to educational participation as a way of 'raising the race' (Mirza, 2005). This commitment to educational participation by black Caribbean women goes some way towards explaining their significant levels of participation in HE. For Asian women in the study, strong parental commitment to higher education was also evident, with some young Asian working-class women explaining that they had no choice – their parents expected them to go to university (Archer and Leathwood, 2003).

However, for those who do go to university, pressure to adapt one's behaviour, for example to appear less working class by changing one's accent (as some students in the study noted above described) or by hiding one's sexuality (Epstein et al., 2003) where it does not conform to the requirements of compulsory heterosexuality, is evident. In a study of undergraduate experiences of gender inequality at an elite British university, women reported pressure to behave in a way that conformed to traditional notions of femininity, for example not being too outspoken or boisterous and to dress in feminine ways, whilst men reported pressure to conform to traditional dominant forms of masculinity, for example to be strong, macho and not too sensitive (Morrison et al., 2005). Morrison and colleagues argue, however, that women are in a 'double-bind', in that they are required to be feminine but femininity is derided: 'activities or spaces where women predominated were often viewed as negative, inferior, marginalised, and even mysterious . . . for example, the only women's college in the University, women's sports and clubs, even a sole female student in a tutorial – all these things were generally reported in a negative way' (p. 153). One woman from a women's college, for example, noted she was seen as 'a lesbian or a tart' (p. 153). Barata, Hunjan and Leggatt (2005) discussed how stereotypically masculine traits were valued in graduate school in Canada, and hence had to be accommodated, with a concomitant loss or repression of aspects of femininity. Racism is reported more often on predominantly white campuses (Bagguley and Hussain, 2007), and is gendered, with Tyrer and Ahmed (2006) reporting that Muslim women students wearing the hijab were particularly targeted.

Sexual harassment was widely reported in Morrison and colleagues' UK study discussed above, replicating findings in other countries. Morley notes that across the Commonwealth, sexual harassment 'is rife on campus' (Morley, 2005b) and she cites a study in Zimbabwe by Zindi in 1998 where all the respondents of a large survey (over 2500) knew lecturers who were sexually exploiting women students, although 93 per cent said they would not report it. In the Canadian graduate school (Barata et al., 2005), sexist encounters were regularly discussed amongst the women graduates, as was the assumption that women felt they had to take responsibility for avoiding being sexualized by men on the campus. Similarly, in a survey of undergraduate students in Hong Kong, 35 per cent of women (and 19 per cent of men) indicated they had been subjected to sexual harassment (France-Presse, 2002). Research has shown that sexual harassment of LGBT students, mostly from other students, is prevalent on campuses in the US (Joyce, 2007), whilst Epstein et al. (2003: 118) report that whilst experiences of being queer vary on different UK campuses which are 'differentially heterosexist and homophobic', students often do face harassment and violence. Rich's (1986) analysis of compulsory heterosexuality is still relevant to UK campuses in the early twenty-first century, despite legislation that has placed a duty on educational organizations and others to ensure that they do not discriminate against students and staff on the basis of sexual orientation (as well as gender, ethnicity, disability, religion and age) in their provision of services and employment practices. Harassment and violence, or the threat of violence, are about power and control. As Morley (2005b: 215) notes, 'the existence of male violence can regulate all women. . . . It is one of the many prices that women are expected to pay for entering traditional male reserve spaces. It marks out and reinforces gendered territory and emphasises women's femaleness in male domains.'

Conclusions

In this chapter we have discussed various constructions of 'the university student' that can be observed in the field of higher education in the contemporary context. All students are engaged in processes of identity making and re-making at university, as they differently take on and move between different constructions of identity at home, university, family and peer group. For those who differ from the white male middle-class norm, such processes also require the negotiation of their differences, in a context in which such difference is marked and continually reasserted, not only socially and culturally, but structurally too, through, for example, the time and energy required to deal with physical barriers to access for people with some disabilities, or to manage childcare around university timetables. Mature students entering higher education face potential challenges to existing gender identities and roles in their families when, for example, male partners of women students still expect their partners to do the domestic work in the house (Baxter and Britton, 2001). In contrast, women partners of male students in this study adjusted their lives to support their partners, for example, by taking on paid employment.

Whilst in some cases negotiation of one's differences involves a repression of aspects of the self, there are also very positive accounts in the studies discussed above. For example, the working-class students in a recent UK study of 'the socio-cultural and learning experiences of working-class students in higher education'[3] demonstrate high levels of resilience and determination, as well as a sense of working-class pride through which they strongly resist the idea that their difference makes them inadequate or inferior (Crozier, 2008; Reay, 2008). Similarly, the Muslim women in Tyrer and Ahmad's (2006) research, who reported high levels of support from parents and family, asserted a Muslim identity to both reject dominant racial classifications and as a positive assertion of their rights. For many, university provided a valuable opportunity to think through their gender, ethnic and religious identities. The women at the Canadian graduate school described developing a feminist identity as one of the positive and pleasurable aspects of their university experience (Morrison et al., 2005) whilst for LGBT students, higher education provided a space in which to explore their sexuality (Epstein et al., 2003).

Similarly, in our discussion of the independent learner and 'needy' student identities earlier in this chapter, it is possible to see how students both resisted and reconstructed their learner identities in a way that made sense of their own experiences. We have also shown how some students adopted a student consumer discourse as a form of resistance, and we have highlighted the identity processes taking place in the re-construction of graduate

---

[3] See http://education.sunderland.ac.uk/our-research/sehe

worker identities. As Quinn (2003) has articulated in her study of women undergraduates at two British universities, students are making their own spaces and identities in the university context, and whilst that has particular challenges and costs for many, resistance to dominant constructions of the university student is very much alive.

7
Academic identities and gendered work

For many academics, the occupation is central to our self-identity, due to a sense of 'vocation', a valuing of the prestige and status the occupation (sometimes) enjoys, and/or due to the years of hard work and struggle merely to be able to *enter* academia, let alone achieve acceptance and security. As Becher and Trowler (2007: 47) note, 'being a member of a disciplinary community involves a sense of identity and personal commitment'. Geertz describes such membership as constituting a whole 'way of being in the world . . . a cultural frame that defines a great part of one's life' (Geertz, 1983, cited in Becher and Trowler, 2007). Yet academia is changing. Academic 'freedom' and 'collegiality' in higher education has been undermined by new managerialist emphases on 'efficiency', 'transparency' and 'accountability', as countries around the world implement policies designed to increase student participation and develop 'mass' higher education (Coaldrake, 2000; Deem, 2003; Barry et al., 2007). The complex relation between such changes and teachers' and lecturers' ongoing constructions of professional identity have increasingly become the focus of research (Parker and Jary, 1995; Dent and Whitehead, 2001; Thomas and Davies, 2002; Harris, 2005; Clegg, 2008).

However, as we shall be exploring in this chapter, for some in the academy such identification with academia has *always* held tensions and ambivalence. For the dominant social construction of the academic, just as for the student, is one that is white, middle class and male (see Morley, 1997b; Aguirre, 2000; Alfred, 2001; Stanley, 2006), and these associations also extend to the concept of the 'professional' more generally. The legitimacy of claims to a 'professional' identity has changed over time in response to the struggles of different occupational groups (Hanlon, 1998, 2000). Traditionally, the term 'professional' was confined to an elite body of White middle-class men working in fields such as medicine and law. Restricted entry ensured protected and impervious boundaries between these elite positions and others, with professionals considered to have scarce specialist knowledge and autonomy over their work. These exclusionary and demarcatory strategies were, argued

Witz (1992), embedded within patriarchal power relations and used to exclude women from the traditional professions. Teachers and lecturers have traditionally been seen as 'public service professionals', operating with 'licensed' autonomy and particular definitions of the 'good teacher' (Seddon, 1997).

A number of challenges to public sector professionalism developed through the 1970s and 1980s, not least of which was the new right's attack on the state (Clarke and Newman, 1997), the increasing marketization of education and the development of the new managerialism noted above. New managerialist initiatives have heralded what has been argued to be a 'de-professionalization' of the academic in terms of status, expertise and autonomy. For example, Randle and Brady (1997: 126) argue that in order to achieve efficiency gains:

> control over the conception and design of academic work is increasingly being taken away, by management, from practitioners responsible for its delivery in the classroom, and placed in the hands of specialist managers or external agencies. This reflects the process of deskilling that Braverman (1975) asserts craft labour has undergone during the twentieth century.

In research conducted by one of the authors in a further education college in the UK (Leathwood, 2005b) it was evident that many lecturers felt that they were being deskilled and de-professionalized, although some managers argued that they were concerned to enhance lecturer professionalism. Such a position reflects an assertion of re-professionalization whereby lecturers were seen to benefit from opportunities to develop new areas of expertise and responsibility. Competing discourses of professionalism, or what Randle and Brady (1997) refer to as a managerial and professional paradigm, were very evident, supporting Seddon's (1997) suggestion for a conceptualization of professionalism as discourse, thereby enabling us to theorize both de-professionalizing and re-professionalizing processes occurring simultaneously.

Some have argued that whilst problematic in many ways, new managerialism may provide a way for women to challenge traditional 'masculinist' academic cultures (see, for example, Luke, 2001a). Others argue that the increasing numbers of women employed as academics in higher education points to a 'feminized future' for staff as well as students (see Chapter 4). In this chapter, we will be exploring gendered notions of academic professional identity against the backdrop of such changing forms of academic culture. How is the construction of the 'academic' gendered both in relation to academic culture and wider social culture? How does this impact on women's academic identities, and what are the implications of such identity processes and cultural change for the feminization thesis?

We will be focusing on several interrelated aspects of gender and academic identities. First, we will be building on the analysis of traditional constructions of the student in Chapter 6 by exploring the ways in which women have historically been placed as 'Other' to Enlightenment constructions of the intellectual, and how the continuing influence of such discourses contribute to women's continued sense of 'Otherness' in the university. Secondly, we will be looking at the ways in which the 'genderedness' of academic identities are constructed and re-constructed through particular and related 'masculinized' aspects of academic culture – competitiveness and individualism – and how these aspects have been *exacerbated* rather than challenged by the increasing dominance of new managerialist cultures. We conclude with a look at some of the ways in which feminists and pro-feminists continue to challenge such cultures and construct alternative identities within the academy.

Women as the intellectual 'other'

In a piece entitled 'Women and transgression in the halls of academe', Bronwyn Davies constructs a 'synopsis for an opera', a 'collective biography' with scenes relating to women and academic life from the 1960s to the present day. In the piece she describes how women used to 'transgress' the norms of academic culture merely by their *presence* as academic faculty:

> A different frame. In the halls of academe in the first half of the twentieth century. At first women were transgressive just by virtue of being there. Their very presence transgressed the boundaries of 'correct practice'. Their actions, too, were transgressive, either because no one told them what correct practice was, or else the practices were designed with men in mind. Women were out of place; out of their depth; in becoming academics they had somehow taken the wrong part in an ideological theatre that had no major parts for them to play. (Davies, 2006: 500)

As we have seen in Chapter 4, at the beginning of the twenty-first century, academia in many countries across the world is a different place for women. Substantial numbers of women are employed as lecturers in universities in countries such as the UK, USA and Australia, nearly equalling men at junior lecturer level. That 'nearly' is telling – men still currently outnumber women in all levels of academic position, and the disparity in numbers grows significantly the further up the academic tree we climb. However, projections by John Pratt of the University of East London (cited in Oxford, 2008) have suggested that women will outnumber men at researcher and junior levels by 2009. Despite going on to forecast that it will be 2070 before the numbers of women professors equal the numbers of men, this prediction has triggered alarmist news pieces that women are poised to imminently 'take over' the academy, with a concomitant victory for a 'feminized' academic culture. In a piece in the UK's *Times Higher Education Supplement* the writer proclaims: 'Figures from the Higher Education Statistics agency suggest that at researcher and lecturer levels, women are poised to take over. . . . Already British universities and their staff are working to come to terms with a feminization of the academy.' This echoes similar pieces since the mid-1990s relating to the rise in numbers and success of women students (as we have seen in earlier chapters), and can be seen in other pieces relating specifically to academic staff – for example a review of greater representation of women academics in Canadian universities in the 1990s was greeted in the popular press with the headline 'Women storm Canada's ivory towers' (Brown, 2005, cited in Acker and Webber, 2006). According to this rhetoric, the moment women statistically creep ahead of men in any area of the education or working world they immediately send in shock troops to stage a 'coup'. Women victors then set about cementing a radically different and alien feminized culture, which may have been insidiously growing during the previous benign (masculinized) regime. Academic men are then immediately cast as the 'losers' or 'prisoners of war' to this new order, who might feebly continue to struggle against the inevitable. For example, Fisher's (2007) ethnography of a business school in the UK found that the appointment of a female Dean provoked ongoing complaints by men staff that 'you need tits to get on around here', despite the continuing dominance of male lecturers in the department, and perceptions by women interviewees that the Dean was not particularly supportive of women's issues. Fisher argues that academic women in the department (23 per cent of academic staff) were 'instantly visible in a way that men, as the dominant group, are not' (p. 508). This was exemplified in the way that men colleagues would often joke or comment about visible groups of women in the department ('I didn't come over because it looked like a meeting of the ladies circle'; 'Aha, it's the witches coven!'; 'The WI is here again'), whilst 'a group of men in the canteen or in a committee meeting will not be remarked upon, presumably because it is the unconscious norm' (p. 509). As we have discussed, the hyper-visibility and exaggeration of women's presence or achievements experienced in the (masculine) social imagination seems to be related to a high degree of 'fear' or 'resistance' to any perceived erosion of male social dominance.

However, as we have shown throughout this book, this picture of a 'feminization' of the culture of the academy is one that is rather difficult to pinpoint when we actually look at academic culture(s) in depth, especially as many women, working-class and minority ethnic academics are concentrated in 'casualized' short-term contract research and teaching (Reay, 2000; Hey, 2001). As Reay (2000) notes, women contract researchers are often described as doing the 'leg work' or the 'spade work' for a research project, 'the presumption being, I suppose, that the head work goes on elsewhere' (p. 15). Moreover, she points to the greater value placed on academic work conducted by those in secure lecturing positions over work produced by contract academics, whether this is academic writing, or other aspects of a contract researcher's job:

> The values of distance – a very male construction – lead to the day-to-day work of the contract researcher – all those 'female' things – making

contact, establishing relationships, talking and listening – being down-graded, as if analysis and theorisation are detached and compart-mentalised from daily engagement with the research field. (Reay, 2000: 16)

As feminists have pointed out, there seems to be a link between the per-ceived 'feminization' of the profession and its de-professionalization and casualization (Hey, 2001). As we have noted elsewhere, the Enlightenment philosophical thought that is still dominant in Western culture constructs rationality, objectivity, and culture as 'masculine', in opposition to the 'feminine' spheres of 'emotionality', 'subjectivity' and 'nature' (Jordanova, 1980; Lloyd, 1984; Hekman, 1990). In all of these binary pairs that which is seen as 'masculine' is seen as superior. Rather interestingly, in an article that suggests that women are 'taking over' the academy, the writer interviews a sociologist, Catherine Hakim, who puts forward the argument that women will never succeed over men in the highest echelons of academia, because women's inherent 'natural' differences imply that they are not able to reach the heights of 'genius' that can be achieved by men: 'there are more male idiots and more male geniuses' (cited in Oxford, 2008b). Another popular conception is that girls'/women's success is pri-marily due to their 'hard work', whilst boys/men are more likely to be per-ceived as 'naturally talented', with poor performance put down to individual 'laziness' or distracting influences (Clarricoates, 1989; Francis and Skelton, 2005).

Feminists have long criticized the gendered notion of 'genius' and its equation with the masculine (see, for example, Battersby, 1990). Closely linked to the notion of genius as embodied by the 'male' is the exclusion of women from the category of 'intellectual'. Moi, for example, in her analy-sis of 40 years' worth of critical engagement with the work of Simone de Beauvoir, notes the 'striking hostility' and 'surprising number of condes-cending, sarcastic, sardonic or dismissive accounts' (Moi, 1994: 74) in these appraisals of de Beauvoir's oeuvre. Moi argues that a number of common themes emerge, including the reduction of de Beauvoir's work to her womanhood and femininity, and accusations of naivety, so that de Beauvoir is presented as a 'false intellectual'. This 'mocking our minds' (Spender, 1982: 24) has a long history which has been central to the exclusion of women from higher education as both students and academics, and must also be seen within a matrix of other subjectivities, for example in relation to class and ethnicity (e.g. Reay, 2000; Mirza, 2006b; Maylor, forthcoming; Maylor, under review). For example, Hill Collins argued in relation to black feminism: 'Reclaiming the Black feminist intellectual tradition involves much more than developing Black feminist analysis using standard epi-stemological criteria. It also involves challenging the very definitions of intellectual discourse' (Hill Collins, 1990: 15).

Gender and marginalization in the academy

The association of the academic with the masculine has profound consequences for women's constructions of an academic self-identity. Those who find they do not 'fit the mould' often find themselves feeling a sense of marginality, dissonance and displacement (Dent and Whitehead, 2001). As Dent and Whitehead note:

> the notion of the professional suggests an embodied discursive subject which is not woman/female, but is indeed man/male/masculine.... For all those positioned as the 'Other' in white male-dominated work organizations, be they women, gays, lesbians or people of colour, the taking up of professional identification is a process constrained by numerous gates, most of which remain formally and informally 'manned' by white male gatekeepers. (p. 6)

As we have discussed in Chapter 1, we do not conceptualize identities as unitary and fixed, but rather as fluid, shifting, and constructed through difference and exclusions. Anthias (2001: 638) notes that:

> What has been thought about as a question of identity (collective identity) can be understood as relating to boundaries on the one hand and hierarchies on the other. Not only do 'identities' such as ethnicity/'race' (as well as gender and class) entail categories of difference and identity (boundaries), they also construct social positions (hierarchies), and involve the allocation of power and other resources.

However, although they are socially formed, such identity constructions are not completely arbitrary, but are constrained in a number of ways. First, they are constructed through, and infused with, particular historically and socially specific discourses that are socially present at the place and time of construction (see, for example, Gadamer, 1975; McGann, 1983; Francis, 2002). We have utilized Foucault's (1977) conceptualization of power in discourse that sees all discourses as having a certain degree of 'power'. However, some discourses have more power than others to legitimize themselves through particular 'regimes of truth', for example, those that are able to be legitimized by the socially constructed authority of the academy. Therefore, socially '*dominant*' discourses concerning the professional and the academic – such as those legitimated by aspects of the social and political establishment, including the academy itself – will be more likely than other less prevalent and powerful discourses to influence an individual's conception of themselves as a 'professional' or 'academic'. As such dominant discourses construct the academic in relation to socially privileged subject positions such as 'white', 'male' and 'middle class', such a construction often fits less comfortably with those who hold other less privileged subject positions.

A growing body of literature has discussed the ways in which women academics have struggled, and continue to struggle with a sense of injustice at such marginalization, and sometimes continue to feel self-doubt or ambivalence at taking on an 'academic' professional identity due to the influence of an academy and wider social culture that places them as 'other'. This is often complexly entwined with other 'non-hegemonic' identities in relation to class, ethnicity and sexuality (Morley, 1997b; Reay, 1997; Walker, 1998; Hey, 2003; Marchbank, 2005; Marchbank and Letherby, 2006). For example, Reay (1997) discusses how her sense of identity with her working-class origin 'conflicts powerfully with a contemporary identity which consequently often feels both fictional and fraudulent' (p. 18). Mirza (2006b: 107) draws on work from other black academics to describe the psycho-social costs of being one of a small minority in a white world, and argues that 'being a curiosity, a "special case", "one in a million" can be an emotional and professional burden to black women in the academy.' A sense of injustice due to seeming invisibility, cultural 'alienation' and exclusion by others is also strong in accounts by Alfred (1997; 2001), Williams (2000) and Stanley (2006) in relation to the marginal positioning of minority ethnic hetero-sexual and lesbian women. A pilot study (AUT, 2001) conducted in 2001 in six universities in the UK found considerable evidence that LGBT staff did not feel comfortable in the university, with only 20 per cent of gay men and 13 per cent of women being 'out' at work. A glass ceiling for LGBT staff also seemed to be in evidence, as well as reports of discrimination and harassment.

Such marginal positionings are related to another important constraint on an individual's identity construction: the power of 'others' to ascribe identity. According to Jenkins (1996) 'what people think about us is no less important than what we think about ourselves. It is not enough to assert an identity. That identity must also be validated (or not) by those with whom we have dealings. *Social identity is never unilateral*' (p. 21, original emphasis). In many of the above accounts, the struggle is not (or not only) *self*-perceptions of 'inauthenticity' but that *others* do not perceive the writers to be 'truly' professional/academic. For example, a minority ethnic further education lecturer in a research project conducted by one of authors (Leathwood, 2005b) described how she came up against challenges to her authority as a professional not only from lecturer colleagues but also from men students, echoing Osler (1997), Stanley (2006), Maylor (under review) and others who found that Black teachers' and lecturers' professional identities were often challenged by students. She felt it was partly about being in a men-dominated department, emphasizing experiences of sexism she experienced as a woman, but also said 'I think if I was perhaps an English woman you see then I probably wouldn't have had so much trouble . . . you know they cannot accept that I can actually be a lecturer' (Leathwood, 2005: 399). Fordham (1993) notes that gender 'passing' is a prerequisite for the success of African-American and white women in the US academy: 'Indeed, it could be debated that the first – and some would argue the only – commandment for women in the academy is "Thou must be taken seriously". "Thou must be taken seriously" is a euphemism for "thou must not appear as a woman" ' (p. 4).

In a study of academics' experiences of speaking and writing also conducted by one of the authors[1] (Read, 2003; 2005), one white woman senior
lecturer with a working-class background described the audience reaction to
her first presentation:

> The first research presentation I gave was a pretty awful experience. In
> fact it makes me blush thinking about it. . . . I over-prepared and then
> read from a written paper which I think is disastrous. The audience prob-
> ably just wanted a really basic introduction to the background literature.
> The upshot was that the group (about 100 male engineering students)
> became quite unruly as the talk went on and had to be asked to keep quiet
> several times by the faculty member who had organized it. The bit that
> makes me really blush is that, at one point I noticed a piece of paper
> going around the room, and at the end the faculty member demanded to
> see it and then handed it to me which I wish he hadn't. It said something
> pretty rude (obscene-rude rather than impolite-rude) about the way I was
> sitting and I couldn't then get the image out of my head that all the time
> I'd been sweating to get through this obviously misjudged paper, all these
> young men had been looking at me with this particular image in mind (as
> I gather nearly everyone in the room saw the paper!).

Usually, as Bourdieu and others have described, the greater cultural and
symbolic capital the lecturer has acquired in relation to the student (through
academic qualifications and occupational status) leads to the former holding
greater 'authority' to communicate than the latter (Bourdieu, 1988, 1991;
Grant, 1997; see Chapter 8). However, for the participant above, members of
the mainly male audience worked collectively to construct themselves in a
'superior' hierarchical position. By calling attention to her gendered 'otherness' through sexualizing her identity performance in a denigrating way,
they worked to undermine the status of the speaker and her 'right' to speak
as a (supposedly gender-neutral) academic. However, interestingly, this
particular participant went on to describe how she now feels comfortable in
'combative' academic environments. As Brooks (1997) argues, it is important
to note the diversity and difference *between* women's interpretation of their
experiences as well as noting similarities. For example, in a questionnaire
sent to academic women relating to gendered experiences in the workplace,
Brooks received a number of replies adding positive comments about the
research and its resonance with their own political views and experiences,
but also some stating that they did not 'care about feminist issues', or that

---

[1] This study was based on email interviews with 52 academics (28 women, 24 men) in
the discipline of sociology, in a variety of pre-1992 and post-1992 universities. Twenty-
nine identified themselves as middle or professional class, and 16 identified themselves as of working-class origin. The vast majority of the sample identified themselves
as white, white British, or white European. The questions (relating to participants'
views and experiences of speaking and writing in the academy) were designed to be as
open ended as possible to encourage detailed answers.

they themselves had never noticed any discrimination in their careers. Experiences are different, and more importantly, interpreted in diverse ways, by different women, complicated of course by myriad other subject positions that come into play at any one time, which can complexly work to construct, mitigate against, or exacerbate feelings of 'otherness' (Walker, 1998; Halford and Leonard, 2001).

Despite such variation, it is still possible, and indeed necessary, to 'tease out' and explore commonalities of experience amongst different women relating to gender (Francis, 2001). And indeed, research indicates that it is often women (at all levels of the career ladder, and of different classes and ethnicities) who are feeling the most pressures over the increased evaluation and surveillance of their work, and the pressure to 'perform' (see, for example, Acker and Armenti, 2004). The pressures of such performativity in academia (i.e. the need to be seen and judged to perform as well as merely producing the performance) has been compared to Foucault's (1977) model of the self-regulation of behaviour produced by the 'panopticon' (Shore and Wright, 2000; Davies et al., 2005; Davies, 2006). The panopticon was an historical form of surveillance of prisoners, in which the possibility of total surveillance by both guards and other prisoners led, Foucault argued, to the prisoner often 'self-regulating' 'his' own behaviour. Similarly, academics in the new managerialist climate often put the most pressure on themselves to perform in ways that are seen as valued and appropriate to the higher education institution, and it is women academics who experience more fear, anxiety and sleeplessness over their own self-perceptions of their performance (Acker and Armenti, 2004; Acker and Webber, 2006). Acker and Armenti's (2004) study showed that issues to do with self-esteem and self-presentation were key concerns for the academic women they interviewed, especially worries over not being 'smart enough', and a felt need to continually justify their worth as women in a 'masculine' culture – to prove that they were 'one of them' (p.16; p.13). However, as we have discussed throughout this section, being 'one of them', the socially dominant conception of the academic, is ultimately impossible for women. Walker, discussing Walkerdine (1990) and her assertion that 'the struggle to perform academically and to perform as feminine must at times seem almost impossible' (p. 144), states.

> Women's intellectual success threatens masculine rationality so that it is dangerous for women to construct transgressive identities which step over the gender divide or challenge acceptable ways of being, such as the 'good girl'. The contradictions may well be unbearable . . . Women are then left with the near-impossible dilemma of balancing 'feminine' attributes, which are seen as inappropriate for the job, and 'masculine' ones seen as unacceptable in women. (Walker, 1998: 337)

As we shall discuss below, many women academics have challenged the dominance of masculine conceptions of the academic, and have worked individually and collectively to resist their marginalization (see also Chapter 10). First though we will be looking in more detail at particular aspects of 'dominant' academic culture and how they work to (re-) assemble and re-enforce Enlightenment constructions of the academic as embodied in the 'male'.

Academic cultures: the ruthless, competitive academic

In contrast to the popular cultural argument that women are 'naturally' less suited to academia, many feminist and pro-feminists have argued that women's relative lack of 'success' in the academy in relation to men is actually related to wider cultural discourses concerning gender (Thomas, 1996; Acker and Armenti, 2004; Acker and Webber, 2006). As Currie et al. 2003 state, as more formal and official discriminatory practices are phased out, 'the constraints on women's careers become more subtle' (Currie et al., 2003: 2., cited in Kjeldal et al., 2005). Varying significantly between countries, between institutions and between disciplines, it is nevertheless possible to speak of an institutional academic 'culture' comprising the dominant discourses of knowledge, communication and practice in higher education institutions (see Bartholomae, 1985; Ballard and Clanchy, 1988; Lea and Street, 1998). And as Acker and Webber (2006: 486) note, this 'culture' is highly masculinized:

> Women academics in universities find themselves in a university that was created and developed by men and with men in mind. This is not to buy into an essentialist take on men, as we know that, historically, only a minority of men have been fortunate enough to gain a university education, let alone occupy the professoriate. Yet there are certain values and styles commonly associated with men that can be easily discerned in today's universities, such as competitiveness, success, individualism, hierarchy and assertiveness.

Characteristics such as those described by Acker and Webber above are not innate, essential traits but are socially constructed concepts, which are conceptualized and experienced differently by different groups of people (see Fülöp, 2004; Read, 2006). As Fülöp (2005) argues, in countries such as Japan that do not have a strong 'individualist' culture, it is not seen as 'appropriate' for either men or women to compete openly – they are more likely to self-present competition in the guise of cooperation in order to avoid censure.

Competitiveness and assertiveness are also deeply gendered constructions. Social constraints may often make it harder for individuals to feel comfortable appropriating characteristics or acting in ways that are deemed to fall under the remit of the 'opposite' gender. Doing so risks social censure. The dominance in the West of cultural associations of competitive behaviours with masculinity means that in many western countries the 'performance' of competitive characteristics or acts by women may be 're-constructed' by themselves or others in more 'gender-appropriate' ways. For example, 'a woman might behave in competitive and aggressive ways, but her behaviour might be constructed as "manipulative" or "bitchy", stereotypically feminine characteristics' (Francis, 2000: 17). Moreover, the way in which behaviour is interpreted as competitiveness or assertiveness by others is also racialized as well as gendered. African-Caribbean women are more often perceived in white majority culture as aggressive, domineering and thus 'unfeminine' (whilst Asian women tend to be constructed as 'too' passive, quiet and overly-feminine (see Hill Collins, 1990; Fordham, 1993; Pyke and Johnson, 2003). Such 'majority' perceptions are also found in relation to working-class and lesbian women. 'Proper' non-competitive passive femininity seemingly resides only with the White, heterosexual middle classes.

A number of studies do show that there can be identifiable gender-appropriate differences in the way men and women act in relation to competition and cooperation in educational settings (e.g. Schick Case, 1990; Kelly, 1991; Kimbell et al., 1991; Sommers and Lawrence, 1992). (However, such acts or 'performances' are also constructed through the eyes of researchers who may indeed at times re-construct behaviour gender appropriately.) Such practices in relation to students are explored further in Chapter 8. Jefferson (1996) specifically links masculinity with competition when he describes the 'masculine will to win' and a conception of the 'triumphant man' that is quite commonly held as a male fantasy ideal. Indeed ambition or the 'desire to succeed' has traditionally been attributed as a masculine trait in Western societies (Gilligan, 1987).

As we shall be exploring further in Chapter 8, writers on language have argued that the most favoured and valued styles of communicating in academia – both in 'professional' speaking and writing – is assertive, unemotional and confident (Harding, 1991; Martin, 1997; see also Farr, 1993; Francis et al., 2001). Academics are also encouraged to act individualistically and competitively in order to 'make a name' for themselves and present 'their' views and opinions in favour of others (see, for example, Doherty, 2000). Although academics are widely judged by their *written* communication, particularly in the forms of journal articles and books, their facility in utilizing academic language orally (for example at interview, or in presentations given at conferences) is also important in terms of their own self-conception of their 'authenticity' as a member of the academy, and how their worth is judged by their peers. Not much research has been conducted on academic oral as opposed to written communication. However, a study by Schick Case (1990) on conversations between academic men and women found that men tended to use more assertive, aggressive speech styles, and that women were more socially facilitative. However, Schick Case's study was focused on informal conversations rather than formal presentations or seminar communication.

The competitive/ aggressive culture of speaking in the academy can be particularly uncomfortable for those that feel they do not 'fit the mould' of the classed raced and gendered construction of the 'ideal' academic. A study by one of the authors investigating 52 men and women academic's views on speaking and writing found that whilst two-thirds of the sample stated they generally felt confident and comfortable when speaking at lectures or seminars, descriptions of feeling nervous or uncomfortable were more often recounted by younger women academics and younger academics of working-class origin (Read, 2003; 2005). Unfortunately, due to the low numbers of minority ethnic participants it was not possible to make any meaningful analysis by ethnicity – reflecting the continued paucity of minority ethnic staff in academia (see Chapters 3–4).

The 'question and answer' section that is customarily held at the end of conference or seminar presentations was singled out by 13 women – and also 7 men – as the most disliked and 'nerve-wracking' element of speaking in the academy. For these academics this section provoked some notably strong emotional reactions for an activity so central to academic practice. Some of the descriptions men and women used in the sample in relation to this 'ritual' included: 'quite anxious', 'a bit nervous', 'a bit panicked', '[it is] a bit daunting', 'dread', 'hate', 'it used to strike terror into my heart'. Such emotions often related to a conception that this practice was particularly competitive and aggressive. For example one junior lecturer in the study, a white woman from a middle-class background, stated 'I always dread the questions part . . . I'm always relieved to get it over with. I guess my anxiety comes from the fact that I've seen academics pretty much torn apart at that stage of the presentation and am dreading the same thing happening to me.' Another white, middle-class woman lecturer said 'I really hate the aggressive style of questioning where there is an impetus to "prove you wrong", and I also dislike the fact that questions are used as an opportunity for questioners to advertise their own research area and eloquence, not always on directly related subjects!'

A number of participants in the study specifically described the more 'competitive', 'aggressive' style of questioning as a 'masculine' style of communication, and the more socially facilitative, supportive style as more 'feminine'. Examples can be seen in the following two descriptions, both from white women senior lecturers, the first of whom is of working-class origin, the second middle class:

> I think here at my university we have quite a combative style of questioning because we had two speakers cry last a couple of years ago during one season (term) of talks . . . . outside though, I realize that often (this is especially true in some gender-focused conferences) people always preface a question – however critical it is in implication – with a thanks and a 'that was really fascinating' or something.

> The culture of HE is highly gendered and many academics seem to have confrontational styles of communication, disrespect for others and unwillingness to listen to another point of view rather than focus on articulating their own . . . the nuances of how people are feeling, or what they are thinking are overlooked.

Interestingly, it is precisely the 'right' for academics to be 'disrespectful' to other colleagues that writers such as Hayes (2005) believes is being eroded in the academy. Noting with incredulity that 'at research conferences, poor or boring papers are listened to with respect', he sees such tolerance as the imposition of 'emotional freedom' at the expense of academic freedom. He argues 'surely the watchwords of academic freedom are respect nothing, tolerate nothing, criticise everything', advocating a rather 'tougher' communicative style that is (explicitly) culturally associated with both 'traditional' academia and (implicitly) 'macho' masculinity. The association of the 'question and answer' section of presentations with 'machismo' is neatly illustrated by Doherty (2000), who describes overhearing a conversation between two male colleagues after a university lecture: 'one of them had asked the speaker a hostile question, and his admiring friend said, "You landed a good clean punch. She was reeling"' (p. 351). Despite some participants stating they believed that the 'macho' aggressive style of questioning has become less common in recent decades, the 'threat' of being at the receiving end of such verbal 'punches' was a common source of concern amongst participants (Read, 2003; 2005).

The finding that women academics and those of working-class origin felt the most uncomfortable in such environments seems to supports the argument that performing the 'academic' fits more comfortably for those with middle-class and male identities, who are more able to move through academic culture like 'a fish in water' (Bourdieu, 1987). However, it needs to be stressed that this finding needs to be read in the context that it may be easier for women to articulate feelings such as lack of confidence or self-doubt, as this fits more easily with culturally 'acceptable' constructions of feminine identity (see Woodfield et al., 2005). Many described how such nerves and discomfort would be 'covered up' in order to be able to present in the 'favoured' academic style that positions the speaker as the calm, confident emotionally detached 'expert' (Read, 2003; 2005), that, as Davies has pointed out is at the heart of the masculinized conception of the professional (Davies, 1996). A number of studies have shown how women and others who hold non-hegemonic identities 'perform' in the academy in ways that are more characteristic of the white, male, middle-class 'norm' – for example, Rosa, a Professor of Architecture in Lester's (2008) study, describes how she hides what she sees as the 'essence' of her 'compassionate and loving' self to perform a 'tough' persona in order to be taken 'seriously' in the workplace (p. 277, 279). These lecturers' continued presence in the academy suggests that despite discomfort they have been successful in 'performing' in a role that does not 'fit' the 'habitus' of their other subject positions, although this might place extra inner strain or discomfort that might not be perceived by others:

> All members of oppressed groups have to work hard at ventriloquizing
> establishment culture in academia, and this 'mimicry' can produce a
> self-division and painful lack of convergence between the initial culture

of family and neighbourhood, and the acquired culture. (Morley, 1997b: 113)

Ivanic (1998) points out that it is important to note that there *are* alternative 'ideologies of knowledge-making' within the academy – some of which emphasize and value characteristics such as cooperation and collectivity more highly than 'traditional' discourses (see below). However, it is fair to say that in general the high value placed on self-confidence, assertiveness and competitiveness can be seen to be a central strand running through 'dominant' discourses of academic culture (see Francis et al., 2001; Acker and Armenti, 2004).

Such characteristics are widely held to have been exacerbated by the emerging dominance of 'new managerialist' cultures and systems of 'quality' audit in universities in many parts of the world (Thomas and Davies, 2002; Deem, 2003; Barry et al., 2007; Fisher, 2007). Academics in Australia, for example, have their research regularly judged in external reviews, and many academics in other countries have their output regularly evaluated in appraisals, leading to greatly increased stress and pressure for university academic staff, particularly those whose outside commitments prevent them working 'above and beyond' in terms of producing the expected 'outputs' (see below; Acker and Webber, 2006).

In the UK, systems of quality audit are focused on both teaching and research. Government funding for academic research in HE institutions in the UK has been allocated since 1986 through the RAE; see Chapter 4). In this system, each university puts forward a submission detailing its research output and is awarded scores meant to indicate their degree of 'excellence' in each subject area (Harley, 2003). Since the system was established many universities (especially 'pre-1992' institutions) have placed a substantial emphasis on the need for academics to produce output that is 'worthy' of being entered into the exercise, with some academics finding themselves feted and headhunted, whilst others have struggled to achieve promotion or hold onto contracted posts if they have not been deemed to have produced 'the goods' (Willmott, 1995; Swain, 1999; Harley, 2000). Women in the UK as elsewhere continue to face the constraints on their time described above, affecting their ability to achieve the high levels of output in 'prestigious' journals by which academics are judged. As Jackson (2002: 28) notes:

> It is clear . . . that with teaching as well as with research male academics are taken as the norm. The 'capable teacher' who also contributes positively to the RAE, and who works competitively and individually in a market-led academy is not a model that many women would recognise of themselves.

Academics in some post-1992 universities in the UK have less pressure placed on them to 'perform' for the RAE, as the focus of many schools and departments is on teaching rather than research, with the institutions not expecting to 'win' funding for research from the exercise (see Clegg, 2008).

However, as Thomas and Davies (2002) point out, many of these institutions also place high importance on other forms of accountability measures and academics in these institutions also face the stress of 'performativity' in other ways, for example, performance-related pay schemes and teaching performance evaluation measures, also experienced by many colleagues in the 'pre-1992' sector.

Therefore, whilst mitigating against some forms of discrimination, the dominance of new managerialism has nevertheless worked to maintain and exacerbate the maculinized culture of individualism and competitiveness in the academy. Harley (2003) describes this transition as the erosion of a more collegiate 'gentleman's club' in favour of a culture of aggressive individualism she labels 'smart macho', borrowing the term from a study by Maddock and Parkin (1993) of public sector cultures – 'smart macho' being a regime whereby 'women are included as long as they compete on equal terms with men and are "needy and greedy" enough to win' (Harley, 2003; see also Le Feuvre's, 1999, analysis of conceptions of 'femininization', discussed in Chapter 2).

Needless to say many academics, both men and women, feel acutely out of place in such an environment, and feel deleterious effects as a result:

> The highly intrusive nature of the [RAE] . . . and the continual measurements . . . is a mutilating experience. All academics are subject to these criteria and regulate their work accordingly. The academic, at once subject and object, produces the work by which his or her authority will be judged. Because these criteria are mostly hidden from view, except the exhortation to produce a quantity of research, the academic experiences acute anguish and stress. (Howie and Tauchert, 2002: 68).

Blackmore (1999) describes how many women educational leaders in her research study tried to buffer their colleagues from the worst excesses of the new market led approach. However, they were often isolated in their roles, and acutely aware they were judged (by men and women) differently from male colleagues as 'being too female or not female enough, too feminist or not feminist enough' (p. 206), showing how women are often judged more negatively than men if they are successful in a masculinized environment (see Thomas and Davies, 2002; Fisher, 2007). In her research Fisher notes how male criticism of a female Dean in the Business School was 'demeaning, personal and highly sexualised. Either she has a voracious sexual appetite and is desperate for a man ("she's always looking at my flies") or she is asexual, possibly a lesbian, and therefore undesirable ("she looks like Dierdre Barlow", "she looks like a man")' (Fisher, 2007: 512). Moreover, whilst women's comments about the Dean were not sexualized, they also contained essentialist expectations of gendered behaviour, remarking, for example, that the Dean 'doesn't give the warm buzzes expected from a woman' (p. 513).

New posts related to development and quality may offer opportunities for promotion for women – and/or to move away from marginalized positions – something Morley found in her research (Morley, 2003b). The danger, as

Morley noted, is that women get further squeezed out of more high status research posts, and have less time to conduct their own research. Deem and colleagues (Deem et al., 2000), in a discussion of further education (FE), suggest that there has been some social and cultural as well as demographic feminization of FE management, but this is much more marked at the middle management level whilst senior management remains more men's work than women's albeit tinged with changing notions of masculinities. Elsewhere, Prichard and Deem (1998) suggest that women may be brought into middle management positions to 'smooth the passage' of new managerialism – and perhaps this is also applicable to HE with notions that women's 'people skills' will enable them to make stroppy academics comply with new bureaucratic and quality procedures. This can be seen as an example of what Walkerdine (2003) argues is the new professional femininity of the neo-liberal subject. This new subject is not only 'created in the image of the middle class', but also embodies the qualities of 'emotionality, caring and introspection' associated with middle-class femininity: 'they are to look the part, sound the part and, moreover, they can make themselves and their homes over to conform to this middle class aesthetic' (p. 242).

However, as we discuss in Chapter 6, we would question whether the neo-liberal subject can be described as feminized – for as we have seen throughout this chapter the dominant cultural construction of the 'professional', who occupies the highest most secure place in the academy, is still embodied as masculine (see Leathwood, 2005b). This can be seen further in the strong continuing cultural association of the academic with the (masculinized) 'individual'.

Academic cultures: the 'objective', neutral, duty-free academic

As we have seen, the 'ideal' academic in the culture of the university is one that is 'competitive' and self-confident – characteristics that arguably fit most comfortably with men's constructed gender identities. Moreover, the academic is also often implicitly constructed as a lone *individual* – 'man' *is* an island in academia. Such an identity is more difficult to accommodate by those balancing other identities as parents or carers with time-consuming duties and responsibilities of care to others, or those with a sense of duty (and desire) to care for students and other colleagues in an emotional and pastoral sense as well as providing purely 'detached' academic support.

The difficulties of arranging childcare, or planning if or when to have children in combination with an academic career that does not take into account such needs, has been a common issue in studies of academic women with (or desiring to have) children (Walker, 1998; Raddon, 2001, cited in Ramsay and Letherby, 2006; Acker and Armenti, 2004). Some of the 'younger' (under 40) women in Acker and Armenti's research described planning children to fit in with the demands of the academic timetable – one of their interviewees states 'for the women my age almost all the babies were born in May and June because that seemed like the only safe time to have a child' (Acker and Armenti, 2004: 10). Theirs and other studies (e.g. Finkel et al., 1994; Coiner and George, 1998; Wolf-Wendel and Ward, 2003) have shown that some women are reluctant even to take the time legally allowed them in terms of maternity leave, or to try to mask or keep silent any difficulties they are experiencing in terms of combining childcare and academic work: 'the fear seems to be that colleagues will learn that the parent is not coping, and not coping is equivalent to not being an acceptable academic' (Acker and Armenti, 2004: 11).

With these difficulties it does not seem surprising that Bagilhole (1993) found in her sample of women academics in the UK that only 56 per cent were married or were living with a partner, and only 30 per cent had children, and other studies have confirmed this pattern in the US (Mason and Goulden, 2004) and Australia (Probert, 2005). Probert found that for some women, especially in their 40s, the difficulties of increased care responsibilities for parents and relatives were not alleviated by university policies such as day care or maternity leave, as they were still expected to manage workloads and publish at a rate that was incompatible with official working hours (Probert, 2005). As a senior male academic in Harris et al.'s Australian study noted, it is older men who are most likely to advance in the culture of academia:

> Very clearly, males, largely between the ages of 40 and 60 [are most likely to get ahead]. They are people who don't have major family responsibilities. If they have families, the wife would be taking the substantial load of raising the children. They are people who can afford 60 plus hours [work per week] because they don't have outside responsibilities. They are normally males in that age range who have obsessional characteristics who are willing to put in high workload time, that includes both research and career advancement. (Harris et al., 1998: 144)

As Howie and Tauchert note, while most higher education institutions are supposedly and officially gender neutral, they actually work with the preconception that its faculty possess 'male' bodies, with the accompanying cultural assumption that the bulk of the time-consuming care of children or other relatives will be performed by their own satellite women dependants:

> A quiet departmental expectation to be available to teach twilight hours; accrual of pastoral care duties; problems with committee selection and roles; toilets with no provision of sanitary bins or baby changing facilities; sexist jokes in the lecture room and staff room; local struggles to maintain parity in pay and promotion. These represent diverse, and sometimes trivial, consequences of latent structures and practices concealed beneath the skin of the androgynous university body. (Howie and Tauchert, 2002: 62)

As the above quotation recognizes, women are not only more likely to take on extra caring relationships in their personal lives, they are also more often culturally positioned as carers in the academy itself – by other colleagues, by students, and also by their own desire to provide such care and support (Skeggs, 1995; Acker and Armenti, 2004). As Ramsay and Leatherby (2006) note, it is important to remember that women who are not mothers are also positioned as 'natural' carers by staff and other students, and are also expected to work extra hours that mothers cannot. A number of studies have found that academic women were more likely to take on administrative, committee and responsibilities related to students – and often be encouraged by managers to do this – than men (Acker and Feuerverger, 1996; Brooks, 1997; Letherby and Shiels, 2001; Kjeldal et al., 2005). Studies have shown that this is a pattern also visited on women administrative staff (see Makebola, 2003; Acker and Webber, 2006) and minority ethnic staff of both genders (see Tierney and Bensimon, 1996; Stanley, 2006).

Such 'support' and advisory work however continues to be undervalued in the academy. The values of caring have no place in masculinist managerial-ism (Leathwood, 2000; Hebson et al., 2007), and Adkins and Lury (2000) note that 'emotionally appeased customers and men co-workers . . . cannot be claimed through performance as indicators of personal effectivity' in the context of performativity (p. 158). Caring therefore goes unrecognized and unrewarded, with women who spend 'too much' time caring never able to meet the ideals of performance. If women are not seen to care, however, their femininity comes under question (Leathwood, 2005b). Performance indicators based on research outputs also do not recognize time spent on committee or advisory boards. Stanley (2006), citing Gregory (2001), notes that women academics of colour are more likely to be involved in advisory or committee work (and also have a heavier teaching workload) than white men or women academics. Mirza describes how the increasing drive towards 'diversity' initiatives in higher education as part of 'cost-effectively [meeting] the needs and aspirations of the greatest number of stakeholders' (HEFCE, 2000, cited in Mirza, 2006b: 102) has meant that some minority ethnic staff have found themselves becoming 'hot property' in the academy – as long as they 'stay in their place' (p.103) – however, they must also work harder to remain 'research active'.

Despite the dominance of the individualistic ethos in academia, a number of feminist scholars have nevertheless noted how career advancement in the university is and always has been strongly based on collective networking, 'collegiality' and the building of a 'reputation' amongst one's peers, which can help provide crucial aid in areas such as winning research funding, gaining promotion, being appointed on prestigious committeees or boards, and opportunities to publish, as well as mentoring and encouragement (Bagilhole, 2002; Harley, 2003). This network of reputation is something that has been historically, and still is, very much a masculinized (as well as classed and 'raced') aspect of academic culture, with women less likely to have access to, and the support of, such networks of influential colleagues (O'Leary and Mitchell, 1990; Bagilhole, 1993; Bagilhole and Goode, 2001; Mavin and Bryans, 2002; Harley, 2003; Kjeldal et al., 2005). As well as often being marginalized or excluded from particular opportunities, women can find their own work (and hence reputation) being judged more negatively by the collective standards of a masculinized culture which values both forms of knowledge itself, and the favoured ways in which to communicate such knowledge, through a gendered lens:

> There seems to be an undervaluing and stereotyping of women as part of the male institution. This is more problematic than overtly discriminatory behaviour. Often inadvertent, sometimes well-intentioned, it often seems so 'normal' as to be virtually invisible, yet creates an environment that wastes women's resources, takes time and energy to ignore or deal with, undermines self-esteem, and damages professional morale.
> (Bagilhole, 2002: 50; see also Bryson, 2004)

Compounding this is a tendency for women, due to the influence of culturally dominant constructions of gender-appropriate behaviour, to be less likely to wish to 'self-promote' their activities and put themselves forward for positions that will advance their careers (Bagilhole, 2002). Those who do succeed often find themselves needing to 'play the game' and assimilate into the masculinized culture of the university in order to keep their positions in the playing field and retain their construction (to themselves and/or to others) as a 'valid', 'authentic' academic (Bagilhole, 2002; Mavin and Bryans, 2002). Indeed, it should be stressed that whilst such competitive and individualistic behaviours can be culturally ascribed as 'masculine', and are therefore arguably easier for men to 'take up' and adopt, they can nevertheless can be (and often are) practised by both men and women. Morley (2003), Skelton (2005) and others have noted the struggles and tensions that occur *between* women (including feminists) as well as between men and women in the academy. hooks argues competitive university cultures combined with the high degree of marginalization of academic women of colour can sometimes cause tensions and competition between black women academics: 'Often in white settings we are like siblings fighting for the approval of "white parents" whose attention we now have' (hooks, 1991: 92). Maguire (forthcoming) has also described ageism in relation to the competition for academic status and promotion on the part of younger women academics towards more mature women academics.

As we have noted, it has been argued that the rising dominance of 'new managerialist' working practices in the academy can be of benefit to women – its emphasis on transparency and accountability working to make women academics' achievements more visible, and minimize the influence of nepotism and the 'old boys' network' in academics' career trajectories (see discussions in Harley, 2003; Acker and Webber, 2006; Davies, 2006). However, whilst it has worked to challenge some traditional patriarchal practices, and opened up opportunities for some women, this does not mean the new managerialism is fundamentally changing gendered inequalities, or the gendered construction of the academic. For example, a study of new managerialist appraisal systems in three Scottish universities (Wilson and Nutley,

2003) found that many women wanted to be appraised, in order to discuss their career, get feedback, be listened to, and to highlight what they had managed to achieve, in a supposedly neutral and transparent process (see also Brooks, 1997). However, the model of the ideal successful academic that such supposedly 'neutral' systems are appraising is still the highly gendered model discussed above – the competitive, individualistic worker who puts in long hours. And with new managerialist regimes of productivity, the 'ideal' academic is now expected to produce even more quantifiable output in terms of publications, at the expense of more 'caring' and feminized concerns such as teaching and pastoral care (Harley, 2003).

Conclusions

In this chapter we have explored changing constructions of academic identities, and the ways in which these constructions are gendered. Such an exploration needs to take into account the massive changes taking place in the higher education arena in many parts of the world, in terms of new managerialist structures and initiatives, and the 'massification' of the university in terms of student numbers. We have seen how the new managerialism has had a particularly strong impact on both women and men's experiences of the academy and their own professional identities. We have also discussed the importance of highlighting the many ways in which academics that do not 'fit the mould' of the white, middle-class, heterosexual man have always felt a degree of tension and ambivalence in the academy – exploring this specifically in relation to gender. In Chapter 6 we looked at the ways in which the historically and culturally dominant conception of knowledge in the West as a 'masculine' arena has meant that women students have always struggled to challenge or subvert the dominant construction of the 'student' as male. As we have seen in this chapter women lecturers and researchers often face the same struggles. Many aspects of both 'traditional' and 'new managerialist' academic cultures can be seen to be infused with culturally dominant discourses associating the 'academic' with the 'masculine', with detrimental effects on many women's academic careers and academic/professional identities.

However it needs to be stressed that the degree to which cultural practices are masculinized will vary greatly in different departments, universities and countries, and are not blanketly universal, providing space for alternative experiences: 'the academy, like any other organization is full of contradictions – structures are both fixed and volatile, enabling and constraining. There are gendered sites of opportunity and constraint' (Morley, 2003b).

As feminists such as Hey (1997), Morley (1997b) and Reay (1997) note, there are many privileges to working in academia that should not be forgotten in a concentration on the detrimental aspects of academic culture: 'working as a researcher in higher education in an elite institution is a lot more privileged than working on the tills at Tesco's supermarket' (Hey,

1993: 145). Moreover, it should also be stressed that there have been, and continue to be, sustained challenges to dominant academic cultural practices. As we will be discussing further in Chapter 10, many women (including some who do not identify themselves as feminists) and pro-feminist men in higher education around the globe have resisted and challenged aspects of masculinized culture, and have worked individually and collectively to provide alternative practices (Goode and Bagilhole, 1998; Walker, 1998; Morley, 1999; Deem and Ozga, 2000; Barry et al., 2007). Many have identified particular aspects of academic professional culture that should be (and are) challenged by feminists. For example Doherty (2000) and the Social Justice Group at the Centre for Advanced Feminist Studies, University of Minnesota, argue the pressing need to challenge individualism in dominant academic culture:

> Resisting individualistic notions of human life and maintaining substantive connections with and accountability to our communities are necessary to transform the university, where current efforts to achieve social justice are at loggerheads with the university's efforts to maintain the status quo. (Doherty, 2000: 262)

Entwined with this, many women have challenged socially dominant conceptions of what it means to be an academic, and constructed alternative identities: for example, a Black South African academic in Walker's (1998) study challenged students' and lecturers' perceptions by forming a women's soccer team, and worked collectively with other Black women colleagues to challenge the lack of encouragement for Black women to do research in her institution. Another white academic in her study spoke of constructing a 'new model' of what it means to be a 'female academic':

> Her research, she says, will be done 'my way' against the grain of established scholarship in her field, even though 'I don't know what that's going to be'; she is determined to 'own' her work so that 'if I write a good book now, it's not going to be at the cost of my interior life, it's going to be with it', because 'I want to be known for something that's female, I don't want this artificial separation between self and the published'. (Walker, 1998: 345)

Despite these resistances, and despite some increases in the number of women in the academic workforce in some countries, there is little evidence to support the conception that academic culture is, or is becoming, 'feminized' – at least in a way that feminists and pro-feminists would desire. The dominant construction of the academic is still predominantly a 'masculine' one. Unless the wider (and seemingly almost universal) cultural 'devaluing' of the feminine is challenged, the realm of the intellectual will still be equated with the superior/masculine. Whilst this association is culturally dominant, it is not surprising that an increase in numbers of women participating in academia (even if it *is* in the 'lower', more casualized and temporary, ends of the hierarchy) is accompanied by a perceived loss of status and a 'de-intellectualization' of the profession. For a continuing cultural equation of the realm of the 'intellectual' with the masculine means that any perceived 'erosion' of masculine dominance in HEIs will inevitably lead universities to be associated more strongly with the 'feminine', due to the cultural association of the feminine with inferiority. As Husu and Morley (2000: 138) note in the context of Europe: 'the time is now ripe for the changes sweeping throughout . . . higher education to incorporate a recognition of the need for *gendered* change.' As we have outlined here, such change needs to be substantial: unravelling and 'deconstructing' the very notion of the individualized, masculinized academic subject.

8
Academic practices: assessment, speaking and writing

> [T]he content of courses and programs is only the more concrete form of undermining experienced by the woman student. More invisible, less amenable to change by committee proposal or fiat, is the hierarchical image, the structure of relationships, even the style of discourse, including assumptions about theory and practice, ends and means, process and goal. (Rich, 1980: 136)

As we have discussed throughout this book, academic practices in many countries are increasingly being constructed through new managerialist discourses. There has also been a substantial increase in the assessment practices utilized to monitor and evaluate such practices, to maintain academic 'standards' and to assess both students' and academics' 'performance' in the academy (Broadfoot, 1999; Leathwood, 2005a). Indeed, Broadfoot notes that in the case of England, assessment may come to be seen as a 'defining principle of English education policy in the late twentieth century' (Broadfoot, 1999: 2). This chapter is the first of two focusing specifically on academic practices. Changes in the form of assessment, specifically the increased use of coursework, are often used to explain the higher levels of achievement of women students at university. This chapter will examine these issues and draw on the authors' and others' research on speaking, writing and application to study to assess the extent to which contemporary cultures and practices of the academy can be said to have been 'feminized', and the implications for women and men students.

In Chapter 6 we looked at various constructions of the university student, and noted that despite the slight majority of women students in the academy, such discourses are in many ways 'masculinized'. We also noted in Chapter 7 that the academic is also discursively constructed as masculine – and that a masculinized academic culture both reflects and constrains, not only the kinds of knowledge that are seen to be valued in the academy, but also the favoured ways in which such knowledge can be communicated. This not only affects academics themselves, but also has a profound impact on students' lives – for, as we shall see in this chapter, in order to succeed at university students must learn the 'rules of the game' of communication in the academy – both orally in seminars and tutorials, and in written form in the language they are encouraged to use when writing essays. And finally, a gendered academic culture infuses the value judgements of academics when they come to assess not only the *content* of students' essays or seminar presentations, but also the *style* in which they are written or spoken.

What is academic language?

So what is academic language, and what are the favoured styles of speaking and writing in the academy? Despite their cultural and institutional specificity, dominant pedagogical practices in the academy such as the lecture, the examination and the essay become 'naturalized': they come to be seen as the only or 'natural' way of communicating, acting and learning (Grant, 1997; Wisniewski, 2000). Perhaps partly due to their 'naturalization', these 'conventions' are rarely explicitly examined, leaving students scrambling in the dark for an understanding of the 'rules of the game' they have found themselves playing (see Bartholomae, 1985; Lea and Street, 1998; Francis et al., 2001; Read et al., 2001; Robson et al., 2002). Students are aware that a certain style of writing is required, but are often uncertain of the specific details (Bartholomae, 1985; Lillis, 1997; Lea and Street, 1998; Read et al., 2001). The 'conventions' of the academic writing style can therefore be seen metaphorically as a type of 'code' to be 'cracked', a form of knowledge that students must uncover for themselves. A number of studies have highlighted the difficulties students face in acquiring this crucial cultural knowledge. A survey on essay-writing conducted with over 100 psychology students at the University of Keele found that the students' single greatest difficulty was not being able to understand what was required of them when writing an essay (cited by 28 per cent of students; Hartley and Chesworth, 2000).

For many students, the sole guidance in essay-writing is given in the form of scribbled notes in the margins of essays from the individual tutors marking their work. Such notes (often brief) point out instances where the lecturer believes a necessary 'rule' has been broken, for example, a sentence might lack relevance to the question set; a series of points may lack structure; a term may lack definition (Ballard and Clanchy, 1988). The long painstaking process of acquiring essay-writing skills through repeated practice and occasional 'guidance' can be seen in some ways as a form of learning by 'apprenticeship'. However, learners such as the apprentice tailors in Jean Lave's (1982) study acquire their skills through attempting to copy examples of work that are clearly and generally held to be exemplary. In contrast, the standards set for academic essay writing are far from obvious, for students and tutors alike. Tutors differ considerably in their interpretation of academic conventions and the importance they attach to them, causing students much confusion (Anson, 1988; Ballard and Clanchy, 1988). Students who study more than one discipline are further confused by contradictory inter-disciplinary variations in accepted style (Ballard and Clanchy, 1988; Nightingale, 1988). Moreover, unlike a craftperson's apprenticeship, it is not fully clear – either to the learner or the tutor – that a process of learning is, or should be, taking place. Often, academic conventions such as the need to evaluate a variety of views before coming to a conclusion, or the need to reference other people's ideas, are unproblematically seen as 'common sense' knowledge that the student should already be familiar with. Failure to correctly utilize these 'rules' can be put down to general illiteracy on the part of the student rather than a failure to grasp an extremely demanding and complex style of writing unfamiliar in the world outside the university (Ivanic, 1998; Lea and Street, 1998; Lillis, 2001). It is not surprising in this context then, that the increasing moves towards providing more detailed, clear guidance and support to students on these topics (especially in 'newer' universities) has been taken as an example of universities 'dumbing down', rather than acknowledging that such supposed 'common sense' skills are more easily acquired by those with middle-class social, cultural and educational capital (Bourdieu, 1988, 1991).

The complex style of writing required at university involves a combination of boldness, caution and 'rational' evaluation distinct to academia (Branthwaite et al., 1980; Ballard and Clanchy, 1988; Martin, 1997; Francis et al., 2001). Ballard and Clanchy (1988), Prosser and Webb (1994), Hounsell (1997) and Crammond (1998) all point to the importance of the demonstration of 'reasoned argument' in academic essay writing. This 'reasoned argument' is often expected to be expressed in a self-confident and bold style (Ainley, 1994; Martin, 1997). Indeed, a study by Branthwaite et al. (1980) on the essay-writing strategies of students demonstrates that a self-confident assertive style will be rewarded with higher grades. However, assertions are usually expected to be supported by 'evidence' and/or the citation of supporting arguments of other academics (Bartholomae, 1985; Ballard and Clanchy, 1988). Several studies have shown that students who present assertions or statements that are 'unsupported' and/or use 'extreme' language (e.g. the use of intensifiers or superlatives) will achieve lower grades (Hays, 1983; Hounsell, 1987; Francis et al., 2001).

Therefore, students are expected to be assertive (but not *too* assertive) in their language, and they are expected to support their assertions with supporting arguments or evidence. Moreover, students should include a critical evaluation of a variety of contrasting viewpoints on a subject, linked to the high value placed in academic 'culture' on 'objective' rational argument rather than emotional subjectivity (see Harding, 1990; 1991).

As we have noted in Chapter 7 in relation to academic staff and communication practices, such characteristics are deeply classed, racialized and gendered. Noting the social and cultural context of academic practices, educationalists have increasingly been taking a more critical look at the 'culture' of the academy, rather than focusing attention on the perceived inadequacies of individual students. Lea and Street (1998) and others have advocated a critical 'academic literacies' approach that highlights the use of power in the construction and legitimization of the discourses that comprise academic culture. Such discourses can be seen to reflect and reproduce social inequalities of power, including those centred on class, gender and ethnicity (Spurling, 1990; Lillis, 1997, 2001).

Class, gender, ethnicity and academic language

As we will describe in more detail throughout this chapter, work by linguists and other writers in the field of the sociology and anthropology of communication have noted that dominant, 'traditional' forms of academic writing and oral communication in HE often privilege traits culturally presented as 'masculine', such as boldness, individualism and competitiveness (traits also valued in the performance of academics, as we have seen in the previous chapter). For example, Martin (1997) asserts that university marking criteria favour culturally 'masculine' characteristics such as self-confidence, detachment, risk and challenge when awarding first class grades. 'Traditional' academic writing is expected to be characterized by a form of 'reasoned' argument that rewards demonstrations of assertiveness mixed with 'detached' caution and 'objectivity', characteristics associated by Harding and Martin as 'masculine' (Harding, 1990; Martin, 1997). Due to culturally dominant discourses of gendered behaviour, women students may arguably be less able to communicate in ways that are seen as oppositional to their gendered identity (Francis, 2000; Francis et al., 2001).

These forms of gendered communication comprise dominant 'traditional' forms of academic 'culture' – that is the dominant discourses of knowledge, communication and practice in higher education. These discourses influence (and are influenced by) the ways in which students and lecturers think, speak and write in the academy. And, as we have shown in previous chapters, this academic culture is not uniformly accessed or experienced. Despite the marked increase in students from working-class and ethnically diverse backgrounds attending university since the mid-1990s, such 'traditional' forms of academic culture predominantly reflect the dominant discourse of the student learner as white, middle class and male (Mirza, 1995; Grant, 1997). Therefore, as we shall see, becoming comfortable with the 'traditional' culture of academia, including the favoured ways of speaking and writing in the academy, could be slightly more difficult for those who do not fit neatly into these categories.

In this chapter we will be looking more specifically at two ways in which students' utilization of such language is presented – in verbal form in academic tutorials and seminars; and in written form in essays. Then, finally, we will look at the genderedness of the assessment of these students' utilization of language. In doing so, we will be drawing heavily on two research projects one of us was involved with, focusing on the gendered writing styles of academic students[1] (Francis et al., 2001; Read et al., 2001; Francis et al., 2002; Read et al., 2002; Robson et al., 2002) and the assessment of such writing by lecturers[2] (Francis et al., 2003; Read et al., 2004; Robson et al., 2004; Read et al., 2005).

Gender and speaking in the academy

It is not surprising that much work in this area has focused on written rather than oral forms of communication – for many subject areas the essay (either coursework or examination) is the primary method of assessment and is thus most directly linked to the academic success of students. However, forms of oral communication such as participation in seminars or tutorials are increasingly also contributing to a student's grades, and it could be argued that the degree of 'fluency' a student possesses in 'speaking' as well as writing 'academically', in seminars or informal discussions with peers or tutors may affect tutors' conceptions as to the 'ability' of that student. Moreover, it may well affect the students' self-conception of their own 'worth' or 'authenticity' as a member of the university and thus their conception of 'belonging' at university and their likelihood of completing their course. In a

---

[1] This project, entitled 'Gendered Patterns in Undergraduate Writing in the Context of Achievement' took place in 1998–9. The principal investigator was Becky Francis, and the team also comprised Jocelyn Robson and Barbara Read, all based at the University of Greenwich. The first part of the study involved a textual analysis of 87 essays written by final year undergraduate history students (40 men and 47 women) from four London-based universities. Two institutions were 'pre-1992' universities and two were 'post-1992' universities. Following on from the essay analysis, 45 of the authors of the essays also consented to be interviewed. Interviews were semi-structured and conducted over the telephone. The sample comprised 27 women and 18 men; 16 were from pre-1992 universities and 28 from post-1992 universities. All interviews were conducted in the summer after the students' graduation (1999).

[2] This ESRC-funded project (R000239187), entitled 'University Lecturers' Constructions of Undergraduate Writing' was conducted from 2000–2001, and involved Becky Francis (principal investigator, then based at London Metropolitan University) Jocelyn Robson (University of Surrey) and Barbara Read (London Metropolitan University). The project methods involved the assessment of sample essays, and individual interviews with academics from history and psychology departments. Of the 50 participants in the discipline of history, 25 were men and 25 were women. Participants were drawn from 24 different HE institutions across England and Wales, of which 14 were 'old' (pre-1992) and 10 were 'new' (post-1992) universities. They were each asked to mark two standardized sample essays from their discipline in advance of the interview. One had been written by a male and one by a female final year undergraduate student, and had already been assessed by a lecturer in their department/institution of origin. In each discipline, the two essays were of an approximately equal standard: each history essay had been graded as lower second by the original assessor.

study on social class and widening participation in HE in which one of us was involved (Archer et al., 2003)[3], a number of students, in particular minority ethnic, mature working-class women, spoke of the difficulties they had understanding academic language and the contribution this made to their feelings of isolation and distance from academic staff, as discussed for example by two mature Black Caribbean students in a group interview:

> Paula: They assume that because you're in university you know, you . . .
> Violet: That you should know, you know what I'm saying. Because when he's giving the lecture and he's like talking, talking, talking, saying those words and things. I said my God, I don't know what you saying! I'm lost! [laughter]
> Paula: I think that's another culture shock in a sense, the language. It is a different language, from being at college, from being at school. It is a totally different language.

These students were discussing their experiences in a 'new' university with large numbers of 'non-traditional' students. Yet the presence of students of similar age, class, gender or ethnicity was not sufficient to enable them to feel comfortable in the environment of the university – to make them feel like they 'belong', as the culture of the university, and in particular the language the lecturers used, very much reflected the 'norm' of the student (and lecturer) as white, middle class and male (Read et al., 2003).

Some studies have been conducted by feminist academics which do indicate a strong link between gender and students' confidence and 'comfort' when speaking in the academy. There is some evidence to suggest that women students communicate less assertively than men in the 'competitive' environment of the university seminar (Sternglanz and Lyberger-Ficek, 1977; Kelly, 1991; Sommers and Lawrence, 1992) and in other public contexts. Mann (2003), in her study of why fewer women get firsts at the University of Cambridge, also discovered that because of women's desire for a deep understanding of their subject, they were more likely to ask questions than men, be a bit more tentative in their assertions and initially more receptive of the authority of the teaching staff. In contrast, men made more suggestions, moved forward rapidly and tended to be more challenging of both other students and of staff. Mann argued that this 'intellectual muscle-flexing' was more likely to be interpreted as a sign of excellence by men teaching staff

---

[3] This project, entitled 'Social Class and Widening Participation in Higher Education' explored working-class students' (and non-students') constructions of higher education and their views on the barriers to participation in a post-1992 university in the UK. The project was directed by Alistair Ross and Bob Gilchrist, and also comprised: Louise Archer, Merryn Hutchings and Carole Leathwood. It was funded by the University of North London (now London Metropolitan University). As part of the study 17 focus groups were conducted with a total of 85 first year undergraduates (51 women, 34 men; 30 per cent White British, 20 per cent Asian, 20 per cent Black, 27 per cent European and other) predominantly from working-class backgrounds.

(who were the majority) than the readiness to listen and understand that women were more likely to demonstrate. Research one of us conducted with undergraduate students in a post-1992 university (see, for example, Leathwood and O'Connell, 2003) also brought up some examples of women students feeling intimidated and silenced in seminars by what one described as 'arrogant men' who acted like they 'know it all'.

A number of academics in the study of lecturers' assessment practices (Francis et al., 2003; Read et al., 2004, 2005; Robson et al., 2004) also stated that they believed men students to be much more confident in such settings. For example a woman historian stated:

> I've got a class in which one male student has joined five women and he's destroyed the atmosphere. He's bullish, he's aggressive, the girls don't know how to hold him back. I'm close to telling him to shut up. There's six phenomenally intelligent women but none of them want to challenge him though sometimes their behaviour suggests, you know, that he's talking nonsense (. . .) They sat back . . . they didn't have the confidence or maybe think it was the done thing (. . .) but we were wasting a class.

Women were described as less confident, for example in the following quotation, this time by a male historian:

> Women do tend to hold back too much; (. . .) if there's one man present, he'll tend to talk more than the women.(. . .) It's very unfortunate. We do get women students who are very conscientious, they attend better, are more punctual and more responsible and they won't speak up, you know. That is a problem.

However, some respondents did feel that this pattern had changed in recent years, and that women, especially mature students, were now much more assertive, as discussed by another male historian:

> When I first started here [it used to be the case that] females were a lot more diffident, modest and shy when it came to expressing themselves (. . .) You'd have a few chopsy males in front who'd hog the discussion; that was quite common in the 70s and 80s; it's less common now. But now women in the class tend to be as talkative as men; certainly mature women are very talkative and the position is almost reversed. You get two or three mature women sort of clicking together as a small group (. . .). Once they get into a class they can hog the discussion amongst themselves (. . .). They're certainly speaking out, speaking out now.

In the social class and widening participation in HE study (see above; Archer et al., 2003), we found instances of women's assertiveness in seminars that was explicitly linked to resistance and challenge. A number of black women students described the necessity to not only to feel confident but to *act* confidently at university, in order to 'play the game' (Read et al., 2003). For example, in the following discussion, Siobhan, a 33-year-old white Irish student, is given advice by Janet, a 22-year-old black Caribbean student, on acting confident in the 'intimidating' competitive atmosphere of the seminar:

> Siobhan: I find [seminars] really intimidating. It's all right to speak in front of a few people but especially in front of some of these guys, oh you're not in the same one are you? (Janet: no) There are some guys who are really political, comments on everything. I think they are gonna just slate me, they're going to pick me apart.
>
> Janet: Oh no, don't talk like that! They can sense this. People sense when you are feeling intimidated. If you go out boldly then you know, say you can't knock me down! (laughing). That's my feelings.

Grant (1997) details other acts of student 'resistance', such as the act of studying in groups to challenge the discourse of the 'independent learner'. However, such 'resistances' are carried out within the constraints of the dominant academic culture: the emphasis is placed on the student learning to adapt (or at least to act as if they have adapted) to the culture of the university: the culture itself remains unchanged (see Mirza, 1995; Quinn, 2003).

Gender and writing in the academy

An emphasis on 'dispassionate' boldness is also what is required in academic writing, where the 'rules of the game' of utilizing academic language are even more fine-tuned. Feminist theorists, poststructuralists and other anti-realists have questioned the supposed 'value neutrality' of academic research and its explicit or implicit goal of 'objectivity' (Hammersley, 1992), yet academic writing predominantly continues to aim for detachment, presented through 'neutral', dispassionate tones. For example, the use of personal experience as a support to assertions is discouraged, as is the use of personal pronouns and the identification of authorship within the text (Farr, 1993; Geertz, 1998; Ivanic, 1998). Harding (1990) and others have described how the modernist goal of objectivity is also gendered, in that objectivity is seen as the preserve of the masculine, whilst (devalued) emotion and subjectivity is linked to the feminine 'other'. Some feminists have indeed argued that abstract rationality, divorced from emotion and subjective experience, runs counter to women's socially dominant ways of reasoning (Gilligan, 1982; Gilligan and Attanucci, 1988). Some have argued further for the promotion of 'experience' as a valid tool for the support of arguments and positions (see Harding, 1991; Skeggs, 1994).

Interestingly, other facets of academic writing that emphasize 'neutrality' and 'objectivity' are also those that are sometimes linked to socially prevalent discourses of 'women's' communication. Assertions in academic writing are often combined with hedges and qualifiers such as 'it could be argued that . . .; it can be seen that . . .' (Farr, 1993; Martin, 1997; Francis et al., 2001). Lakoff (1973) argued that the prevalent use of hedges and qualifiers in academic language associated academic expression with 'feminine' language, related to the relative lack of status of the academy in the United States. However, sociolinguists such as Holmes (1984) have argued that hedges in academic writing do not necessarily denote lack of assertion. Indeed, forms of 'caution' are often used to emphasize the 'detachment' of the argument being put forward, and the acknowledgement of the possible validity of other views (Francis et al., 2002). The need to include a critical evaluation of other arguments rather than putting forward a single view (Hounsell, 1987) has also been argued by some to be culturally easier for women to do. A number of studies of gender and language have found that women tend to write in a more affiliative than confrontational style, and are more likely to acknowledge other viewpoints in their writing (see, for example, Rubin and Greene, 1992).

It could be argued that such patterns are solely related to culturally learnt communication behaviours that lie outside the university (e.g. Tannen, 1990; Maltz and Borker, 1998) and thus not directly connected to academic culture. However, many feminists in the field of linguistics have challenged the gender 'difference' theories of communication advocated by writers such as Tannen for downplaying the socio-political context of language practices and the unequal power relationship between men and women constructed through discourse (see, for example, Cameron, 1998). Additionally, as discussed above, 'academic literacies' theorists such as Lea and Street (1998), Ivanic (1998), Lillis (2001) and the contributors to Lea and Stierer (2000) argue that such a position leaves the power relations constructed through academic practices in higher education unproblematized.

Interestingly, a study by Lynch and Stauss-Noll (1987) demonstrates that where discernable gender differences occur in student writing, they are more pronounced in informal than formal writing. Indeed, a study one of us was involved with, concerning gender differences in history undergraduates' essay-writing styles, showed there to be far more similarity than difference between genders (see Francis et al., 2001; Robson et al., 2002). Eighty-seven essays by final year history students from four different London universities were analysed. Sentences that did not directly reference the work of others (and therefore appeared to present the student's own opinions or assertions) were placed into a number of categories ranging from 'very bold' to 'very tentative' (for a fuller discussion of the categories and methodology in analysing the essay-writing, see Francis et al., 2001). Both men and women students wrote equal numbers of (and very few) statements we characterized as 'tentative'. In contrast, students predominantly adopted a mildly 'assertive' style when presenting their own 'voice' in essays. We characterized this style as clear assertions of viewpoint which followed a linear line of argument and (crucially) built on previous arguments or evidence already presented in the essay and referenced to others. As writers such as Bartholomae (1985) and Ballard and Clanchy (1988) note, the need always to 'back up' assertions with evidence is a distinct characteristic of academic persuasive writing. Students who are less successful in maintaining this style can lapse into the presentation of assertions which are statements of unsupported opinion, which can be seen as a retreat into the adoption of an assertive style more familiar to the student, such as the absolute authority of 'facts' presented by the school teacher (Bartholomae, 1985: 136) or the unsupported assertions and extreme language characteristic of media journalism (Nightingale, 1988: 69). Men students tended to write more of these types of statements. It could be suggested from this that even though many facets of academic writing style are traditionally ascribed as masculine (such as the air of self-confidence and 'rationality'), men students find it slightly harder than women students to *adapt* to certain constraints of academic writing (Francis et al., 2001; Wartchow, 2001; Robson et al., 2004).

In contrast however, the interviews we conducted with the students high-lighted marked differences between genders in relation to confidence in the value and usefulness of their own opinions when writing essays. Whilst some students 'pragmatically' modified or silenced their own views and opinions due to a lack of trust in their fair evaluation, others felt unable to present their own views and ideas through lack of confidence. Students must write for an audience that (usually) knows far more about the subject than they do, but they must do so in a style that assumes an equality of knowledge and status between the two (Bartholomae, 1985; Anson, 1988; Hounsell, 1997; Lea and Street, 1998). As Bartholomae (1985: 135) states:

> The student has to appropriate (or be appropriated by) a specialised discourse, and he [sic] has to do this as though he were easily and comfortably one with his audience. . . . He must learn to speak our language. Or he must dare to speak it or to carry off the bluff, since speaking and writing will most certainly be required long before the skill is 'learned'.

However, despite the presumed equality in the utilization of academic language, hegemonically dominant constructions of academia construct a hierarchy of status in relation to (perceived or actual) 'possession' of knowledge. Bourdieu notes that the cultural and symbolic capital acquired by the tutor through the status of their occupation and qualifications gives their communications a greater 'authority' than the student (Bourdieu, 1988, 1991; see also Grant, 1997). This inequality of power may translate into a lack of confidence on the part of the student in the validity and importance of their ideas (Wolffensberger, 1993; Lea and Street, 1998; Read et al., 2001; Robson et al., 2004).

In our interviews, seven students talked of a lack of confidence in their views and opinions when writing essays, and all but one of these students were women. This articulated lack of confidence centred on the students' perceived lack of knowledge compared to their tutor and the academic 'establishment'. Kate stated she felt that she 'didn't know enough' to adopt a bold style, and this inhibited her from achieving first class grades: 'I think [in a first class essay] they're just looking for maybe something more from yourself, and I don't really have the confidence to, not so much gamble. I tend to, tend to play safe'. Although the importance of presenting one's own argument in an essay was clearly recognized by many students in the study (see above), these students nevertheless felt unable to criticize 'established' academics in their essays. Denise stated 'you can't turn round to someone like that and say "sorry, I think you're rubbish!"'. Vanessa stated similarly: 'I felt that at my stage of knowledge I hadn't the right to "lay down the law", and also I might say a tiny bit in feeling that who am I to question all these established writers'.

Characteristics such as 'confidence' need to be understood in their socio-cultural context (Bartky, 1990), and 'admissions' of self-doubt and lack of confidence are arguably harder for men participants to articulate than women, due to the connection between outward confidence and culturally 'appropriate' constructions of masculinity. This might lead to gender differences in relation to statements about self-confidence amongst participants being exaggerated in the data. Nevertheless, many participants themselves believed that men students were more confident and comfortable with speaking and writing in the academy, with both men and women participants repeatedly alluding to the greater 'boldness' and confidence of men students. For example, when they were asked why they thought men students received more 'first-class' awards than women students, nine participants (four men and five women) put forward the suggestion that men were bolder in expressing their opinions, and four participants (one men and three women) proposed lack of confidence in women as a contributing factor (Read et al., 2001). In their interviews, many of the students articulated a distinction between the genders in terms of confidence and assertiveness that stands in contrast to the findings of the essay analysis. Paula saw men students' greater assertiveness as contributing to failure as well as success: 'I suppose, well, the lads that I saw at university, they tend to have very strong viewpoints, so they would probably assert themselves more all through the essay, therefore if they're right, they're right, and if they're wrong, they're completely wrong!'

As we have seen, though, the majority of the students linked assertiveness and confidence with success in essay writing. For example Claire stated 'You'll get a couple [of men students] that are, sort of, really confident and they'll come across really confident, and they'll write things confidently, and succeed.'

The interviews therefore highlight that whilst both men and women students may write assertively in their essays, this does not necessarily indicate a confidence on the part of the student in their own views or opinions (with the caveat concerning the gendered 'acceptability' of discussing self-confidence borne in mind). Like Kate above, they will 'play safe' rather than 'gamble' and risk receiving low grades (Read et al., 2001), an issue also brought up in Lillis's study of women student writers (Lillis, 2001).

Gender and assessment in the academy

One of the key areas in which universities (and indeed all sectors of education) are said to have become 'feminized' is in the area of assessment. In an article in the *Spectator* (a UK-based right-wing current affairs magazine) entitled 'How exams are fixed in favour of girls', Madsen Pirie argued that 'girls are doing better than boys in exams, but that does not mean they are brighter. . . . What has happened is that exams have been feminized – and so has the country' (Pirie, 2001).

One of the key debates in this area has been the issue of the increasing practice of continuous/coursework-based assessment in favour of, or alongside, 'traditional' examinations, and whether, as Pirie argued, this privileges women over men. Women, it is argued, perform better in assessment that rewards consistency of application, or as Bleach (1998) described in the context of pre-16 education, the 'diligent and plodding approach that is characteristic of girls' (p.14, cited in Francis and Skelton, 2005). Men are argued to prefer assessment by examination. At Cambridge in 2002, over 26 per cent of men and just 16 per cent of women were awarded firsts, and Mann (2003), supporting Martin (1997), argued that the reason for the gender disparity was due to the examination system at 'Oxbridge' favouring 'aggression, singularity and the ability to maintain a coherent, if dogmatic, argument' (Mann, 2003: 67), thus favouring traits culturally constructed as masculine. Mann's study of students at Cambridge suggested this was because women were more likely to seek 'understanding' and wide knowledge of their subject in contrast to the tendency for men students to strive for performance and public recognition. She found that men targeted their learning primarily to achieve success in examinations, whilst women's motivation in examinations was more related to demonstrating what they understood about their subjects rather than an instrumental desire for public success. Men were also reported to have more confidence in their 'innate' ability and in using examination techniques (Mann, 2003).

However, the argument that the increasing substitution of examinations in favour of coursework assessment is a 'feminized' practice that favours women fails to take into account the complexity of the issue. First, a number of studies have shown that both men and women students tend to say they favour coursework assessment over examinations because they believe that coursework better represents their ability in a subject (see, for example, Woodfield et al., 2005). Secondly, women have historically done very well in examinations. For example, girls regularly outperformed boys in the selective examination known as the '11 plus', required to gain entry into the more 'academic' grammar schools during the tripartite system of education in the UK from 1944 to 1976 (Francis and Skelton, 2005). Francis (2000) notes that girls' success has continued even when the percentage of examination by coursework has been reduced.

Interestingly, a study which examined gender and exam performance in one university found that men performed less well than women, and were less likely to complete their degrees than women, due to women students working harder and fulfilling the identity of the compliant 'good girl' (Saunders and Woodfield, 2003), again indicating that women students are possibly more used to having to 'adapt' to the constraints of masculinized academic culture.

Therefore, often women's harder work, and their greater desire to adapt and 'play the game' of academia, might well contribute more to their increasing success at degree level than a supposed 'feminization' of assessment techniques. Moreover, for a more complete understanding of the way in which assessment practices in HE are gendered, we need to look at the way in which assessment itself is a socially constructed practice that both reflects and reinforces social inequalities of power, including those based on gender.

The social construction of assessment

Both the grade a coursework essay is given and the accompanying feedback are of crucial importance to undergraduate students. The marks for coursework essays frequently contribute to a student's final degree grade. Moreover, both the mark the essay receives and the nature of the feedback given is known to greatly affect a student's self-esteem and motivation to study (Broadfoot, 1996; Elwood, 2001).

However, despite its importance, the assessment of essays is far from being an objective 'scientific' process. One of the key factors in any form of assessment is the notion of reliability: that the system of assessment should allow the same mark to be awarded to a piece of work regardless of the marker (Newstead, 1996). Nevertheless, a number of studies have shown that there is a wide margin of variation in the marks awarded to essays at undergraduate level (Cox, 1988; Newstead and Dennis, 1994; Baume and Yorke, 2002). One study by Newstead and Dennis looked at the assessment of six sample essays by a group of 14 external examiners in the discipline of psychology. They reported sizeable discrepancies in marks awarded by different examiners, including a case where an essay was awarded an excellent First from one participant, and a borderline Lower Second/Third from another (Newstead and Dennis, 1994). This can cause acute stress and anxiety for students, as was apparent in the interviews with students in our study of gendered writing styles (see above), for example Clara and Penny:

> I really didn't like writing essays. I hated it, because it was different for . . . that's the thing, it was different for every tutor. So you could write one essay for someone and they'd like it, [and] write the same style for another and they wouldn't like it. . . . Even to the last *day* I still didn't know [what was expected].

> I could get a 70, you know, a first, from one tutor and a 60 from another, when I thought I would be deserving of more. . . . I never, you know, and

> this goes for some of my colleagues as well at university, we never really <laughs> understood *why*, you know, there was such a difference in the marking.

Quite a few of the students discussed the 'detective work' they felt needed to be done in response to these perceived differences, for example Tim stated:

> Different tutors seem to have different ideas, you see, and sometimes it was hard to 'second-guess' what they wanted. So the first – maybe you did two essays over the whole year, the first essay you did for a particular tutor would be trying to find out what they want.

In recent years there have been challenges to the reliability of traditional forms of assessment by approaches that emphasize the socio-cultural and situated aspects of cognition, and therefore of both learning itself and the assessment of that learning (Wertsch, 1991; Elwood, 1999). There has also been a move towards emphasizing the socio-political context of assessment practices (see, for example, Leathwood, 2005a). As Connell, Johnson and White note, all forms of assessment are 'social techniques which have social consequences' (Connell et al., 1992: 23, quoted in Elwood, 1999: 206). Bias cannot be removed from the assessment of essays, for the quality of a piece of academic writing cannot be objectively determined but is ultimately constructed by the assessor. This is not to say that such assessment is completely arbitrary, or that we should not attempt to minimize bias, but that assessment is inextricably influenced by a number of factors, including both the author's and the assessor's own 'ways of understanding the world', which is in turn influenced by their social positionings, such as class and gender.

Gender and the assessment of written texts

Whilst one of our previous studies has seemed to show there to be far more similarity than difference in academic style according to gender (see above), another study we conducted involving analysing men and women academics' marking of undergraduate essays showed that *socially constructed* conceptions of such differences are quite strongly held. Conceptions of gender difference can influence the reception of essay texts by the reader. As Schick Case (1990: 97) notes:

> Since women are thought to be emotional, indecisive, submissive, supportive, and interpersonally oriented, their speech is rated likewise; similarly, since men are seen as behaving aggressively, instrumentally, bluntly, and decisively, their speech is also rated consistent with that role image.

A number of studies have shown that without anonymous marking, biases relating to gender of essay author can be found. For example, Bradley (1984) hypothesized that external markers who knew the gender of the authors of essays (but had no other experience of the performance of particular students) might be more likely to decide borderline upper second/ first class essays were first class in the case of men students, and more likely to give third class marks to men students whose essays were initially judged as borderline lower seconds, due to an assumption that women students are more likely to conform and 'play safe'. Her findings confirmed this hypothesis. A study by Newstead and Dennis (1990) did not find the bias reported by Bradley. However another study by Dennis, Newstead and Wright (1996) found bias in favour of men students by their supervisors rather than external examiners. Other studies have confirmed a tendency for gender bias in forms of assessment where the gender of the author is known (Spear, 1984; Murphy and Elwood, 1998).

However, in our study we were concerned with the possibility that gender bias might exist even *with* the practice of anonymous marking, due to socially prevalent discourses relating to academic constructions of quality, to gender and other aspects of identity, that infuse the way in which the essay is read and judged by the assessor. As the project team related elsewhere (Francis et al., 2003; Read et al., 2005), we found that many participants in our own study held quite strong views of gender differences in the academic writing styles of students. Several discursive patterns could be identified in their interviews, with men students regularly characterized as writing in a more self-confident and bold style, but with more 'carelessness', whilst women students' writing was often characterized as more articulate than men, and showing a greater conscientiousness and concern with aesthetic style (Francis et al., 2003). However, when they were asked to guess whether men or women students were the authors of the sample essays they had been given to *mark* as part of the study, the results showed that a majority of them were unable to assign gender accurately (Read et al., 2005).

We also found slight gender differences in the characteristics men and women lecturers stated they valued when marking essays: there was a tendency for women academics to say they rated presentation and effort more highly than men, while men stressed issues around argument more often than did their women colleagues (Read et al., 2004). However, when we analysed their appraisals of the *actual* essays we gave them, such gendered constructions are actually either not borne out or were even contradicted (Read et al., 2005).

In any case, both men and women lecturers generally rated most highly the forms of academic language most favoured in the academy, a style we have shown in this chapter to be overwhelmingly masculinized. Murphy and Elwood (2002) note that until GCSE stage, girls are positioned as closer to the constructions of 'success' in terms of literacy skills, particularly in relation to descriptive and empathetic writing. However, such positioning is reversed from A levels onwards, where abstract impersonal writing is more valued, favouring forms of literacy (and the preferred reading matter) that are closer to dominant constructions of masculine gender identity. The assessment of an essay, like the interpretation of any text, is not 'objective' or 'true' but merely one of a plurality of interpretations, 'constrained' to a certain extent by the discursive and material positioning of both the author and reader, and more widely by the forms of communication most valued by the academy (Gadamer, 1975; McGann, 1983; Francis, 2002a). As Wolf (1993: 213) notes, 'any assessment is . . . a head-on encounter with a culture's models of prowess. It is an encounter with a deep-running kind of "ought". Assessments publish what we regard as skill and what we will accept or reject as a demonstration of accomplishment.'

Conclusion

In this chapter we have focused specifically on the 'genderedness' of academic cultural practices in the academy in relation to both the language utilized in speaking and writing, and the way in which such language (particularly in the form of student essays) is judged and valued by assessors. In contrast to conceptions that academic practices, particularly in relation to assessment, are becoming 'feminized', we have shown how academic language and assessment practices are complexly gendered, and in many ways have – and still do – favour behaviours and practices associated with the 'masculine'.

'Traditional' forms of academic writing and oral communication – still often culturally dominant in many universities and departments worldwide – often privilege traits culturally presented as 'masculine', such as boldness, individualism and competitiveness. Whilst many feminists have argued that such behaviours may be harder to 'pick up' and adopt by women due to the dissonance between such practices and dominant constructions of 'femininity', women students may actually be more successful than some men students at 'adapting' their language practices to the dictates of the academy, despite reporting a greater sense of self-doubt in relation to their ability to do so.

Moreover, there is no evidence to suggest that the rise in assessment by coursework favours women students, who have historically also fared well in examinations. Research we have been involved with shows that both men and women lecturers rate most highly the forms of 'masculinized' academic language favoured in the academy, and women students' success seems to be primarily related to women students' hard work at adapting to the masculinized cultural discourses relating to speaking, writing and assessment in the academy, rather than signs that academic practices are themselves becoming feminized.

9

Academic practices: curriculum, knowledge and skills

> Is there anything more glorious than a professor? ... a professor is the only person on earth with the power to put a veritable frame around life ... He organizes the unorganizable. Nimbly partitions it into modern and postmodern, renaissance, baroque, primitivism, imperialism and so on. Splice that up with Research Papers, Vacation, Midterms. All that order – simply divine ... Consider a Kandinsky. Utterly muddled, put a frame around it, voilà – looks rather quaint above the fireplace. And so it is with the curriculum. That celestial, sweet set of instructions, culminating in the scary wonder of the Final Exam. (Pessl, 2006: 11)

The circumstances of the formation of the disciplines taught and studied at university are rarely explicitly examined, so they come to take on the form in the public imaginary of something 'natural', something organically grown into distinct separate entities. However, as historians and sociologists of knowledge have documented, the academic disciplines are *socially constructed* categories of knowledge, legitimated by academic tradition to become 'taken-for-granted' and seemingly 'natural' categories (Thomas, 1990; Becher and Trowler, 2001; Howie and Tauchert, 2002). Moreover, the actual *content* of these subjects, that which is deemed to be valid and valued knowledge in all of these disciplinary areas, is also socially constructed, changing continuously through time and in different places over the world. These social constructions are not arbitrary, however, but reflect and reinforce dominant power relations, for example, the historical and contemporary hierarchical dominance of 'western' thought and of 'white' ethnicity, of middle-class and upper-class values, and of men over women (Evans, 1983; 1997).

In Chapter 4 we recounted how, despite higher education having been open to women on equal terms to men in the UK since the 1940s, there are still major gendered patterns in terms of participation, achievement and subject 'choice', and this is replicated globally. As we will be exploring in this chapter, the choices students make as to which subjects they study are not simply down to individual taste or aptitude – they are constrained to a high degree by culturally constructed gendered conceptions of knowledge, which influence ideas as to how far certain subjects 'fit' with culturally dominant conceptions of gender identity. Many studies have shown that students' conceptions of their own ability and desire to take on certain subjects over others are greatly influenced by the degree to which such subjects are socially deemed 'appropriate' for their gender (see, for example, Francis and Skelton, 2005).

We will be looking in this chapter at the ways in which university sanctioned constructions of knowledge have historically been, and continue to be, gendered, and the ways in such forms of knowledge have been challenged. As we have seen in Chapter 2, the increasing dominance of the 'skills agenda' in higher education has been conceptualized as one aspect of the feminization of the sector, as demonstrated by the increasing prevalence of the construction of the student as the neo-liberal worker of the future. Others have argued that feminist research has been sufficiently 'mainstreamed' to be considered to have successfully overturned 'traditional' masculinized knowledge. This chapter will explore these conceptualizations of knowledge in the light of arguments that perceive the university curriculum to be feminized. In what ways has the curriculum in the past and present been gendered? What are the implications for the popular conception that higher education has become 'feminized'?

The 'traditional' university curriculum: knowledge as 'truth'?

As many post-structuralist and/or feminist scholars have outlined, the dominant construction of academic knowledge as the disinterested pursuit of 'truth' is a central feature of Enlightenment thought, with roots that stretch back to Ancient Greek philosophy (see Foucault, 1971; Derrida, 1976; Harding, 1984; Irigaray, 1985). However, this construction of knowledge has come under sustained attack from the 1960s onwards, especially by post-structuralist and/or feminist academics and thinkers. In this part of the chapter we will be exploring both the ways in which 'traditional' forms of knowledge have been attacked by such thinkers, and the degree to which women individually and collectively might be said to have 'feminized' knowledge in the disciplines, using examples from the fields of the sciences, of history and of art criticism/art history.

'Masculinised' disciplines of knowledge and the marginalization of the 'feminine'

Following Nietzsche (1964), a number of influential writers have argued that the stable conceptual binary in Enlightenment thought of the active autonomous 'subject' (the knower), and the passive 'object' of knowledge to be studied (the known) is an untenable fiction (Foucault, 1971; Gadamer, 1975; Derrida, 1976; Rorty, 1979). These and other critics have called into question the very pillars of Enlightenment thought itself – the conception of an ultimate 'truth' that is able to be 'discovered' and objectively and dispassionately studied (Hekman, 1990). For example, Rorty asserts:

> There is nothing deep down inside us except what we have put there ourselves, no criterion that we have not created in the course of creating a practice, no standard of rationality that is not our appeal to such a criterion, no rigorous argumentation that is not obedience to our own conventions. (Rorty, 1979, quoted in Hekman, 1990: 12)

It has generally been specifically feminist research, however, that has noted that the 'subject' of Enlightenment thought is, crucially, a 'masculine' one. Indeed, as we have seen in earlier chapters, the binaries that are such a central aspect of Enlightenment philosophy – subject/object, rational/irrational, culture/nature – are deeply gendered, the first 'half' of each pair being associated with the masculine, and the second with the feminine (Cixous, 1981; Harding, 1984; Hekman, 1990). Moreover, in virtually all Enlightenment writings the concepts defined as 'masculine' are also the most revered and valued. As Cixous notes:

> [E]very theory of culture, every theory of society, the whole conglomeration of symbolic systems – everything that is, that's spoken, everything that's organised as discourse, art, religion, the family, language, everything that seizes us, everything that acts on us – it is all ordered around hierarchical oppositions that come back to the man/woman opposition. (Cixous, 1981: 44)

The long historical dominance of Enlightenment thought in the university has had specific consequences for women in academia:

> Because only subjects can constitute knowledge, the exclusion of women from the realm of the subject has been synonymous with their exclusion from the realm of rationality, and, hence, truth. Although this characterisation of women has defined their status in all aspects of cultural life it has had a particular impact on women's efforts to engage in intellectual pursuits. (Hekman, 1990: 94)

Not only has the Enlightenment 'metanarrative' affected women's representation as students and academics in particular fields (and for a long time barring them from the university as a whole) and thus hindering them from taking up the role of 'subject' or knower, it has also affected the ways in which women are presented and described as 'objects' of knowledge across the disciplines (Thomas, 1990). As Thomas (1990), Becher and Trowler (2001) and others have noted, these socially constructed disciplines have formed academic 'cultures' of their own, and are represented in cultural discourses as having particular implicit essentialized attributes (Trowler,

1998). This includes essentialized conceptions of genderedness – for example, it is often presented that scientific subjects such as physics and chemistry are 'hard' sciences, which are seen to be 'masculinized', whereas the arts and humanities are seen as 'softer', more 'feminized' subject areas – and needless to say, couched as inferior to the 'harder' sciences (Spender and Sarah, 1980; Smith, 1992; Bagilhole and Goode, 1998; Coate, 2006). As the quotation from Nietzsche below highlights, science, with its especial concern for finding objective 'truth', has historically been couched as antithetical to woman's fundamentally 'irrational' nature:

> Is it not in the very worst taste that woman thus sets herself up to be scientific? . . . But she does not *want* truth – what does woman care for truth? From the very first nothing is more foreign, more repugnant, or more hostile to women than truth – her great art is falsehood, her chief concern is appearance and beauty. (Nietzsche, 1964: 183; see also Hekman, 1990; Thomas, 1990; Bagilhole and Goode, 1998)

A number of feminist historians have charted women's history of exclusion from the scientific arena, cemented in the early nineteenth century and continuing in the UK until the 1970s (Schiebinger, 1989; Mazon, 2003; Fara, 2004; Watts, 2007). Previous to this some women had been involved in science through what was known as 'kitchen physic' – learning and experimenting with chemistry via the cooking of food, treating injuries and burns, and preparing cleaning and hygiene materials (Watts, 2007). By the eighteenth century such 'popular' ways of learning and practising science had been dismissed/degraded by 'learned' scientific men of the day, and it became completely unexpected for middle-class and upper-class girls to learn any subject in depth (as of course, it always had been for working-class children; Watts, 2005, 2007). A small group of white middle-class women around the turn of the nineteenth century were able to have some influence through the writing of educational books primarily aimed at women and children, including the influential Jane Marcet. However, such 'amateur' science was increasingly denigrated and ridiculed by men seeking greater professionalization and status for the sciences: 'Familial science, by "some garrulous old woman or pedantic spinster" as one new male professional scientist termed it, gradually died out in favour of more depersonalised, decontextualized texts, suitable for "the serious thoughts of men"' (Watts, 2007: 392).

Women were excluded from the growing numbers of professional scientific societies – Watts notes how the Royal Society had a bust of the pioneering scientist Elizabeth Somerville in their great hall, yet she had never been allowed through its doors. The twentieth century saw scientific research established throughout UK universities, with a concomitant struggle for women to be allowed equal entry to practise science. They also predominated in areas deemed more appropriate (or at least, less inappropriate), such as medical areas involving women and children (i.e. obstetrics, gynaecology, medical education) and domestic science (Watts, 2007). Even today, as we have seen in Chapter 4, women in science, engineering and technology in the UK are seriously under-represented as both staff and students, with African-Caribbean women (and men) particularly under-represented (Bebbington, 2002). Moreover, the scientific subjects most often pursued by women in higher education in many countries are those seen as 'gender appropriate', for example the social and biological sciences (Watts, 2007).

Whilst the sciences are cast in the social imaginary as the most 'masculine' of disciplines, we can see similar patterns of gendered marginalization even in the 'softer', supposedly more 'feminized' subject areas. In the spheres of art and literature the dominant cultural conception was – and still is, in many ways – that 'creative' works to be studied are the creative product of individuals, the 'expression' of the artist's subjective intention – 'the creation of "genius", transcending existence, society and time' (Barthes, 1977: 146). These ideas form part of the Enlightenment discourse of the autonomous creative subject. Post-structuralists such as Barthes have criticized the notion that a 'work of art' is simply 'the "message" of the Author–God' (Barthes, 1977). The myth of the author legitimizes the myth of the unity of the artwork, which Barthes (1977) and others argue are made up of a variety of unoriginal signifiers that are historically and socially situated. Moreover, feminist theorists have persuasively argued that the myth of the 'artist as genius' dominant in art historical and critical discourse is gender specific (see, for example, Pollock, 1999). Just as with the scientific societies, in the seventeenth and eighteenth centuries the emerging influential Academies of Art (established in 1648 in Paris and 1768 in London) effectively excluded women from being accepted as artists by banning them from life-drawing classes (Wolff, 1981). Much more recently, a member of the all-male selection panel of the Arts Council in 1980 criticized feminist demands for proportional representation for the awarding of grants, commenting 'women don't have enough depth to be artists' (Parker and Pollock, 1987: xiv).

As Lovibond (1993) and others have noted, history as a discipline has also historically seen the dominance of Enlightenment thought. Linked to notions of absolute reason and absolute truth, Enlightenment philosophy centres on the notion of society's progression towards an absolute 'ideal' – hence the term 'Enlightenment'. Central to this was Descartes' conception of the 'centred' human subject that has managed to transcend the world of nature in order to control it. Similarly, the mastery of the 'object' world depends on the ability of the human subject to rise above irrational thought in order to achieve autonomy – a philosophy inherited from Plato. These ideas combine to form a conception of the past as the acts of great and powerful individuals who rose above their surroundings to 'change the course of history', a history that progresses to today's 'pinnacle of achievement': the modern West. And as feminist post-structuralists have argued, the Cartesian subject that progresses surely through the annals of history is not only socially constructed but also gendered (see Read, 1996) – as is the Enlightenment notion of time itself.

The perception of time as a unidirectional flow from past, present to future is by no means universal – social anthropologists and historians have shown how societies conceive of time and therefore 'history' in different ways (Leach, 1971; Vernant, 1987). The Enlightenment discourse of unilinear time borrows from Aristotle, who broke from Platonic notions of the reincarnation of souls (Vernant, 1987). Moreover, the notion of history as progression toward a particular ideal was a rationalist secularization of the Judeo-Christian conception of history as the movement towards a divine goal, the 'perfection of man's estate on earth' (Carr, 1986: 105). The stress within this notion of time on the progression of history towards an 'ideal' state links it to notions of 'culture' and the 'active subject' that are equated in Enlightenment thought with the 'masculine': in this discourse, therefore, time itself is gendered, as well as classed and racialized. As Jordanova states:

> The ideology of progress which was so deeply entrenched in Enlightenment thought meant that the growth of a humane, rational and civilised society could also be seen as a struggle between the sexes. . . . Human history, the growth of culture through the domination of nature, was the increasing assertion of masculine ways over irrational, backward-looking women. (Jordanova, 1980: 61)

This ethnocentric, racialized, classed and masculinized conception of history derives legitimacy and authority by its acceptance and dominance in the academy itself. And although distanced from the 'hard' sciences, history as a discipline has grown from the same Enlightenment stem as the sciences, with a belief in the ability to objectively find the 'truth' about the past. Moreover, the 'framing' of history into neat periods evolved as part of the Enlightenment desire to organize the world rationally into a series of defined and researched categories (Horne, 1984), a masculinized hierarchical conception of knowledge constructed by the 'glorious' and (white male) professors described by Pessl in the quotation at the beginning of this chapter. Derrida and others have argued that whilst some form of categorization is necessary in order to interpret the world coherently, nevertheless this is an artificial process of 'framing' that serves to mark chaos and disunity (Derrida, 1987).

However, these artificial 'orders' are implicitly presented by the curriculum as 'natural' and inevitable by the aid of discourses such as scientific 'objectivity' and the idea of the incontrovertibility of the proven 'fact'. These scientific discourses have heavily influenced 'traditional' history, and continue to prevail in the fields of 'positivistic' archaeology and 'strong' empiricist history. Moreover, whilst few historians believe that the past can be unproblematically and transparently 'discovered', the notion that with enough reflexivity concerning bias one can reach an understanding about 'what really happened' still underpins much historical work today (Shanks and Tilley, 1992; Munslow, 1997; Scott, 2000).

Feminist challenges to 'malestream' knowledge

As we have already described, women students have in many countries gradually increased in numbers in the academy over the last century. This increase has been uneven and not replicated in all countries – though this has not stopped a media 'moral panic' that women are going to 'take over' the academy. Women have also increased greatly in number as academics as well as students, although they continue to be in a minority and to be concentrated in more junior and less secure posts (see Chapter 3). As well as the rise in numbers of women as both students and staff in the academy, feminist academics in a huge variety of disciplines have increasingly challenged the gendered construction of knowledge itself. In this section, we will be outlining some of these challenges. Inevitably, space precludes more than a very brief overview of such a heterogenous, wide-ranging body of work, and again here we have limited ourselves to drawing predominantly from work in some 'example' areas: the sciences, the sociology of science, art criticism/history, and history.

Feminists in the sciences continue to struggle against the conception that scientific knowledge is 'neutral' and that the only arena for feminist concern is in terms of increasing the numbers of women taking part in science (Bagilhole and Goode, 1998). Historically, 'objective' scientific knowledge has often been utilized in order to 'prove' women's inferiority. For example, Schiebinger (1989) recounts how in the emerging science of anatomy at the turn of the nineteenth century men's larger skull size was taken to prove men's greater intelligence. However, when the German anatomist Samuel Thomas von Soemmerring discovered that women actually had larger skulls than men in relation to their body size, the anatomist was first charged with inaccuracy, and then scientists began to assert that larger skull sizes in women were, like children, associated with incomplete growth (see also Mazon, 2003). Today, feminists have similarly critiqued research into brain lateralization that seems intent on 'proving' biological differences in analytical reasoning, visual-spatial ability and intuitive thought that has not so far been consistently shown in scientific experiments (Anderson, 1987; Francis and Skelton, 2005).

The feminist critique of knowledge in the social sciences, arts and humanities has been stronger and more widespread (Hekman, 1990). The 'neutrality' of knowledge in the disciplines has long been challenged by modernist political movements such as Marxism, socialism, and 'second wave' feminism (see, for example, discussions in Holloway, 1998; Thornham, 2000; Vander Stichele and Penner, 2005). In terms of the arts and humanities, a large body of modernist work criticized aspects of Eurocentric 'Enlightenment' discourse – for example the conception of the individual 'artist as genius'. Such critiques emphasized the influence of socially situated ideas and practices on the work of the artist, including Marxist analyses (e.g. Wolff, 1981), and the 'first wave' of feminist critique and activism in the art world, towards the end of the 1960s (see Parker and Pollock, 1987). This period saw an attempt to attack the androcentrism of the art world by protesting at the then near-total exclusion of women artists from contemporary exhibitions and academic studies, and providing space for and staging women-only exhibitions (Gourma-Petersen and Mathews, 1987; Parker and Pollock, 1987; Nead, 1992). Feminist artists continue to be a strong force outside of, as well as inside, the academy – for example, in the collective art and performance by the Guerrilla Girls (www.guerrillagirls.com).

Feminist artists and art historians within the academy soon realized it was not enough just to attempt to 'add women and stir' into the masculinized 'canons' of revered work in the arts and humanities. For example, feminist art historians began looking into the social circumstances surrounding artistic production, in order to see how the social status of women in particular historical and cultural locations affects both their ability to produce art, and how that work is received and judged (Nochlin, [1971] 1988; for discussion see Frederickson, 2003). Like their counterparts in art history, feminist historians have critiqued the androcentrism of history by writing about the lives of historical women other than the anomalous few already visible (Southgate, 1996; Vander Stichele and Penner, 2005). However, as Lerner (1979), Scott (2000) and others noted, although valuable, these surveys ultimately remain 'innocuous supplements' which leave mainstream history – the history of men – untouched, or at least scarcely grazed. Increasingly feminists began to challenge the androcentric construction of history itself (Vander Stichele and Penner, 2005). Moving away from attempts to 'insert' women into mainstream (or 'malestream') knowledge, some feminist writers sought to promote and valorize an alternative 'feminized' form of knowledge (see e.g. Daly, 1978; Griffin, 1978). Both perspectives, however, leave the dualism of Enlightenment thought unchallenged (Grimshaw, 1986; Hekman, 1990).

Such challenges in their academic form were predominantly by white and middle-class academics, reflecting the sparse numbers of appointments of minority ethnic academics and those of working-class origin that is still a crucial issue in universities today (see Chapters 3 and 4). As bell hooks points out, black cultural criticism has historically proliferated outside the academy (and still does): 'unfortunately, all that counter-hegemonic cultural criticism that had been honed and developed in black living room kitchens, barber shops and beauty parlors did not surface in a different form' (hooks, 1991: 4). In the last few decades however, Western BME feminist academic work around the world has increasingly flourished in the academy, and the concerns of the feminist movement itself have been the subject of sustained critique and challenge by BME, working-class and lesbian women, who have argued that many white, and/or middle-class and heterosexual feminists were presenting their own specific interests and viewpoints on the assumption that they related to all women. For example, hooks argued back in 1982 (p.7):

No other group in America has so had their identity socialized out of existence as have black women. We are rarely recognized as a group separate and distinct from black men, or as present part of the large group 'women' in this culture. When black people are talked about, sexism militates against the acknowledgement of the interests of black women; when women are talked about racism militates against a recognition of black female interests. When black people are talked about the focus tends to be on black men; and when women are talked about the focus tends to be on white women. Nowhere is this more evident than in the vast body of feminist literature.

More recently, since the 1990s postcolonialist scholarship has been increasingly influential, including a strong feminist strand, that has itself influenced the direction of feminism in terms of the contemporary academic curriculum (see, for example, Rajan, 1993; Spivak, 1996; Spivak, 2006). Feminism has also been increasingly influenced by the development of 'queer theory', and queer theorists have continued a sustained critique on the marginalization of LGBT perspectives in the curriculum (Epstein et al., 2003; Stewart, 2007). For example Epstein et al. (2003) note how queer sexualities are silenced and marginalized in the curriculum in schools and universities, or included as an 'add-on' extra that homogenizes the complex different identifications and experiences within 'queerness'. The normalization of heterosexuality and homophobia are often not challenged in the classroom, contributing to a sense of marginalization for queer students and staff.

The last few decades have also seen a sustained critique of Enlightenment philosophies in the form of feminist poststructuralism: often – especially in the arts and humanities – combined with Lacanian psychoanalytic theory (Whelehan, 1995). Since the 1980s academic feminists have been wrestling with the challenges and opportunities thrown up by post-structuralist philosophies for feminism as a movement. For example, the influential critic of 'masculinist' science, Donna Haraway argued in a 1981 essay that a complete rejection of the notion of objectivity is incompatible with feminist political goals: 'An epistemology that justifies not taking a stand on the nature of things is of little use to women trying to build a shared politics' (Haraway, 1981, cited in Hekman, 1990: 130). The compatibility of post-structuralist perspectives with the political/emancipatory goals of feminism, and the degree to which we can still 'believe in access to knowable truths' (Munslow, 1999: 231) continues to be a major debate amongst feminists in a wide variety of disciplines (see, for example, Holloway, 1998 in relation to the discipline of history). Increasingly, the role of feminist theory and practice has been one of critique and subversion instead of attempts to breach the mainstream, concentrating on challenging the conception that constructions of knowledge can ever be neutral, value free and apolitical (Gourma-Peterson and Matthews, 1987; Whelehan, 1995).

Since the 1970s, then, constantly changing and proliferating forms of feminism have posed challenges to dominant forms of knowledge across a whole spectrum of disciplines. As well as its growth within the 'traditional' subject areas, the challenge of feminist knowledge in the curriculum has been focused in the emergence of a specific new academic 'field' – women's studies.

The field of women's studies

Growing alongside other new fields in the 1970s and 1980s such as race and ethnicity studies and development studies (Becher and Trowler, 2001), women's studies was daring in its interdisciplinary scope (Bird, 2004). Anderson (1989: 225) states its explicitly political objectives, in its challenge to 'traditional' constructions of knowledge: 'Women's Studies seeks to make radical transformations in the systems and processes of knowledge creation and rests on the belief that changing what we study and know about women will change women's and men's lives.'

Bird (2004), Coate (2006), Stake (2006) and others have provided detailed accounts of the development of women's studies in various countries – from the first programmes established in the US in the late 1960s to more than 700 programmes established worldwide in 2006. Developed from the women's movement and influenced by the civil rights and Black studies movements (see Butler, 1991), it included not only challenges to sexism in relation to women's lives, but also critiques of power relations in relation to other marginalized groups. It has also developed a strong focus on sexualities, and of masculinities as well as femininities, in conjunction with the growing influence of feminist poststructuralist work on the deconstruction of 'sex' as well as gender (Bird, 2004). Reflecting this change, some women's studies programmes were renamed as 'gender studies' (Stake, 2006), although this has been problematized as diluting the political radicality of the field.

Another major area of innovation was in the development and promotion of specifically 'feminist' pedagogies, such as the focus on the 'personal' as a valid area of academic exploration, springing from the famous feminist concept of the 'personal is (always) political' (see, for example, David, 2006). Another key area was a critique of the 'traditional' hierarchical power relations between the lecturer and student, and the development of 'liberatory' teaching and learning practices that aimed to 'empower' the woman student (Marchbank and Letherby, 2002). The concept of 'empowerment', however, and the possibilities for such individual agentic challenges to power relations itself became a subject of critical feminist debate (see, for example, Luke and Gore, 1992; Morley, 1998).

The history and development of the field has varied greatly in relation to the specific political, educational and cultural contexts of different countries. For example, Stake, (citing Bollac, 1996) describes how academics in former Communist states in Eastern Europe were not allowed to offer women's studies under the Communist regime, but now have a growing number of programmes in a variety of universities. Universities in some conservative Muslim countries have yet to offer women's or gender studies classes, which are often seen as part of a Westernized, anti-Islamic movement, although this has not stopped some academics teaching feminist materials in other courses (Elsadda, 2002, cited in Stake, 2006). Pappu (2002) describes how the development of women's studies in India in the 1970s was initially supported by many male academic colleagues as a 'safe' way to develop politically driven content in a difficult political climate. However, it soon became clear that 'mainstream' 'masculinized' academia was marginalizing feminist knowledge, failing to engage with feminist scholarship in the 'traditional' academic disciplines. Like many other countries around the world, Indian feminists are also challenging the Eurocentrism of Western feminism and focusing attention on issues more directly relevant to their own cultural concerns (Talwar, 1997, cited in Stake 2006). However, Stake notes that as well as strong differences there have also been strong similarities in the development and present situation of women's and gender studies internationally:

> The position of WGS [Women's and Gender Studies] has been and continues to be fragile in most educational institutions, even in western countries in which WGS has been relatively well accepted. Underfunded programmes, insufficient and overworked staff, unsupportive colleagues and administrators, and lack of power in the academy have been recurring challenges. (Stake, 2006: 201)

Bird (2004) describes how the setting up of an MSc in gender and social policy at the University of Bristol, UK, in the late 1980s was challenged by a male Professor of Economics, who queried whether there was a 'responsible' academic literature in the area, and expressed concerns that the course would be no 'more than a forum in which certain preconceived attitudes and value judgments are aired and rehearsed' (p. 54). As we can see from this quotation, one of the main challenges to women's studies in the academy is an attack on its 'validity' as an area of knowledge. In a study of the establishment of women's studies in the UK and USA, Bird (2004) found many more tales of criticism and outright hostility in the UK than the US, noting that the US have a history of greater flexibility and innovation in the curriculum. Coate (2006) adds that women's studies was undoubtedly aided in its establishment in the US through a shared political solidarity amongst many academics in the aftermath of Vietnam. However, Stake (2006) describes how today 'critics in the US have charged that Women's Studies is overly focused on political issues and on providing false reassurances of women's worth, overemphasising students' personal feelings and experiences in place of serious scholarship' (p. 201; see also Butler, 1991). The criticisms described here detail explicitly 'masculinist' conceptions of what 'knowledge' should be: apolitical, uncaring, unemotional. The marginalization of women's studies as a discipline is epitomized in the UK by the lack of a panel related to women's or gender studies in the research assessment exercise (Jackson, 2002; Coate, 2006), a system for assessing research in the UK described in more detail in Chapter 4.

A study by Marchbank and Letherby (2006) showed that the conception that women's studies is not a 'valid' subject area was quite common in the public arena: 86 per cent of women's studies students in their survey had heard people saying 'women's studies is easy' and 90.5 per cent had heard it described as a 'Mickey Mouse subject'. Another common description was that it is (homophobically perceived as) 'a haven for lesbians' (so much so that the working title for Marchbank and Letherby's paper was 'Mickey Mouse is a lesbian'). This association thus explicitly sexualizes both valued and unvalued forms of knowledge, reinforcing the dominant cultural connections of 'valid' 'authoritative' knowledge as the realm of both the masculine and the normative heterosexual.

Women's studies in academia has also been challenged from the 'left', by Black and minority ethnic women academics and/or by lesbian academics for privileging the experiences and concerns of white and heterosexual women – as described above in relation to feminism in 'mainstream' subject areas (Wilton, 1995; Appleby, 1997). It has also been criticized by activists who believe incorporation of feminism into the academy has diluted feminism's radical roots (see Bagilhole, 1995, cited in Bagilhole and Goode, 1998). Moreover, the popularity of post-structuralism and the 'cultural turn' towards gender studies and queer theory has led to some tension between advocates and those feminists who believe that such 'deconstruction' of sex and gender undermines the reality of women's lived experiences and continuing social and cultural oppression (see, for example, the debate in Richardson et al., 2006).

Since the 1990s women's studies as a separate field of study has been in decline in the UK and some other countries, although it remains strong in countries such as the USA and Australia (Coate, 2006; Marchbank and Letherby, 2006). The last remaining undergraduate degree in women's studies in the UK, at London Metropolitan University, will no longer be taught after the summer of 2008 (Lakhani, 2008). Some have argued that this decline is related to the increasing 'marketization' of education (see below). However, another perception – and one that Marchbank and Letherby (2006) conclude with, is that the decline of women's studies is also related to feminism's success in challenging the masculinized constructions of knowledge in 'mainstream' disciplinary areas – something that in 1984 the feminist biologist Bonnie Spanier envisaged would happen across the curriculum:

> The integration of women's studies scholarship within and across disciplines has initiated a far-reaching and perhaps revolutionary transformation of traditional knowledge. . . . The very canons of literature, art, the natural sciences, and the social sciences are called into question as women's studies scholars expand the boundaries of their fields of inquiry and as integration efforts bring this new scholarship into traditional courses. (Spanier et al., 1984, cited in Hughes et al., 2001)

As we have seen, however, whilst feminist academics have made significant challenges to 'traditional' forms of knowledge in many arenas (and have particularly influenced the validation of personal, qualitative knowledges in the social sciences – see David, 2006) they are still struggling against marginalization and devaluation. Many feminists are also concerned that feminist knowledge will be diluted of its radical potential by 'assimilation' into the mainstream curriculum (see Coate, 2006).

Nevertheless, as Evans states, feminism – through and alongside women's studies courses – remains a challenging 'thorn in the side of' hegemonic mainstream knowledge:

> Women's Studies . . . [questions] the very ways in which 'knowledge' is constructed and assessed . . . [making] feminism an inherently destabilising force in both intellectual life and the academy. Even if at times the sheer strength of the academy to absorb and limit debate is more than able to limit the more critical and subversive elements of the subject. (Evans, 1997: 107)

Continuing marginalization in the disciplines

Despite much work from feminists in this area, the continuing marginalization of women in the artistic and literary canons of the academy speaks volumes for the endurance of the masculinized curriculum in the arts. As Anderson (1987: 241) notes, many lecturers in these fields argue that the 'great' works of art and literature focused on in the curriculum 'speak to universal themes and transcend the particularities of sociocultural conditions like race, class and gender' with the implication that academic knowledge can be neutral and value free.

Examples of the continuing marginalization of feminist research in the disciplines are numerous. For example, Sue Jackson, an educationalist, describes how her work was excluded from a departmental book on higher education because 'Sue's interests are in gender, which is not relevant to the topic'! (Jackson, 2002: 23). Fredericksen (2003) notes that when she proposed a course in 'Women artists from Impressionism to the present' her department head proposed instead that she teach it in the women's studies department. Noting that nearly all monographs written about women artists are by women authors, Fredericksen asks: 'Does there still lurk an unspoken perception that while male artists are relevant to us all, female artists are important only to other women? Is it assumed that in writing about male artists one is writing about art, whereas in writing about women artists one is writing about women?' (2003: 7).

In a study of women and feminism in two subject areas, environmental studies and American studies, Quinn (2003) found that feminism had made very little impact on the former, and only some impression on the latter. Moreover, whilst there had been some moves to include discussions on Black cultures and experience in the American studies course at one university, this had been instigated and presented by white faculty in a way Quinn described as 'white voyeurism', rather than a full transformation of the curriculum away from its ethnocentric traditions.

Higher education is, however, experiencing a gradual transformation of the curriculum in many countries around the world, although not in a form that most feminists would support. In the final section of this chapter, we take a brief look at the ways in which the 'skills and employability' agenda in higher education is impacting on the HE curriculum, and the gendered implications of these changes.

Knowledge as commodity: the emphasis on 'skills' and 'employability'

Just as the 'knowledge' constructed and presented in academia has always been politically motivated rather than 'objective' and neutral, it has always, either directly or indirectly, had a relationship with the marketplace and the world of work. Traditional 'elite' higher education, just like public schooling, was traditionally the arena for schooling the future (white, upper-class, male) 'captains of industry' and rulers of the Empire, although such an agenda was implicit, 'hidden' in a curriculum that was ostensibly 'traditional' in its pursuit of knowledge 'for its own sake'. Universities have varying relationships with (and generally it is the 'newer' non-elite institutions maintaining the closest ties to) the commercial sector (Naidoo, 2003). Moreover, many disciplines have always been wholly or partially vocation oriented, with such 'applied' knowledge areas viewed as categorically distinct from their 'pure', disinterested counterparts.

However, since the 1980s there has been a growing movement towards constructing *all* forms of knowledge in the academy *explicitly* in relation to the needs of 'industry' and the commercial world. A number of writers in the field of education have tracked the increasing development of the conception of knowledge in academia as a 'commodity' to be sold to the student consumer, in the form of 'bite-sized' internationally transferable 'modular' courses:

> Modularisation serves to fragment knowledge ... self-contained as they are, modules constitute a cafeteria-style menu rather than a balanced and properly varied and contrasting diet: the rich varieties of knowledge, with all their inter-connections and uncertainties, are thus transformed into the politically far safer business of gathering and reproducing information. (Brecher, 2005)

There is also an increasing emphasis on the 'skills' that will make graduates more 'employable' in the world of work (see Chapter 6; see Morley, 2003b; Barnett, 2004; Moreau and Leathwood, 2006b; Singh, 2006). As Singh points out, the needs of industry are increasingly being specifically catered to, in contrast to other specified 'stakeholders' in 'civil society':

Benefits to industry or 'the economy' are increasingly expected as direct outcomes to be delivered by universities while benefits to other non-corporate stakeholders continue to be viewed as indirect possibilities, trickling eventually down unspecified societal pathways to address the more abstract purposes of higher education. (Singh, 2006: 60)

In the UK, the Leitch Report (Leitch, 2006) stated that unless the country became a 'world leader' in terms of 'our nation's skills . . . we would condemn ourselves to a lingering decline in competitiveness, diminishing economic growth and a bleaker future for all', concluding that 'we need to be much more ambitious . . . the UK must "raise its game"' (p. 1). The Report recommended that employers should be much more closely involved in the funding and design of higher education courses in areas where they would achieve 'the best returns'. The government would invest in 'market failures', therefore 'ensuring a basic platform of skills for all' (p. 3). An emphasis would be placed on developing 'economically valuable' skills that 'provide real returns for individuals, employers and society' (p. 3). In a letter to higher education institutions in early 2008 John Denham, Secretary of State for Innovation, Universities and Skills, confirmed the UK Government would be acting on the recommendations of the Leitch Report, with the aim of 15,000 full-time additional students being co-funded by employers and government by 2010/11 (Denham, 2008).

In contrast to the development of the curriculum in terms of transformative 'capabilities' for the student in liberal arts colleges such as Alverno College (Barnett, 2004), this skills-as-commodity approach ties the 'outcomes' expected for the student very much in commercial terms that can be quantifiably assessed. Increasingly attempts to 'measure' the successful 'delivery' of such skills to consuming students have been instituted by quality assessment systems such as the practice of subject 'benchmarking' – statements of expected 'learning outcomes' for the student of particular subject areas, now mandatory in UK higher education (Morley, 2003). As part of the process, the content of each proposed taught course in HEIs needs to provide a 'descriptor' of the generic as well as subject-specific skills the student will be expected to have acquired on completion. Some academics have noted that benchmarking is the nearest development yet so far to a 'national curriculum' in the UK higher education sector (Morley, 2003). The Quality Assurance Agency (QAA) specifically states that 'it was not the intention of the QAA to identify something like a national curriculum in terms of the content of a degree in a given subject. This remains a matter of academic freedom' (QAA, 2000: 1). However, as Blackmore (1997), Barnett (2004) and others have pointed out, the construction of knowledge in terms of definable outcomes such as graduate 'skills' has inevitable implications for curriculum:

The professionalization of the academic community is tipping into a skills, standards and outcomes model of curriculum rather than a reflexive, collective, developmental and process-oriented model. It is a model overly concerned with the skills level of students and with the effectiveness of programmes in driving up those skills. (Barnett, 2004: 18)

The relation of expected teaching of 'skills' to curriculum content can be clearly seen in HEFCE's 1999 document where it provided guidance to all HEIs in the UK on constructing a required 'learning and teaching strategy'. Barnett (2004) points out that curriculum is hardly mentioned in most of the document, which he argues to be a deliberate attempt to construct knowledge performatively in terms of learning outcomes such as 'skills'. However, it *is* present in a section on national priorities, stating that institutions 'may wish to address . . . Promoting innovation in the curricula, particularly activity to increase the employability of graduates . . . including work experience and developing key skills' (HEFCE, 1999, point 46c, cited in Barnett, 2004).

Such limited parameters are based on 'traditional' masculinized conceptions of knowledge as something that can be objectively 'reached' and assessed: 'benchmarking is a positivistic concept of knowledge based on objective truths to be communicated, memorized and measured' (Morley, 2003: 44). Moreover, as Blackmore and others have argued, the assumption is that 'skills are concrete, can be readily categorized, are technically defined and neutral', whereas the generic 'skills' often mapped out for a student to 'acquire' are socially constructed and complexly gendered (Blackmore, 1997), as discussed earlier in Chapter 6.

It will be disciplinary teaching in 'lower status' rather than 'elite' institutions, already more explicitly dedicated to the 'needs' of business and the commercial sector, that is most affected by these changes. Thus students in post-1992 institutions who generally already possess less social, economic and cultural capital will form the majority of those receiving such explicitly 'skills-based' education. As Naidoo (2003: 256) argues: 'Rather than gaining access to powerful forms of knowledge, the majority of disadvantaged students will receive an education that has been reduced to narrowly defined core competencies which have been legitimated on the bandwagon of consumer choice.'

And as we have outlined in Chapter 4, the majority of these students, at least in the UK, are not only working class and/or minority ethnic, but also women.

The demand for modular courses designed to be 'economically valuable' to employers as well as students will have inevitable consequences for the forms of knowledge deemed most 'worthy' to be included in the higher education curriculum. Women's studies, and courses in 'traditional' subjects focusing on women and gender, will be increasingly vulnerable, as will other knowledges based on challenge and critique of political, economic and cultural forms of hegemonic dominance. Indeed, many smaller, less 'prestigious' and less explicitly vocational subject areas are increasingly vulnerable in the marketized world of education (Jackson, 2000), and the perception that subjects such as women's studies will not further graduate students' job prospects will not help student recruitment to the field

(Letherby and Marchbank, 2001; Marchbank and Letherby, 2006). The future development of feminist knowledges within the higher education sector in the face of the marketization of the sector remains to be seen.

Conclusion

In this chapter we have explored some of the ways in which the 'traditional' curricula in higher education have historically been, and continue to be, highly gendered, as well as classed and racialized. We outlined some of the ways in which 'traditional' forms of knowledge are predicated on an 'Enlightenment' concept of knowledge as the realm of the 'masculine', ensuring the historical exclusion of women from the university, and contributing to the continuing marginalization of feminist knowledges in the disciplines today. However, we also documented some of the ways in which feminist academics have challenged such marginalization, including a sustained critique of the gendered binaries of masculinity/rationality and femininity/emotionality predominant in Enlightenment thought. As well as outlining some of these challenges in relation to work in the 'traditional' disciplines, such as the sciences, history and art criticism, we have also focused particularly on women's studies as a primary site of feminist challenge to 'malestream' knowledges.

Women's studies is currently in decline in the UK, although it continues to flourish in other countries such as the USA. This has been attributed by some to the success of feminism in integrating with the wider curriculum. However, despite some degree of success and influence, as we have outlined, feminist knowledges are still often marginalized in the mainstream curricula of higher education. Often women's studies and feminist courses are perceived by non-feminist academics (and also by students) as too 'emotional', too 'politically charged' to be 'valid' knowledge – demonstrating the continued cultural dominance of gendered Enlightenment conceptions of knowledge as 'neutral', 'objective', and concerned with the 'disinterested pursuit of truth'.

The higher education curriculum in the academy is thus far from becoming a 'feminized' arena. Whilst such Enlightenment discourses of knowledge remain culturally dominant in, and legitimated by, the academy, the curriculum will remain predominantly 'masculinized'. Moreover, whilst some have pointed to the developing dominance of 'skills'- and 'employability'- focused knowledges in higher education as an example of the 'feminization' of the curriculum, such constructions of knowledge are complexly gendered. As we have seen in Chapter 6, whilst some forms of personal and social 'skills' favoured in such curricula are those that are culturally associated with 'femininity', such as collaborative working and communication skills, others such as 'self-confidence', assertiveness and 'independent learning' are culturally 'masculinized'. Moreover, the 'rational' commodification of learning into 'skills' packages for the consuming students is a masculinized, marketized model of knowledge construction that few feminists would advocate. As Apple states, 'while most economics textbooks may give the impression that markets are impersonal and impartial, they are instead highly political as well as inherently unstable' (Apple, 2005a: 12).

It is no surprise, then, that many feminists and other academics interested in social justice issues are increasingly working to challenge and subvert the new 'audit culture' of higher education. One example is a recent initiative by the University of Warwick, which has established a 'Reinvention Centre' (Lambert and Parker, 2006), designed to support and develop critical pedagogies, which, according to two of the academics involved, has 'brought about a cultural shift within our immediate intellectual environment, making shared involvement in certain forms of academic activism (more) possible' (p. 470), including a student led anti-sexism initiative (see Chapter 10). In the final chapter of our book, feminist resistances and challenges to both 'new' and 'traditional' forms of masculinized culture will be further explored, as part of an overview of our critique on the popular conception of higher education as a 'feminized' arena.

10

Conclusions: re-visioning the academy

So, are women storming the ivory tower? Can we talk seriously about a feminized future for higher education? As we have shown throughout this book, such conceptions have been challenged by a wealth of academic studies, contesting both the conception that academia is 'feminized' either in numerical or cultural terms.

In Chapter 2 we discussed what we termed the 'feminization thesis' through an analysis of the various discourses of feminization that construct the argument that society, education, and, specifically, higher education, have become a 'feminized' space. In contrast, in Chapter 3, we describe how patterns of access to higher education for women have been uneven and patchy around the world rather than a happy progress towards equal access for all, relating to complex social, economic and cultural contexts (with the UK context described in more detail in Chapter 4). Women academics also remain seriously under-represented in higher education, with vertical and horizontal stratification and lower pay seemingly ubiquitous worldwide. An equal opportunities discourse is often articulated in order to claim that there is no systematic discrimination in higher education – an argument that ignores the myriad structural and cultural barriers that women academics face, relating to the dominant cultural construction of the academic as 'masculine', which we outlined in detail in Chapter 7.

In Chapter 5 we turned our attention to a discursive analysis of the construction of the 'university' in university websites. We explored the ways in which such sites discursively represent the university, authority/knowledge and the 'academic' as masculine, in contrast to the 'good' student, apprentice learner and welcoming 'guide' as feminine. As we describe in Chapter 6, a number of culturally dominant discourses in higher education construct the 'typical' student rather differently – such as the masculinized construction of the 'independent learner' and the complexly gendered student as 'consumer', influencing students' own experiences and identities in the academy. Chapters 8 and 9 focused on the various ways in which the 'culture' of the academy is gendered, and the implications for staff and students. In

Chapter 8, we looked at the genderedness of academic language and speaking and writing practices in higher education, as well as the assessment of such practices, and in Chapter 9 we explored some of the ways in which the 'traditional' curricula in higher education have historically been, and continue to be, highly gendered, as well as classed and racialized. We also discussed the ways in which academic feminists (both within particular 'traditional' subject areas and through the field of women's studies) have challenged and critiqued the masculinized construction of academic knowledge. However, in the predominant climate of the 'skills and employability' agenda for higher education, feminist pedagogies and practices face increasing challenges.

Therefore, the arguments underpinning the 'feminization thesis': first, that there are greatly increasing numbers of women 'taking over' the academy, and secondly, that such numerical 'dominance' has led to a 'feminization' of the *culture* of the academy, have not been borne out by academic analysis. There is also little evidence that men/masculine subjectivities are becoming feminized. It is clear from the evidence we have presented that women are not forming a substantial majority in numerical terms, either as students, or, especially, as academic staff, a sphere which remains firmly male dominated. Moreover, the 'cultures' and practices of the academy remain highly masculinized, as well as reflecting other cultural matrixes of power in relation to class, 'race', sexuality, and dis/ability. Far from having a 'feminized future', then – at least in *feminist* terms – higher education remains solidly masculinized, with the chances for developing critical resistances and challenges constrained by the dominance of a neo-liberalist ethos and technicist, new managerialist practices in many aspects of HE, in many parts of the world.

Nevertheless, as Hey, Quinn (Hey, 2001; Quinn, 2003; Hey and Bradford, 2004) and others have demonstrated, and as we have discussed in earlier chapters, many women students and academic staff continue to construct a 'space of their own' within academia that provides many pleasures, comforts and rewards. Moreover, since the latter decades of the twentieth century the academy has been influenced by major legal reforms tackling social inequalities, established in response to pressures by social movements such as the women's and civil rights movements. There have been moves internationally to address gender inequality throughout the culture of organizations with a policy of 'gender mainstreaming', an initiative that has been adopted by organizations such as the European Union, the Commonwealth Secretariat and UNESCO (Morley, 2006), along with similar strategies in relation to 'diversity' mainstreaming (Mirza, 2006b). Initially derived from feminist arguments that gender equality needs to be pervasive in the culture of organizations, gender mainstreaming requires that the implications of gender equality for any planned policy or programme throughout an institution needs to be assessed before their implementation. The practice however is controversial, with many feminists arguing that it dilutes radical feminist goals to a new managerialist 'checklist' concerning 'best practice' (Morley, 2006).

Moreover, Brooks (1997) and others have found the implementation of legislative policies are very uneven and that some staff find such policies more useful symbolically than in practice. Morley (2006) argues that there has been little effort to implement gender equality measures into mainstream higher education policy, due to a 'post-feminist' conception that the battles have 'all been won':

> In terms of gender, post-feminist rather than feminist theory shapes UK higher education policy. ... [Post-feminism] reconceptualises gendered power and suggests a new type of citizenship in which agency and individual choice are explanatory variables rather than structures, social relations and hegemonies. (Morley, 2006: 135)

As more critical feminists have noted, liberal feminist initiatives to challenge inequality through increasing 'equality of opportunity' will ultimately fail if the wider cultural thinking underlying institutional cultures is left unchallenged. For example, as Brooks (1997), Morley (2005b) and others have commented, despite formal policies, sexual harassment and violence is 'rife' in HEIs in many countries internationally. It remains under-reported, as women are often too intimidated to speak out against such practices for fear of retaliation. In a number of US studies women academics are reported to experience sexual harassment at far greater rates than men (see Lester, 2008). Pereira (2007: 11) states that 'sexual harassment has become embedded in the malgovernance of the university system and the general spread of corruption' in Nigeria. She reports both passive and active resistance to gender reform programmes in Nigerian universities ranging from the ignoring of mandates to ridicule and sexual harassment. She argues that wider cultural expectations of women to be subservient infuse Nigerian academic culture, undermining attempts at reform.

In any case, Morley (2003) Leonard (2001) David (2006) and others have noted that most change in the academy has not come from gender mainstreaming initiatives or equality policies, but through the practices of lecturers involved in social movements such as the women's movement. In a study on resistance by women in Irish higher education, O'Connor (2003) found that where resistance occurred, counter-resistance was common, including:

> the stigmatisation of any initiative in favour of women; the demonization of prominent women; the starving of women of resources (individually or collectively); the establishment of organizational 'roadblocks' and the rendering of hard-won procedures irrelevant by the introduction of new ones containing implicit positive discrimination in favour of men. (p. 23)

Nevertheless, we would like to conclude this chapter with some more positive examples of what women academics and students have been achieving in terms of challenges to dominant forms of academic culture. This is not simply because we cannot conceive of finishing this book without a modernist Hollywood-style 'happy ending', but also because we wanted to celebrate what women continue to achieve individually and collectively in higher education, providing inspiration in the face of an educational climate that can engender an almost inevitable, and often immobilizing, sense of pessimism and fatalism in many concerned with issues of social justice.

As well as myriad disciplinary and institutional women's networks and campaigns, there also exist national networks in many countries for women to make connections with each other and campaign on particular issues of regional or international importance – for example the Women in Higher Education Network (WHEN) in the UK, and the European Network on Gender Equality in Higher Education (see, for example, Barry et al., 2007). Many groups have been founded on feminist principles and are designed specifically to challenge particular masculinized forms of academic culture, for example the London, UK based 'Feminist Salon' organized by women academics in the field of education was designed specifically for women to talk informally about academic ideas away from the competitive arena of formal conferences and seminars (see London Feminist Salon Collective, 2004). In New Zealand, women academics from a variety of disciplines and universities on the North Island regularly meet for 'writing retreats' away from the academy, in a spirit of collaboration and support. These retreats have taken place despite the organizer being challenged as to why she would organize events that would help academics from 'rival' universities, highlighting the continuing individualistic, competitive climate in which academics work (Grant, 2006). However, in myriad different ways, feminist academics all over the world are individually and collectively working to challenge dominant cultural practices in higher education and providing alternative ways of teaching, learning and working in the academy.

Ultimately, as we noted in the introduction, change within the academy can only be accompanied by wider social change to dominant cultural discourses that construct and perpetuate inequalities, as Gqola (2002) acknowledges in the context of African higher education. She describes the decision to make a new e-journal, 'Feminist Africa', accessible to the public, therefore ensuring that African feminist constructions of knowledge are available to others outside the academy, through 'contesting the hierarchies of access and circulation both in content and form' (Gqola, 2002: 2). We have found this a particularly valuable resource in researching this book, but are conscious that our own work, published in journals requiring a subscription, is not similarly available to our African colleagues.

Groups have been established by students as well as academic staff: Lambert and Parker (2006) describe how a postgraduate woman student set up the 'Warwick Anti-Sexism Society' (WASS) in 2004 which is now thriving as an activist and social group, and with almost as many men as women members. Lambert and Parker argue that 'students are far from indifferent when it comes to gender politics amongst the shadows of the masculinist new-managerialism to which UK higher education has succumbed' (2006: 470). Interestingly, they explore the ways in which some women WASS members pragmatically chose to present themselves as 'feminine' and (implicitly) heterosexual, playing with the 'ironic possibilities offered by the simultaneous performance of feminism and femininity', in order to 'draw both women and men in, and simultaneously counter the associations of feminism with humourlessness and a lack of femininity' (p. 476). Such strategies demonstrate the continuing popular cultural associations of feminism with (lack of) femininity (as discursively defined) that were also found in Marchbank and Letherby's study on perceptions of women's studies (2006). The implication is that women's contributions will be taken more seriously and valued more highly within mainstream culture if women themselves present such knowledge whilst 'doing' gender within the constraints of normative (heterosexual) constructions of femininity. Moreover, it seems many young women and men may only be able to self-identify with pro/feminism when constructed within such 'safe' constraints. Nevertheless, Lambert and Parker find much to be hopeful for, arguing that such 'fears' around feminism can be taken up in reflexive debate, and stressing the positivity felt by many of the members engaged in WASS activities, many of whom express the desire to continue with anti-sexist campaigning after leaving university.

Clegg (1994), notes that resistance to dominant cultural discourses are more likely to occur 'if a subjectivity formed around a [collective] will to resist' exists, for example through the 'consciously organised resources of a social movement or collective organisation in the pursuit of their agency' (Clegg, 1994, cited in O'Connor, 2003: 12). It seems that in higher education at the beginning of the twenty-first century there still exists such collective wills on the part of feminists and pro-feminists to resist and challenge changing forms of masculinized hegemonic culture, including that of the academy. As we have researched and written this book we have become increasingly aware of the *commonalities* of women's positionalities and experiences in the academy across the world, as well as the many differences. We have also developed a growing sense of outrage at the persistence of gendered, classed and racialized structures and cultures in the global field of higher education. The importance of recognizing, analysing, resisting and challenging both material and cultural inequalities, for both women and men, students and staff, is, we suggest, highlighted by the evidence we have presented. For feminists utilizing poststructuralist perspectives the possibility of being able to collectively instigate change as well as subversion and resistance has been the topic of much debate. However we would agree with Francis (2002b) and others that it *is* possible to operate agentically, within inevitable discursive constraints. Feminists around the world *are* able to, and indeed do, work individually and collectively towards instigating a future for higher education that is centrally based on the tenets of a feminism that fully takes into account matrixes of inequality – a 'feminist' rather than 'feminized' future.

References

ABC (2000) *Feminized Fish Throughout Europe. 2000.* www.abc.net.au/science/news/stories/s173226.htm (accessed 11 October, 2007).

Acker, S. and Armenti, C. (2004) Sleepless in academia, *Gender and Education*, 16(1): 3–24.

Acker, S. and Feuerverger, G. (1996) Doing good and feeling bad: the work of women university teachers, *Cambridge Journal of Education*, 26: 401–22.

Acker, S. and Webber, M. (2006) Women working in academe: approach with care, in C. Skelton, B. Francis and L. Smulyan (eds) *The Sage Handbook of Gender and Education*. London: Sage.

Adkins, L. (2002) *Revisions: Gender and Sexuality in Late Modernity.* Buckingham: Open University Press.

Adkins, L. and Lury, C. (2000) Making bodies, making people, making work, in L. McKie and N. Watson (eds) *Organizing Bodies: Policy, Institutions and Work.* Basingstoke: Macmillan.

Aguirre, A. (2000) *Women and Minority Faculty in the Academic Workplace: Recruitment, Retention and Academic Culture.* San Francisco, CA: Jossey Bass.

Ahmed, S. (1999) *Differences that Matter: Feminist Theory and Postmodernism.* Cambridge: Cambridge University Press.

Ahmed, S. (2004) Affective economics, *Social Text*, 22(2): 117–39.

Ainley, P. (1994) *Degrees of Difference.* London: Cassell.

Alfred, M. (1997) A re-conceptualisation of marginality: perspectives of African American female faculty in the white academy. Paper presented at SCUTREA Conference 'Crossing Borders, Breaking Boundaries: Research in the Education of Adults', University of London, July.

Alfred, M. (2001) Reconceptualising marginality from the margins: perspectives of African American tenured faculty at a white research university, *Western Journal of Black Studies*, 25: 1–11.

Allen, K. (2007) It's arrived: the feminization of the net, *The Guardian*, 23 August.

Anderson, M. (1987) Changing the curriculum in higher education, *Signs*, 12(2): 222–54.

Anson, C. (1988) Toward a multidimensional model of writing in the academic disciplines, in D.A. Joliffe (ed.) *Advances in Writing Research Vol. 2: Writing in Academic Disciplines.* New York: Ablex.

Anthias, F. (2001) New hybridities, old concepts: the limits of 'culture', *Ethnic and Racial Studies*, 24(4): 619–41.

Appadurai, A. (2006) Disjuncture and difference in the global cultural economy, in H. Lauder, P. Brown, J.-A. Dillabough and A.H. Halsey (eds) *Education, Globalisation and Social Change*. Oxford: Oxford University Press.

Apple, M. (2005a) Education, markets and an audit culture, *Critical Quarterly*, 47(1–2): 11–29.

Apple, M.W. (2005b) Are markets in education democratic? Neoliberal globalism, vouchers, and the politics of choice, in M.A. Apple, J. Kenway and M. Singh (eds) *Globalizing Education: Policies, Pedagogies and Politics*. New York: Peter Lang.

Appleby, Y. (1997) Negotiating the narrow straits of education, in G. Griffin and S. Andermahr (eds) *Straight Studies Modified: Lesbian Interventions in the Academy*. London: Cassell.

Archer, L. (2003) 'Knowing their limits'? Identities, inequalities and inner city school leavers' post-16 aspirations, *Journal of Education Policy*, 18(2): 53–69.

Archer, L. and Hutchings, M. (2000) 'Bettering yourself?' Discourses of risk, cost and benefit in ethnically diverse, young working-class non-participants' constructions of higher education, *British Journal of Sociology of Education*, 21(4): 555–74.

Archer, L., Hutchings, M. and Leathwood, C. (2001) Engaging with commonality and difference: theoretical tensions in the analysis of working class women's educational discourses, *International Studies in Sociology of Education*, 11(1): 51–71.

Archer, L., Hutchings, M. and Leathwood, C. (2002) Higher education: a risky business, in A. Hayton and A. Paczuska (eds) *Widening Participation and Higher Education: Policy and Practice*. London: Kogan Page.

Archer, L., Hutchings, M., Ross, A. with Leathwood, C., Gilchrist, R. and Phillips, D. (2003) *Social Class and Higher Education: Issues of Exclusion and Inclusion*. London: RoutledgeFalmer.

Archer, L. and Leathwood, C. (2003) Identities, inequalities and higher education, in L. Archer, M. Hutchings, A. Ross with C. Leathwood, R. Gilchrist and D. Phillips (eds) *Higher Education and Social Class: Issues of Exclusion and Inclusion*. London: RoutledgeFalmer.

Arum, R., Gamoran, A. and Shavit, Y. (2007) More inclusion than diversion: expansion, differentiation, and market structure in higher education, in Y. Shavit, R. Arum, A. Gamoran and G. Menahem (eds) *Stratification in Higher Education: A Comparative Study*. Stanford, CA: Stanford University Press.

Asmar, C. (1999) Is there a gendered agenda in academia? The research experience of female and male Phd graduates in Australian universities, *Higher Education*, 38(3): 255–73.

Assié-Lumumba, N.D. and Sutton, M. (2004) Global trends in comparative research on gender and education, *Comparative Education Review*, 48(4): 345–52.

Attwood, R. (2007) It pays for women to work in post-92s, *The Times Higher Education*, 11 May.

AUT (2001) *Lesbian, Gay and Bisexual Participation in UK Universities: Results from a Pilot Study*. London: Association of University Teachers.

AUT (2005) *The Diverse Academy: The Pay and Employment of Academic and Professional Staff in UK Higher Education by Gender and Ethnicity*. London: Association of University Teachers.

Badran, M. (1995) *Feminists, Islam, and Nation: Gender and the Making of Modern Egypt*. Princeton, NJ: Princeton University Press.

Bagguley, P. and Hussain, Y. (2007) *The Role of Higher Education in Providing Opportunities for South Asian Women.* York: Joseph Rowntree Foundation.

Bagilhole, B. (1993) Survivors in a male preserve, a study of British women academics' experiences and perceptions of discrimination in a UK University, *Higher Education,* 26(4): 431–48.

Bagilhole, B. (2002) Against the odds: women academics' research opportunities, in G. Howie and A. Tauchert (eds) *Gender, Teaching and Research in Higher Education: Challenges for the 21st Century.* Aldershot: Ashgate.

Bagilhole, B. (2007) Challenging women in the male academy: think about draining the swamp, in P. Cotterill, S. Jackson and G. Letherby (eds) *Challenges and Negotiations for Women in Higher Education.* Dordrecht: Springer.

Bagilhole, B. and Goode, J. (1998) The 'gender dimension' of both the 'narrow' and 'broad' curriculum in UK higher education: do women lose out in both? *Gender and Education,* 10(4): 445–58.

Bagilhole, B. and Goode, J. (2001) The contradiction of the myth of individual merit, and the reality of a patriarchal support system in academic careers, *The European Journal of Women's Studies,* 8(2): 161–80.

Bal, M. and Bryson, N. (1991) Semiotics and art history, *Art Bulletin,* 73(2): 174–208.

Ball, S.J. (1999) Global trends in educational reform and the struggle for the soul of the teacher! Paper presented at the British Educational Research Annual Conference, University of Sussex, Brighton. Available on Education-Line at www.leeds.ac.uk/educol/documents/00001212.doc (accessed 2 February, 2001).

Ball, S.J. (2003) *Class Strategies and the Education Market: The Middle Classes and Social Advantage.* London: RoutledgeFalmer.

Ball, S.J., Maguire, M. and Macrae, S. (2000) *Choice, Pathways and Transitions Post-16: New Youth, New Economies in the Global City.* London: RoutledgeFalmer.

Ball, S.J., Reay, D. and David, M. (2002) 'Ethnic choosing': minority ethnic students, social class and higher education choice, *Race, Ethnicity and Education,* 5(4): 333–57.

Ballard, B. and Clanchy, J. (1988) Literacy in the university: an 'anthropological' approach, in G. Taylor, B. Ballard, V. Beasley, H. Bock, J. Clanchy and P. Nightingale (eds) *Literacy by Degrees.* Milton Keynes: SRHE and Open University Press.

Banerji, S. (2006) Aaup: women professors lag in tenure, salary, *Diverse Online,* (26 October).

Barata, P., Hunjan, S. and Leggatt, J. (2005) Ivory tower? Feminist women's experiences of graduate school, *Women's Studies International Forum,* 28(2–3): 232–46.

Barnett, R. (2004) *Engaging the Curriculum in Higher Education.* Maidenhead: McGraw-Hill.

Barry, J., Chandler, J. and Berg, E. (2007) Women's movements and new public management: higher education in Sweden and England, *Public Administration,* 85(1): 103–22.

Barthes, R. (1977) The death of the author, in S. Heath (ed.) *Image-Music-Text.* New York: Hill and Wang.

Bartholomae, D. (1985) Inventing the university, in M. Rose (ed.) *When a Writer Can't Write.* London: Guilford Press.

Bartky, S.L. (1988) Foucault, femininity, and the modernization of patriarchal power, in I. Diamond and L. Quinby (eds) *Feminism and Foucault.* Boston, MA: Northeastern University Press.

Bartky, S.L. (1990) *Femininity and Domination: Studies in the Phenomenology of Oppression*. New York: Routledge.

Battersby, C. (1990) *Gender and Genius: Towards a Feminist Aesthetics*. Bloomington, IN: Indiana University Press.

Baudrillard, J. (1998) *The Consumer Society: Myths and Structures*. London: Sage.

Baume, D. and Yorke, M. (2002) The reliability of assessment by portfolio on a course to develop and accredit teachers in higher education, *Studies in Higher Education*, 27(1): 7–25.

Bawden, A. (2007) Missing male, *Education Guardian*, 31 July.

Baxter, A. and Britton, C. (2001) Risk, identity and change: becoming a mature student, *International Studies in Sociology of Education*, 11(1): 87–102.

Baxter, S. (2007) Will women rule the world? *The Sunday Times*. London, TimesOnline. www.timesonline.co.uk/tol/news/world/article1321476.ece (accessed 14 November, 2007).

BBC (2005) Buerk attacks women broadcasters. *BBC News*. www.newsvote.bbc.co.uk (accessed 4 Novovember, 2007).

BBC (2006) Rape in war 'a growing problem'. *BBC News*: http://news.bbc.co.uk/1/hi/world/europe/5105102.stm (accessed 14 January 2008).

BBC (2008) Tables 'affect university policy'. *BBC News*. http://news.bbc.co.uk/1/hi/education/7336631.stm, BBC MMVIII. 2008 (accessed 9 April, 2008).

Bebbington, D. (2002) Women in science, engineering and technology: a review of the issues, *Higher Education Quarterly*, 56(4): 360–75.

Becher, T. and Trowler, P. (2001) *Academic Tribes and Territories: Intellectual Enquiry and the Culture of Disciplines*. Buckingham: SRHE/Open University Press.

Beck, U. (2000) *What is Globalization?* Cambridge: Polity Press.

Beck, U. and Beck-Gernsheim, E. (2002) *Individualization*. Thousand Oaks, CA: Sage.

Bell, P. and Milic, M. (2002) Goffman's gender advertisements revisited: combining content analysis with semiotic analysis, *Visual Communication*, 1(2): 203–22.

Bing, V.M. and Reid, P.T. (1996) Unknown women and unknowing research: consequencies of color and class in feminist psychology, in N.R. Goldberger, J.M. Tarule, B.M. Clinchy and M.F. Belenky (eds) *Knowledge, Difference and Power: Essays Inspired by Women's Ways of Knowing*. New York: Basic Books.

Bird, E. (2004) The sexual politics of introducing women's studies: memories and reflections from North America and the United Kingdom 1965–1995, *Gender and Education*, 16(1): 51–64.

Blackmore, J. (1997) The gendering of skill and vocationalism in twentieth-century Australian education, in A.H. Halsey, H. Lauder, P. Brown and A. Stuart Wells (eds) *Education: Culture, Economy, Society*. Oxford: Oxford University Press.

Blackmore, J. (1999) *Troubling Women*. Buckingham: Open University Press.

Blackmore, J. (2000) Globalization: a useful concept for feminists rethinking theory and strategies in education?, in N.C. Burbules and C.A. Torres (eds) *Globalization and Education: Critical Perspectives*. London: Routledge.

Blackmore, J. and Sachs, J. (2003a) Managing equity work in the performative university, *Australian Feminist Studies*, 18(41): 141–62.

Blackmore, J. and Sachs, J. (2003b) 'Zealotry or nostalgic regret'? Women leaders in technical and further education in Australia: change agents, entrepreneurial educators or corporate citizens? *Gender, Work and Organization*, 10(4): 478–503.

Bombardieri, M. (2005) Summers' remarks on women draw fire, *The Boston Globe*.

www.boston.com/news/local/articles/2005/01/17/summers_remarks_on_women_draw_fire/ (accessed 14 November, 2007).

Bompard, P. (2004) Only elite need apply, *The Times Higher Educational Supplement*, 13 February.

Booth, A., Frank, J. and Blackaby, D. (2005) Outside offers and the gender pay gap: empirical evidence from the UK academic labour market, *Economic Journal*, 115(51): 81–107.

Bosch, J. (2003) *Women in Spanish Universities*. http://csn.uni-muenster.de/women-eu/ (accessed 23 January, 2008).

Bouchard, P., Boily, I. and Proulx, M.-C. (2003) *School Success by Gender: A Catalyst for the Masculinist Discourse*. Ottawa: Status of Women Canada.

Bourdieu, P. (1987) What makes a social class? On the theoretical and practical existence of groups, *Berkeley Journal of Sociology*, 1–17.

Bourdieu, P. (1988) *Homo Academicus*. Cambridge: Polity Press.

Bourdieu, P. (1991) *Language and Symbolic Power*. Cambridge: Polity Press.

Bradley, C. (1984) Sex bias in the evaluation of students, *British Journal of Social Psychology*, 23: 147–63.

Branthwaite, A., Trueman, M. and Hartley, J. (1980) Writing essays: the actions and strategies of students, in J. Hartley (ed.) *The Psychology of Written Communication*. London: Kogan Page.

Brecher, B. (2005) Complicities and modularisation: how universities were made safe for the market, *Critical Quarterly*, 47(1–2): 72–82.

Brewer, R.M. (1993) Theorising race, class and gender: the new scholarship of black feminist intellectuals and black women's labour, in S.M. James and A.P.A. Busia (eds) *Theorising Black Feminisms*. London: Routledge.

Brine, J. (2001) Education, social exclusion and the supranational state, *International Journal of Inclusive Education*, 5(2/3): 119–31.

Britton, C. and Baxter, A. (1999) Becoming a mature student: gendered narratives of the self, *Gender and Education*, 11(2): 179–93.

Broadfoot, P. (1996) *Education, Assessment and Society*. Buckingham: Open University Press.

Broadfoot, P. (1999) Empowerment or performativity? English assessment policy in the late twentieth century. Paper presented at British Educational Research Association Annual Conference, University of Sussex, September.

Brockes, E. (2003) Taking the mick, *The Guardian*, 15 January.

Broecke, S. and Nicholls, T. (n.d.) *Ethnicity and Degree Attainment: Research Report Rw92*. London: Department for Education and Skills.

Brookfield, S. (1999) Reclaiming and problematising self-directed learning as a space for critical adult education. Paper presented at 29th Annual SCUTREA Conference, University of Warwick, Department of Continuing Education, 5–7 July.

Brooks, A. (1997) *Academic Women*. Buckingham: SRHE/Open University Press.

Brouns, M. (2000) The gendered nature of assessment procedures in scientific research funding: the Dutch case, *Higher Education in Europe*, 25(2): 193–9.

Brown, P. and Hesketh, A. (2003) *The Social Construction of Graduate Employability: Final Report of ESRC Project R000239101*. Online at www.regard.ac.uk (accessed 13 October, 2003).

Brown, P. and Hesketh, A. (2004) *The Mismanagement of Talent: Employability and Jobs in the Knowledge Economy*. Oxford: Oxford University Press.

Brown, R. (2004) English higher education: past, present, future. Lecture at Southampton Institute, 29 April.

Brown, V.B. (1990) The fear of feminization: Los Angeles high schools in the progressive era, *Feminist Studies*, 16(3): 493–519.

Bryson, C. (2004) The consequences for women in the academic profession of the widespread use of fixed term contracts, *Gender, Work and Organization*, 11(2): 188–206.

Bunting, C. (2004) Distinct lack of ebony in the ivory towers, *The Times Higher Education Supplement*, 22 October.

Burman, E. (2005) Childhood, neo-liberalism and the feminization of education, *Gender and Education*, 17(4): 351–67.

Burstyn, J.N. (1980) *Victorian Education and the Ideal of Womanhood*. London: Croom Helm.

Butler, J. (1990) *Gender Trouble*. London: Routledge.

Butler, J. (1991) The difficult dialogue of curriculum transformation: ethnic studies and women's studies, in J. Butler (ed.) *Transforming the Curriculum*. Albany, NY: State University of New York Press.

Cadbury, D. (1998) *The Feminization of Nature: Our Future at Risk*. London: Penguin Books.

Callender, C. (2004) *The Changing Finances of Students Studying in London: Evidence from the 2002/03 Student Income and Expenditure Survey*. London: Greater London Authority.

Callender, C. and Kemp, M. (2000) *Changing Student Finances: Income, Expenditure and the Take-up of Student Loans among Full- and Part-Time Higher Education Students in 1998/9*. London: Department for Education and Employment.

Cameron, D. (1998) *Language: The Feminist Critique*. London: Routledge.

Carr, E. (1986) *What is History?* London: Macmillan.

Carrington, B., Francis, B., Hutchings, M., Skelton, C., Read, B. and Hall, I. (2007) Does the gender of the teacher really matter? Seven- to eight-year-olds' accounts of their interactions with their teachers, *Educational Studies*, 33(4): 397–413.

Carter, J., Fenton, S. and Modood, T. (1999) *Ethnicity and Employment in Higher Education*. London: Policy Studies Institute.

Chanana, K. (2004) Gender and disciplinary choices: women in higher education in India. Paper presented at UNESCO Colloquium on Research and Higher Education Policy 'Knowledge, Access and Governance: Strategies for Change', Paris, 1–3 December.

Chapman, C. (2004) Germany to create elite institution to rival Oxbridge, *The Times Higher Education Supplement*, 16 January.

CHERI (2008) *Counting What is Measured or Measuring What Counts? League Tables and Their Impact on Higher Education Institutions in England*. www.hefce.ac.uk/pubs/ hefce/2008/08_14/08_14.pdf, Higher Education Funding Council for England (accessed 14 April, 2008).

Cixous, H. (1981) Castration or decapitation, *Signs*, 1(4): 875–93.

Clark, L. (2006) Boys are being failed by our schools, *The Daily Mail*, 13 June.

Clarke, J. and Newman, J. (1997) *The Managerial State*. London: Sage.

Clarricoates, K. ([1978] 1989) Dinosaurs in the classroom – the 'hidden' curriculum in primary schools, in M. Arnot and G. Weiner (eds) *Gender and the Politics of Schooling*. Milton Keynes: Open University Press.

Clegg, S. (2008) Academic identities under threat? *British Educational Research Journal*, iFirst article, 1–15.

Coaldrake, P. (2000) Rethinking academic and university work, *Higher Education Management*, 12(3): 7–30.

Coate, K. (2006) Imagining women in the curriculum: the transgressive impossibility of women's studies, *Studies in Higher Education*, 31(4): 407–21.

Cohen, M. (1998) 'A habit of healthy idleness': boys' underachievement in historical perspective, in D. Epstein, J. Elwood, V. Hey and J. Maw (eds) *Failing Boys? Issues in Gender and Achievement*. Buckingham: Open University Press.

Cohen, S. (1972) *Folk Devils and Moral Panics*. London: MacGibbon and Kee.

Cohen, S. (2002) Moral panics as cultural politics. New introduction, in S. Cohen (ed.) *Folk Devils and Moral Panics: The Creation of the Mods and Rockers, 3rd Edition*. London: Routledge.

Coiner, C. and George, D. (1998) *The Family Track: Keeping Your Faculties While You Mentor, Nurture, Teach and Serve*. Urbana, IL: University of Illinois Press.

Committee on Maximizing the Potential of Women in Academic Science and Engineering (2006) *Beyond Bias and Barriers: Fulfilling the Potential of Women in Academic Science and Engineering*. www.nap.edu/catalog/11741.html (accessed 14 November, 2008), National Academy of Sciences, National Academy of Engineering, and Institute of Medicine.

Conlon, G. and Chevalier, A. (2002a) *Financial Returns to Undergraduates: A Summary of Recent Evidence*. London: Council for Industry and Higher Education.

Conlon, G. and Chevalier, A. (2002b) *Rates of Return to Qualifications: A Summary of Recent Evidence*. London: Council for Industry and Higher Education.

Connell, R.W. (1987) *Gender and Power*. Cambridge: Polity Press.

Connell, R.W., Johnston, K. and White, V. (1992) *Measuring Up*. Canberra: Australian Curriculum Studies Monograph.

Connolly, K. (2007) Educated women leave East German men behind, *The Guardian*, 1 June.

Connor, H., Tyers, C., Modood, T. and Hillage, J. (2004) *Why the Difference? A Closer Look at Higher Education Minority Ethnic Students and Graduates. DfES Research Report Rr552*. London: Department for Education and Skills.

Costello, C.Y. (2001) Schooled by the classroom: the (re)production of social stratification in professional school settings, in E. Margolis (ed.) *The Hidden Curriculum in Higher Education*. London: Routledge.

Court, S. (2004) *Gender and Research Activity in the 2001 RAE*. London: AUT.

Cox, R. (1988) Examinations and higher education: a survey of the literature, in L. Elton and J. Gilbert (eds) *Module D: Assessment, Extracts. Diploma in the Practice of Higher Education*. Guildford: University of Surrey Press.

Crammond, J. (1998) The uses and complexity of argument structures in expert and student persuasive writing, *Written Communication*, 15(2): 230–68.

Cronin, A. (2000) *Advertising and Consumer Citizenship: Gender, Images and Rights*. London: Routledge.

Crozier, G. (2008) Social identities in higher education: border crossings and cultural fusions, cultural flows: constructing hybrid identities. SEHE Dissemination Event. Institute of Education, London. www.education.sunderland.ac.uk/our-research/sehe (accessed 23 April, 2008).

Currie, J., Thiele, B. and Harris, P. (2002) *Gendered Universities in Globalized Economies: Power, Careers, and Sacrifices*. Lanham, MD: Lexington Books.

Currie, J., Harris, T. and Thiele, B. (2003) Gendered universities in globalized economies: changing the organization. Paper presented to the Gender, Work and Organization Conference, Keele University.

Curtis, P. (2006) Segregation, 2006 style, *The Guardian*, 3 January.

Curtis, P. (2008) Women take longer to repay student loans, *The Guardian*, 2 January.

www.guardian.co.uk/politics/2008/jan/02/uk.studentfinance (accessed 15 February, 2008).

Daly, M. (1978) *Gyn/Ecology: The Metaethics of Radical Feminism.* Boston, MA: Beacon Press.

David, M. (2006) Personal learning on professional doctorates: feminist and women's contributions to higher education, in M. Danowitz Sagaria (ed.) *Gender Equality and University Change.* Gordonsville, VA: Palgrave Macmillan.

Davies, B. (2006) Women and transgression in the halls of academe, *Studies in Higher Education*, 31(4): 497–509.

Davies, B., Brown, J., Gannon, S., Honan, E. and Somerville, M. (2005) Embodied women at work in neoliberal times and places, *Gender, Work and Organisation*, 12(4): 342–62.

Davies, C. (1996) The sociology of professions and the profession of gender, *Sociology* 30(4): 661–78.

Dayioğlu, M. and Türüt-Aşik, S. (2007) Gender differences in academic performance in a large public university in Turkey, *Higher Education*, 53(2): 255–77.

Deem, R. (2001) Globalisation, new managerialism, academic capitalism, and entrepreneurialism in universities: is the local dimension still important? *Comparative Education*, 37(1): 7–20.

Deem, R. (2003) Gender, organizational cultures and the practices of manager-academics in UK universities, *Gender, Work and Organization*, 10(2): 239–59.

Deem, R. and Ozga, J.T. (2000) Transforming post-compulsory education? Femocrats at work in the academy, *Women's Studies International Forum*, 23(2): 153–66.

Deem, R., Ozga, J.T. and Prichard, C. (2000) Managing further education: is it still men's work too? *Journal of Further and Higher Education*, 24(2): 231–50.

Delamont, S. (2006) Gender and higher education, in C. Skelton, B. Francis and L. Smulyan (eds) *The Sage Handbook of Gender and Education.* London: Sage.

Denham, J. (2007) Speech by the Secretary of State for Innovation, Universities and Skills. Action on Access Conference: 'The Future of Widening Participation'. London, 11 December.

Denham, J. (2008) *Higher Education Funding 2008–09: Letter to HEFCE, 18 January.* London: Higher Education Funding Council for England.

Dennis, I., Newstead, S.E. and Wright, D. (1996) A new approach to exploring biases in educational assessment, *British Journal of Psychology*, 87: 515–34.

Dent, M. and Whitehead, S. (2001) Introduction: configuring the 'new' professional, in M. Dent and S. Whitehead (eds) *Managing Professional Identities: Knowledge, Performativity and the 'New' Professional.* London: Routledge.

Derrida, J. (1976) *Of Grammatology.* Baltimore, CA: Johns Hopkins University Press.

Derrida, J. (1987) *The Truth in Painting.* Chicago, IL: University of Chicago Press.

DfES (2003) *The Future of Higher Education: White Paper.* London: The Stationery Office.

DfES (2007) *Memorandum Submitted by the Department for Education and Skills in Evidence to the Education and Skills Select Committee.* www.publications.parliament.uk/pa/cm200607/cmselect/cmeduski/285/285we02.htm (accessed 14 November, 2008).

Disabilities Task Group (2007) *What Happens Next? A Report on the First Destinations of 2005 Graduates with Disabilities.* www.agcas.org.uk/agcas_resources/17-What-Happens-Next-A-Report-on-the-First-Destinations-of-Graduates-with-Disabilities (accessed 15 March, 2008).

Doherty, S. (2000) To challenge academic individualism in U. of M. Social Justice

Group at the Center for Advanced Feminist Studies (ed.) *Is Academic Feminism Dead?* New York: New York University Press.

Driessen, G. (2007) The feminization of primary education: effects of teachers' sex on pupil achievement, attitudes and behaviour, *International Review of Education*, 53(2): 183–203.

du Gay, P. (1996) Organizing identity: entrepreneurial governance and public management, in S. Hall and P. Du Gay (eds) *Questions of Cultural Identity*. London: Sage.

Dyhouse, C. (1984) Storming the citadel or storm in a teacup? The entry of women into higher education 1860–1920, in S. Acker and D.W. Piper (eds) *Is Higher Education Fair to Women?* Guildford: SRHE and NFER-Nelson.

Dyhouse, C. (2006) *Students: A Gendered History*. London: Routledge.

Ecclestone, K. (2004) Developing self-esteem and emotional well-being – inclusion or intrusion? *Adults Learning*, 16(3): 11–13.

Ecclestone, K. and Hayes, D. (2007) A response to Daphne Loads, *Studies in the Education of Adults*, 39(1): 95–7.

Ecclestone, K., Hayes, D. and Furedi, F. (2005) Knowing me, knowing you: the rise of therapeutic professionalism in the education of adults, *Studies in the Education of Adults*, 37(2): 182–200.

Edelman, M. (ed.) (1977) *Political Language: Words that Succeed and Policies that Fail*. London: Academic Press Inc.

Edelman, M. (1985) *The Symbolic Uses of Politics*. Chicago, IL: University of Illinois Press.

Elwood, J. (1999) Gender, achievement and the 'Gold Standard': differential performance in the GCE A level examination, *The Curriculum Journal*, 10(2): 189–208.

Elwood, J. (2001) Examination techniques: issues of validity and effects on pupil performance, in D. Scott (ed.) *Curriculum and Assessment*. Westport, CA: Ablex.

England, P., Allison, P., Li, S., Mark, N., Thompson, J., Budig, M.J. and Sun, H. (2007) Why are some academic fields tipping toward female? The sex composition of US fields of doctoral degree receipt, 1971–2002, *Sociology of Education*, 80(1): 23–42.

Enloe, C. (1990) *Blue Jeans and Bankers*. London: Pandora.

Epstein, D., Elwood, J., Hey, V. and Maw, J. (eds) (1998a) *Failing Boys? Issues in Gender and Achievement*. Buckingham: Open University Press.

Epstein, D., Elwood, J., Hey, V. and Maw, J. (1998b) Schoolboy frictions: feminism and 'failing' boys, in D. Epstein, J. Elwood, V. Hey and J. Maw (eds) *Failing Boys? Issues in Gender and Achievement*. Buckingham: Open University Press.

Epstein, D., O'Flynn, S. and Telford, D. (2003) *Silenced Sexualities in Schools and Universities*. Stoke on Trent: Trentham.

European Commission (2004) *Women and Science: Indicators and Statistics*. http://ec.europa.eu/research/science-society/women/wssi/downindi_en.html#As (accessed 14 January, 2008).

European Commission (2007) *Key Data on Higher Education in Europe*. Luxembourg: European Commission.

European Monitoring Centre on Racism and Xenophobia (2006) *Annual Report on the Situation Regarding Racism and Xenophobia in the Member States of the EU*. http://fra.europa.eu/fra/material/pub/ar06/AR06-P2-EN.pdf (accessed 14 March, 2008).

Evans, M. (1983) In praise of theory: the case for women's studies, in G. Bowles and D. Klein (eds) *Theories of Women's Studies*. London: Routledge.

Evans, M. (1997) *Introducing Contemporary Feminist Thought*. Cambridge: Polity Press.

Evans, M. (2004) *Killing Thinking: The Death of the Universities*. London: Continuum.

Fairclough, N. (1993) Critical discourse analysis and the marketisation of discourse: the universities, *Discourse and Society*, 4(2): 133–68.

Fara, P. (2004) *Pandora's Breeches: Women, Science and Power in the Enlightenment*. London: Pimlico.

Farr, M. (1993) Essayist literacy and other verbal performances, *Written Communication*, 10(1): 4–38.

Fenton, S., Carter, J. and Modood, T. (2000) Ethnicity and academia: closure models, racism models and market models, *Sociological Research Online*, 5(2): www.socresonline.org.uk/5/2/fenton.html (accessed 29 March 2008).

Ferber, M.A. and Nelson, J.A. (eds) (2003) *Feminist Economics Today: Beyond Economic Man*. Chicago, IL. and London: University of Chicago Press.

Ferguson, K.E. (1984) *The Feminist Case against Bureaucracy*. Philadelphia, PA: Temple University Press.

Finkel, S.K., Olswang, S. and She, N. (1994) Childbirth, tenure and promotion for women faculty, *Review of Higher Education*, 17(3): 259–70.

Fisher, G. (2007) 'You need tits to get on around here': gender and sexuality in the entrepreneurial university of the 21st century, *Ethnography*, 8(4): 503–17.

Fordham, S. (1993) 'Those loud black girls': black women, silence, and gender 'passing' in the academy, *Anthropology and Education Quarterly*, 24(1): 3–32.

Foucault, M. (1971) *The Order of Things: An Archaeology of the Human Sciences*. New York: Random House.

Foucault, M. (1977) *Discipline and Punish: The Birth of the Prison*. London: Penguin.

Foucault, M. (1981) *The History of Sexuality: An Introduction*. London: Penguin.

France-Presse, A. (2002) Nearly 30 per cent of Hong Kong students victims of sexual harassment, *Global Newsbank*: www.newsbank.com (accessed 25 January, 2008).

Francis, B. (2000) *Boys, Girls and Achievement: Addressing the Classroom Issues*. London: Routledge.

Francis, B. (2001) Commonality and difference? Attempts to escape from theoretical dualisms in emancipatory research in education, *International Studies in Sociology of Education*, 11(2): 157–72.

Francis, B. (2002) Relativism, realism and feminism: an analysis of some theoretical tensions in research on gender identity, *Journal of Gender Studies*, 11(1): 39–54.

Francis, B. (2008) Teaching manfully? Exploring gendered subjectivities and power via analyses of men teachers' gender performance, *Gender and Education*, 20(2): 109–22.

Francis, B., Robson, J. and Read, B. (2001) An analysis of undergraduate writing styles in the context of gender and achievement, *Studies in Higher Education*, 26(3): 313–26.

Francis, B., Robson, J. and Read, B. (2002) Gendered patterns in writing and degree award, in G. Howie and A. Tauchert (eds) *Gender, Teaching and Research in Higher Education: Challenges for the 21st Century*. Aldershot: Ashgate.

Francis, B., Robson, J., Read, B. and Melling, L. (2003) Lecturers' perceptions of gender and undergraduate writing style, *British Journal of Sociology of Education*, 24(3): 357–73.

Francis, B. and Skelton, C. (2005) *Reassessing Gender and Achievement*. London: Routledge.

Francis, B., Skelton, C., Carrington, B., Hutchings, M., Read, B. and Hall, I. (forthcoming) A perfect match? Pupils' and teachers' views on the impact of matching educators and learners by gender, *Research Papers in Education*.

Fraser, N. and Gordon, L. (1997) A genealogy of 'dependency': tracing a keyword of the US welfare state, in N. Fraser (ed.) *Justice Interruptus*. London and New York: Routledge.

Frederickson, K. (2003) Introduction: histories, silences and stories, in K. Frederickson (ed.) *Singular Women: Writing the Artist*. Ewing, CA: University of California Press.

Freire, P. (1972) *Pedagogy of the Oppressed*. Harmondsworth: Penguin.

Fukuyama, F. (1998) Women and the evolution of world politics, *Foreign Affairs*, 77(5): 24–40.

Fülöp, M. (2004) Competition as a culturally constructed concept, in C. Baillie, E. Dunn and Y. Zheng (eds) *Travelling Facts: The Social Construction, Distribution, and Accumulation of Knowledge*. Frankfurt/New York: Campus Verlag: 124–148.

Fülöp, M. (2005) The role of gender in competition viewed by Canadian, Hungarian and Japanese young adults. Paper presented to the Elöadás a VII Regional Congress of the International Association of Cross Cultural Psychology, San Sebastian, Spain, July.

Furedi, F. (2003) *Therapy Culture: Cultivating Vulnerability in an Uncertain Age*. London: Routledge.

Furedi, F. (2004) *Where Have All the Intellectuals Gone?: Confronting 21st Century Philistinism*. London: Continuum.

Gadamer, H. (1975) *Truth and Method*. London: Sheed and Ward.

GAO (2007) *Higher Education: Report to the Chairman, Committee on Education and Labor, House of Representatives*. Washington, United States Government Accountability Office. www.gao.gov/new.items/d08245.pdf (accessed 15 March, 2008).

Gee, J.P. (1999) *An Introduction to Discourse Analysis: Theory and Method*. London: Routledge.

Geertz, C. (1983) *Local Knowledge*. New York: Basic Books.

Geertz, C. (1998) *Works and Lives: The Anthropologist as Author*. Stanford, CA: Stanford University Press.

Gilbert, N. (2008) Women scientists face discrimination, says study, *The Guardian*. http://education.guardian.co.uk/gendergap/story/0,,2267022,00.html (accessed 24 March, 2008).

Gilder, G. (2005) The idea of the (feminized) university, *National Review*, 57(24): 26–8.

Gillborn, D. and Youdell, D. (2000) *Rationing Education: Policy, Practice, Reform and Equity*. Buckingham: Open University Press.

Gilligan, C. (1977) In a different voice: women's conceptions of the self and of morality, *Harvard Educational Review*, (47): 481–517.

Gilligan, C. (1982) *In a Different Voice*. Boston, MA: Harvard University Press.

Gilligan, C. (1987) Woman's place in man's life-cycle, in S. Harding (ed.) *Feminism and Methodology*. Bloomington, IN: Indiana University Press.

Gilligan, C. and Attanucci, J. (1988) The moral principle of care, *Merrill-Palmer Quarterly*, 34: 223–37.

Goffman, I. (1979) *The Presentation of Self in Everyday Life*. London: Penguin.

Goldthorpe, J.H. (1997) Problems of 'meritocracy', in A.H. Halsey, H. Lauder,

P. Brown and A.S. Wells (eds) *Education: Culture, Economy, Society.* Oxford: Oxford University Press.

Goode, J. (2000) Is the position of women in higher education changing?, in M. Tight (ed.) *Academic Work and Life: What is it to Be an Academic and How this is Changing.* Amsterdam: Elsevier Science.

Goode, J. and Bagilhole, B. (1998) Gendering the management of change in higher education: a case study, *Gender, Work and Organisation,* 5(3): 148–62.

Gourma-Petersen, T. and Mathews, P. (1987) The feminist critique of art history, *Art Bulletin,* 69(3): 326–57.

Gqola, P.D. (2002) Coming out and being proudly threatening: feminist activists and African academies, *Feminist Africa,* issue 1. www.feministafrica.org/index.php/coming-out (accessed 12 July, 2008).

Grant, B. (1997) Disciplining students: the construction of student subjectivities, *British Journal of Sociology of Education,* 18: 101–14.

Grant, B. (2006) Writing in the company of other women: exceeding the boundaries, *Studies in Higher Education,* 31(4): 483–95.

Griffin, S. (1978) *Woman and Nature: The Roaring inside Her.* New York: Harper & Row.

Griffiths, M. (1995) *Feminisms and the Self: The Web of Identity.* London and New York: Routledge.

Grimshaw, J. (1986) *Philosophy and Feminist Thinking.* Minneapolis, MN: University of Minnesota Press.

Gunawardena, C., Rasanayagam, Y., Leitan, T., Bulumulle, K. and Abeyasekera-Van Dort, A. (2006) Quantitative and qualitative dimensions of gender equity in Sri Lankan higher education, *Women's Studies International Forum,* 29: 562–71.

Gustavsson, E. and Czarniawska, B. (2004) Web woman: the on-line construction of corporate and gender images, *Organization,* 11(5): 651–70.

Halford, S. and Leonard, P. (2001) Airy atriums and cluttered corridors: construction of gender identity in organizational spaces. Paper presented at the Gender, Work and Organisation Conference, Keele University, 27–9 June.

Hall, S. (1996) Cultural identity and cinematic representation in H.A. Baker, M. Diawara and R.H. Lindeborg (eds). *Black British Cultural Studies: A Reader.* Chicago, IL, and London: University of Chicago Press.

Hammersley, M. (1992) *What's Wrong with Ethnography?* London: Routledge.

Hanlon, G. (1998) Professionalism as enterprise: service class politics and the redefinition of professionalism, *Sociology,* 32: 43–63.

Hanlon, G. (2000) Sacking the New Jerusalem? The new right, social democracy and professional identities. *Sociological Research Online,* 5(1): May.

Harding, S. (1984) Is gender a variable in conceptions of rationality? A survey of issues, in C. Gould (ed.) *Beyond Domination.* Ottowa: Rowan and Allanheld.

Harding, S. (1990) Feminism and theories of scientific knowledge, *Women: A Cultural Review,* 1: 87–98.

Harding, S. (1991) *Whose Science? Whose Knowledge?* Buckingham: Open University Press.

Harley, S. (2000) Accountants divided: research selectivity and academic accounting labour in UK universities, *Critical Perspectives on Accounting,* 11: 549–82.

Harley, S. (2003) Research selectivity and female academics in UK universities: from gentleman's club and barrack yard to smart macho? *Gender and Education,* 15(4): 377–92.

Harris, A. (2004) *Future Girl: Young Women in the Twenty-First Century*. Routledge: London.

Harris, P., Thiele, B. and Currie, J. (1998) Success, gender and academic voices. Consuming passion or selling the soul? *Gender and Education*, 10(2): 133–48.

Harris, S. (2005) Re-thinking academic identities in neo-liberal times, *Teaching in Higher Education*, 10(4): 421–33.

Hartley, J. and Chesworth, K. (2000) Qualitative and quantitative methods in research on essay writing: no one way, *Journal of Further and Higher Education*, 24(1): 15–24.

Hatcher, R. (1998) Class differentiation in education: rational choices? *British Journal of Sociology of Education*, 19(1): 5–23.

Hayes, D. (2005) The touchy-feely brigade: coming your way soon, *The Times Higher Education Supplement*, 4 November. www.thes.co.uk/search/story.aspx (accessed 22 November, 2007).

Hays, J. (1983) The development of discursive maturity in college writers, in J. Hays (ed.) *The Writer's Mind: Writing as a Mode of Thinking*. Urbana, IL: NCTE.

Hebson, G., Earnshaw, J. and Marchington, L. (2007) Too emotional to be capable? The changing nature of emotion work in definitions of 'capable teaching', *Journal of Education Policy*, 22(6): 675–94.

HEFCE (2000) *Diversity in Higher Education: HEFCE Policy Statement, 00/33*. www.hefce.ac.uk/pubs/HEFCE/2000/0033main.rtf (accessed 15 March, 2008).

HEFCE (2006a) *The Higher Education Workforce in England: A Framework for the Future. Issues Paper 2006/21*. www.hefce.ac.uk/pubs/hefce/2006/06_21/ (accessed 13 January, 2008).

HEFCE (2006b) *Selection of Staff for Inclusion in RAE 2001: Issues Paper 2006/32*. www.hefce.ac.uk/pubs/hefce/2006/06_32/ (accessed 14 March, 2008).

HEFCE (2007) *Staff Employed at HEFCE-Funded HEIS: Update. Trends and Profiles 2007/36*. www.hefce.ac.uk/pubs/hefce/2007/07_36/07_36.pdf (accessed 15 March, 2008).

Hefner, D. (2004) Where the boys aren't, *Black Issues in Higher Education*, 21(9): 70–5.

Hekman, S. (1990) *Gender and Knowledge: Elements of a Postmodern Feminism*. Cambridge: Polity.

HESA (2007a) *Resources of Higher Education Institutions 2005/06*. London: Higher Education Statistics Agency.

HESA (2007b) *Statistical First Release 112: Destinations of Leavers from Higher Education in the United Kingdom for the Academic Year 2005/06*. www.hesa.ac.uk/index.php/content/view/613/161/ (accessed 15 December, 2007).

HESA (2008) *HESA Data Shows Increase in Proportion of Female Professors, Press Release 118*. www.hesa.ac.uk/index.php/content/view/1120/161/ (accessed 21 March, 2008).

Hey, V. (1997) Northern accent and Southern Comfort: subjectivity and social class, in P. Mahony and C. Zmroczek (eds) *Class Matters: 'Working-class' Women's Perspectives on Social Class*. London: Taylor & Francis.

Hey, V. (2001) The construction of academic time: sub/contracting academic labour in research, *Journal of Educational Policy*, 16(1): 67–84.

Hey, V. (2002) Horizontal solidarities and molten capitalism: the subject, intersubjectivity, self and the other in late modernity, *Discourse: Studies in the Cultural Politics of Education*, 23(2): 227–41.

Hey, V. (2003) Joining the club? Academia and working-class femininities, *Gender and Education*, 15(3): 319–35.

Hey, V. and Bradford, S.J. (2004) The return of the repressed? The gender politics of emergent forms of professionalism in education, *Journal of Education Policy*, 19(6): 691–713.

Higher Education Statistics Agency (2008) *Students in Higher Education Institutions 2006–07*. Cheltenham: Higher Education Statistics Agency.

Hill, P. (2004) Men leave low status academy to women, *The Times Higher*, 25 June.

Hill Collins, P. (1990) *Black Feminist Thought: Knowledge, Consciousness and the Politics of Empowerment*. London: Routledge.

Hilton, M. (2003) *Consumerism in 20th-century Britain*. Cambridge: Cambridge University Press.

Hirsch, E. (1982) The politics of theories of interpretation, *Critical Inquiry*, 9: 235–47.

Hodge, M. (2003) Speech by Margaret Hodge, Minister of State for Lifelong Learning and Higher Education. IPPR seminar, diverse missions: achieving excellence and equality in post-16 education, 13 January, London.

Holland, S. (2004) *Alternative Femininities: Body, Age and Identity*. Oxford: BERG.

Holloway, G. (1998) Writing women in: the development of feminist approaches to women's history, in W. Lamont (ed.) *Historical Controversies and Historians*. London: UCL Press.

Holmes, J. (1984) Hedging your bets and sitting on the fence: some evidence for hedges as support structures, *Te Reo*, 27: 47–62.

Honigsbaum, M. (2006) Changing the world one boy at a time, *New Statesman* 21 August: 29–31.

hooks, b. (1982) *Ain't I a Woman: Black Women and Feminism*. London: Pluto.

hooks, b. (1991) *Yearning: Race, Gender, and Cultural Politics*. London: Turnaround.

Horne, D. (1984) *The Great Museum: The Re-Presentation of History*. London: Pluto.

Hounsell, D. (1987) Essay writing and the quality of feedback, in J.T. Richardson, M. Eysenck and D.W. Piper (eds) *Student Learning: Research in Education and Cognitive Psychology*. Milton Keynes: SRHE and Open University Press.

Hounsell, D. (1997) Contrasting conceptions of essay writing, in F. Marton (ed.) *The Experience of Learning: Implications for Teaching and Studying in Higher Education*. Edinburgh: Scottish Academic Press.

Howie, G. and Tauchert, A. (2002) Institutional discrimination and the 'cloistered' academic ideal, in G. Howie and A. Tauchert (eds) *Gender, Teaching and Research in Higher Education: Challenges for the 21st Century*. Aldershot: Ashgate.

Hughes, M., Stein, K., Harlow, L., et al. (2001) The curriculum in context: campus networks and change, in C. Musil (ed.) *Gender, Science and the Undergraduate Curriculum: Building Two-Way Streets*. Washington, DC: Association of American Colleges and Universities.

Husu, L. (2000) Gender discrimination in the promised land of gender equality, *Higher Education in Europe*, 25(2): 221–8.

Husu, L. and Morley, L. (2000) Academe and gender: what has and has not changed? Introduction, *Higher Education in Europe*, 25(2): 137–8.

Hutchings, M., Carrington, B., Francis, B., Skelton, C., Read, B. and Hall, I. (2008) Nice and kind, smart and funny: what children like and want to emulate in their teachers, *Oxford Review of Education*, 34(2): 135–57.

Illouz, E. (1997) Who will care for the caretaker's daughter? Towards a sociology of happiness in the era of reflexive modernity, *Theory, Culture and Society*, 14(4): 31–66.

Iragaray, L. (1985) *Speculum of the Other Woman*. Ithaca, NY: Cornell University Press.

Iser, W. (1974) *The Implied Reader*. Baltimore, MD: Johns Hopkins University Press.

Ivanic, R. (1998) *Writing and Identity.* Amsterdam: John Benjamins.

Jackson, D. (1998) Breaking out of the binary trap: boys' underachievement, schooling and gender relations, in D. Epstein, J. Elwood, V. Hey and J. Maw (eds) *Failing Boys: Issues in Gender and Achievement.* Buckingham: Open University Press.

Jackson, S. (2000) Women's studies/gender studies 2000 and beyond, *Women's Studies Network Newsletter,* 36: 20–5.

Jackson, S. (2002) Transcending boundaries: women, research and teaching in the academy, in G. Howie and A. Tauchert (eds) *Gender, Teaching and Research in Higher Education: Challenges for the 21st Century.* Aldershot: Ashgate.

Jacobs, S., Owen, J., Sergeant, P. and Schostak, J. (2007) *Ethnicity and Gender in Degree Attainment: An Extensive Survey of Views and Activities in English HEIS.* www.heacademy.ac.uk/projects/detail/Ethnicity_Degree_Attainment_project (accessed 15 March 2008).

Jansen, W. (2006) Gender and the expansion of university education in Jordan, *Gender & Education,* 18(5): 473–90.

Jefferson, T. (1996) From 'little fairy boy' to the 'compleat destroyer': subjectivity and transformation in the biography of Mike Tyson, in M. Mac an Ghail (ed.) *Understanding Masculinities.* Buckingham: Open University Press.

Jenkins, R. (1996) *Social Identity.* London: Routledge.

Jianqi, Z. (2000) Study of the status of women teachers in China's higher education, *Chinese Education & Society,* 33(4): 16–30.

Jordanova, L. (1980) Natural facts: a historical perspective on science and sexuality, in C. MacCormack and M. Strathern (eds) *Nature, Culture and Gender.* Cambridge: Cambridge University Press.

Joyce, T. (2007) Lesbian, gay, bisexual, and transgender issues on campus: making the private public, *Journal of Curriculum and Pedagogy,* 4(2): 31–6.

Kaba, A.J. (2005) Progress of African Americans in higher education attainment: the widening gender gap and its current and future implications, *Education Policy Analysis Archives,* 13(25): http://epaa.asu.edu/epaa/v13n25/ (accessed 15 March, 2008).

Kang, M.-E. (1997) The portrayal of women's images in magazine advertisments: Goffman's gender analysis revisited, *Sex Roles,* 37(11–12): 979–96.

Kaplan, E. (1983) Is the gaze male?, in A. Snitow, C. Stansell and S. Thompson (eds) *Powers of Desire: The Politics of Sexuality.* New York: Monthly Review Press.

Kaplan, E. (2000) *Feminism and Film.* Oxford: Oxford University Press.

Kelly, J. (1991) A study of gender differential linguistic interaction in the adult classroom, *Gender and Education,* 3(2): 137–43.

Kenway, J., Willis, S., Blackmore, J. and Rennie, L. (1994) Making 'hope practical' rather than 'despair convincing': feminist post-structuralism, gender reform and educational change, *British Journal of Sociology of Education,* 15(2): 187–210.

Kimbell, R., Stables, K., Wheller, T., Wosniak, A. and Kelly, V. (1991) *The assessment of performance in design and technology.* London: School Examinations and Assessment Authority.

King, J.E. (2000) *Gender Equity in Higher Education: Are Male Students at a Disadvantage?* Washington, DC: American Council on Education.

Kirby, A. (2007) Pollution blamed for fall in Arctic baby boys, *The Times,* 12 September.

Kirkup, G. (1996) The importance of gender, in R. Mills and A. Tait (eds) *Supporting the Learner in Open and Distance Learning.* London: Pitman.

Kjeldal, S., Rindfleish, J. and Sheridan, A. (2005) Deal-making and rule-breaking: behind the façade of equity in academia, *Gender and Education,* 17(4): 431–47.

Kohlberg, L. (1981) *The Philosophy of Moral Development.* New York: Harper & Row.

Kress, G. and Van Leeuwen, T. (1996) *Reading Images: The Grammar of Visual Design.* London: Routledge.

Kulis, S., Sicotte, D. and Collins, S. (2002) More than a pipeline problem: labor supply constraints and gender stratification across academic science disciplines, *Research in Higher Education,* 43(6): 657–91.

Kwesiga, J.C. and Ssendiwala, E.N. (2006) Gender mainstreaming in the university context: prospects and challenges at Makerere University, Uganda, *Women's Studies International Forum,* 29: 592–605.

Lafferty, G. and Fleming, J. (2000) The restructuring of academic work in Australia: power, management and gender, *British Journal of Sociology of Education,* 21(2): 257–67.

Lakhani, N. (2008) Farewell to 'predictable, tiresome and dreary' women's studies, *The Independent,* 23 March.

Lakoff, R. (1973) Language and woman's place, *Language and Society,* 2: 45–79.

Lambert, C. and Parker, A. (2006) Imagination, hope and the positive face of feminism: pro/feminist pedagogy in 'post' feminist times? *Studies in Higher Education,* 31(4): 469–82.

Lave, J. (1982) A comparative approach to educational forms and learning processes. *Anthropology & Education Quarterly,* 13(2): 181–7.

Lazar, M. (2006) 'Discover the power of femininity!': analyzing global 'power femininity' in local advertising, *Feminist Media Studies,* 6(4): 505–17.

Le Feuvre, N. (1999) Gender, occupational feminization, and reflexivity: a cross-national perspective, in R. Crompton (ed.) *Restructuring Gender Relations and Employment: The Decline of the Male Breadwinner.* Oxford: Oxford University Press.

Lea, M. and Stierer, B. (2000) *Student Writing in Higher Education: New Contexts.* Buckingham: SRHE and Open University Press.

Lea, M. and Street, B. (1998) Student writing in higher education: an academic literacies approach, *Studies in Higher Education,* 23(2): 157–72.

Leach, E. (1971) *Rethinking Anthropology.* London: Athlone.

Leathwood, C. (1999) Technological futures: gendered visions of learning? *Research in Post-Compulsory Education,* 4(1): 5–22.

Leathwood, C. (2000) Happy families? Pedagogy, management and parental discourses of control in the corporatised further education college, *Journal of Further and Higher Education,* 24(2): 163–82.

Leathwood, C. (2004) A critique of institutional inequalities in higher education (or an alternative to hypocrisy for higher educational policy), *Theory and Research in Education,* 2(1): 31–48.

Leathwood, C. (2005a) Assessment policy and practice in higher education: purpose, standards and equity, *Assessment and Evaluation in Higher Education,* 30(3): 307–24.

Leathwood, C. (2005b) 'Treat me as a human being – don't look at me as a woman': femininities and professional identities in further education, *Gender and Education,* 17(4): 387–410.

Leathwood, C. (2006) Gender, equity and the discourse of the independent learner in higher education, *Higher Education,* 52(4): 611–33.

Leathwood, C. (2007) Gender equity in post secondary education, in C. Skelton, B. Francis and L. Smulyan (eds) *Gender and Education.* London: Sage.

Leathwood, C. and O'Connell, P. (2003) 'It's a struggle': the construction of the 'new student' in higher education, *Journal of Educational Policy,* 18(6): 597–615.

Leiss, W., Kline, S. and Jally, S. (1990) *Social Communication in Advertising: Persons, Products and Images of Well-Being*. Canada: Nelson.

Leitch, L. (2006) *Prosperity for All in the Global Economy – World Class Skills*. London: The Stationary Office.

Leonard, D. (2001) *A Woman's Guide to Doctoral Studies*. Buckingham: Open University Press.

Lerner, G. (1979) *The Majority Finds its Past*. Oxford: Oxford University Press.

Lester, J. (2008) Performing gender in the workplace: gender socialization, power and identity among women faculty members, *Community College Review*, 35: 277–305.

Letherby, G. and Marchbank, J. (2001) Why do women's studies? A cross England profile, *Women's Studies International Forum*, 24(5): 587–603.

Letherby, G. and Shiels, J. (2001) Isn't he good, but can we take her seriously? Gendered expectations in higher education, in P. Anderson and J. Williams (eds) *Identity and Difference in Higher Education: 'Outsiders Within'*. Aldershot: Ashgate.

Lihamba, A., Mwaipopo, R. and Shule, L. (2006) The challenges of affirmative action in Tanzanian higher education institutions: a case study of the university of Dar Es Salaam, Tanzania, *Women's Studies International Forum*, 29: 581–91.

Lillis, T. (1997) New voices in academia? The regulative nature of academic writing conventions, *Language and Education*, 11(3): 182–99.

Lillis, T. (2001) *Student Writing: Access, Regulation, Desire*. London: Routledge.

Lingard, B. (2003) Where to in gender policy in education after recuperative masculinity politics? *International Journal of Inclusive Education*, 7(1): 33–56.

Lingard, B. (n.d.) Contextualising and utilising the 'what about the boys' backlash for gender equity goals. *Change: Transformations in Education*: www-faculty.edfac.usyd.edu.au/projects/change/whatabout.html (accessed 14 March 2008).

Lipsett, A. (2007a) Snow queens, *EducationGuardian.co.uk*, 11 December.

Lipsett, A. (2007b) Women miss out on university places, *Education Guardian*. 2007b: http://www.educationGuardian.co.uk (accessed 14 November, 2007).

Lloyd, G. (1984) *The Man of Reason*. London: Methuen.

London Feminist Salon Collective (2004) The problematization of gender in postmodern theory: where do we go from here? *Gender and Education*, 16(1): 25–33.

Lovibond, S. (1993) Feminism and postmodernism, in T. Docherty (ed.) *Postmodernism: A Reader*. London: Harvester Wheatsheaf.

Luke, C. (2001) *Globalization and Women in Academia, North/West – South/East*. Mahwah, NJ: Lawrence Erlbaum.

Luke, C. and Gore, J. (eds) (1992) *Feminisms and Critical Pedagogy*. London and New York: Routledge.

Lynch, C.M. and Strauss-Noll, M. (1987) Mauve washers: sex differences in freshman writing, *English Journal*, 76(1): 90–4.

Mabolela, R.O. and Mawila, K.F.N. (2004) The impact of race, gender and culture in South African higher education, *Comparative Education Review*, 48(4): 396–416.

Mac an Ghaill, M. (1994) *The Making of Men: Masculinities, Sexualities and Schooling*. Buckingham: Open University Press.

Mackinnon, A. (1998) Revisiting the fin de siècle: the threat of the educated woman, in A. Mackinnon, I. Elgqvist-Saltzman and A. Prentice (eds) *Education into the 21st Century: Dangerous Terrain for Women?* London: Falmer Press.

Maddock, S. and Parkin, D. (1993) Gender cultures: women's choices and strategies at work, *Women in Management Review*, 8: 3–9.

Maguire, M. (forthcoming) 'Fade to grey': older women, embodied claims and attributions in HE, *Women's Studies International Forum*.

Mahony, P. (1998) Girls will be girls and boys will be first, in D. Epstein, J. Elwood, V. Hey and J. Maw (eds) *Failing Boys? Issues in Gender and Achievement*. Buckingham: Open University Press.

Mahony, P., Hextall, I. and Menter, I. (2003) 'I'm sorry this is just so painful': the gendered impact of threshold assessment. Paper presented at Gender and Education Conference, University of Sheffield, 14–16 April.

Mahony, P. and Zmroczek, C. (eds) (1997) *Class Matters: 'Working-Class' Women's Perspectives on Social Class*. London: Taylor & Francis.

Makebola, R.O. (2003) 'Donkeys of the university': organisational culture and its impact on South African women administrators, *Higher Education*, 46: 129–45.

Maltz, D. and Borker, R. (1998) A cultural approach to male-female miscommunication, in J. Coates (ed.) *Language and Gender: A Reader*. Oxford: Blackwell.

Malveaux, J. (2008) Perspectives: the status of African-American women, *Diverse Issues in Higher Education* (7 March). www.diverseeducation.com/artman/publish/article_10797.shtml (accessed 14 April 2008).

Mann, C. (2003) *Summary Report of Findings of the Project on Indicators of Academic Performance*. Cambridge: University of Cambridge. www.admin.cam.ac.uk/reporter/2002–03/weekly/5913/6.html (accessed 6 June, 2005).

Marchbank, J. (2005) Still inside, still 'out' – a decade of reflection on exposure, risk and survival, *Women's Studies International Forum*, 28: 139–49.

Marchbank, J. and Letherby, G. (2002) Offensive and defensive: student support and higher education evaluation, in G. Howie and A. Tauchert (eds) *Gender, Teaching and Research in Higher Education: Challenges for the 21st Century*. Aldershot: Ashgate.

Marchbank, J. and Letherby, G. (2006) Views and perspectives of women's studies: a survey of women and men students, *Gender and Education*, 18(2): 157–82.

Marginson, S. (1994) Markets in education: a theoretical note. Melbourne: Centre for the Study of Higher Education, University of Melbourne.

Marshall, B. (2006) The feminization of the school system is a myth, *The Independent Education Section*, 22 June.

Martin, M. (1997) Emotional and cognitive effects of examination proximity in female and male students, *Oxford Review of Education*, 23: 4.

Maslen, G. (2005) Elite want to make a break, *The Times Higher Education Supplement*, 28 October.

Mason, M. and Goulden, M. (2004) Marriage and baby blues: redefining gender equity in the academy, *Annals of the American Academy of Political and Social Science*, 596: 86–103.

Mavin, M.A. and Bryans, P. (2002) Academic women in the UK: mainstreaming our experiences and networking for action, *Gender and Education*, 14(3): 235–50.

Maylor, U. (forthcoming) What is the meaning of 'black'? Researching black respondents, *Ethnic and Racial Studies*.

Maylor, U. (under review) Is it because I am black? A black female research experience. *Race, Ethnicity and Education*.

Mazon, P.M. (2003) *Gender and the Modern Research University: The Admission of Women to German Higher Education, 1865–1914*. Stanford, CA: Stanford University Press.

McCabe, J. (2004) *Feminist Film Studies: Writing the Woman into Cinema*. London: Wallflower Press.

McDowell, L. (1997) *Capital Culture: Gender at Work in the City*. Oxford: Blackwell.

McGann, J. (1983) *The Romantic Ideology: A Critical Investigation*. Chicago, IL: University of Chicago Press.

Mercer, I. (2007) Return to reason. *WorldNet Daily*. www.wnd.com/news/article. asp?ARTICLE_ID=48527 (accessed 14 November 2007).

Miller, J. (1992) *More has Meant Women: The Feminization of Schooling*. London: Institute of Education, University of London.

Mirza, H.S. (1995) Black women in higher education: defining a space/finding a place, in L. Morley and V. Walsh (eds) *Feminist Academics: Creative Agents for Change*. London: Taylor & Francis.

Mirza, H.S. (1997) Black women in education: a collective movement for social change, in H.S. Mirza (ed.) *Black British Feminism*. London: Routledge.

Mirza, H.S. (2005) *Race, Gender and Educational Desire: Inaugural Professorial Lecture*. London: Middlesex University.

Mirza, H.S. (2006a) The in/visible journey: black women's lifelong lessons in higher education, in C. Leathwood and B. Francis (eds) *Gender and Lifelong Learing: Critical Feminist Engagements*. Abingdon: Routledge.

Mirza, H.S. (2006b) Transcendence over diversity: black women in the academy, *Policy Futures in Education*, 4(2): 101–13.

Modood, T. (2006) Ethnicity, Muslims and higher education entry in Britain, *Teaching in Higher Education*, 11(2): 257–50.

Mohanty, C. (2002) 'Under Western Eyes' revisited: feminist solidarity through anticapitalist struggles, *Signs: Journal of Women in Culture and Society*, 28(2): 499–535.

Moi, T. (1994) *Simone De Beauvoir: The Making of an Intellectual Woman*. Oxford: Blackwell.

Moreau, M.-P. and Leathwood, C. (2006a) Balancing paid work and studies: working (-class) students in higher education, *Studies in Higher Education*, 31(1): 23–42.

Moreau, M.-P. and Leathwood, C. (2006b) Graduates' employment and the discourse of employability: a critical analysis, *Journal of Education and Work*, 19(4): 305–24.

Morley, L. (1997a) Change and equity in higher education, *British Journal of Sociology of Education*, 18(2): 231–42.

Morley, L. (1997b) A class of one's own: women, social class and the academy, in P. Mahony and C. Zmroczek (eds) *Class Matters: Working-Class Women's Perspectives on Social Class*. London: Taylor & Francis: 109–121.

Morley, L. (1998) All you need is love: feminist pedagogy for empowerment and emotional labour in the classroom, *International Journal of Inclusive Education*, 2(1): 15–27.

Morley, L. (1999) *Organising Feminisms: The Micropolitics of the Academy*. Basingstoke and London: Macmillan.

Morley, L. (2002) Reconstructing students as consumers: new settlements of power or the politics of assimilation? Paper presented at the Society for Research in Higher Education Annual Conference, University of Glasgow, 10–12 December.

Morley, L. (2003) *Quality and Power in Higher Education*. Buckingham: SRHE/Open University Press.

Morley, L. (2005a) Clare Burton Memorial Lecture 2003 – sounds, silences and contradictions: gender equity in British commonwealth higher education, *Australian Feminist Studies*, 20(46): 109–19.

Morley, L. (2005b) Gender equity in commonwealth higher education, *Women's Studies International Forum*, 28: 209–25.

Morley, L. (2006) Gender and UK higher education: post-feminism in a market economy, in M. Danowitz Sagaria (ed.) *Gender Equality and University Change*. Gordonsville, VA: Palgrave Macmillan.

Morley, L. (2007) The gendered implications of quality assurance and audit, in P. Cotterill, S. Jackson and G. Letherby (eds) *Challenges and Negotiations for Women in Higher Education*. Dordrecht: Springer.

Morrison, Z., Bourke, M. and Kelley, C. (2005) 'Stop making it such a big issue': perceptions and experiences of gender inequality by undergraduates at a British university, *Women's Studies International Forum*, 28: 150–62.

Mulvey, L. (1975) Visual pleasure and narrative cinema, in P. Rosen (ed.) *Narrative, Apparatus, Ideology*. New York: Columbia University Press.

Munford, R. and Rumball, S. (2000) Women in university power structures, in M.-L. Kearney (ed.) *Women, Power and the Academy: From Rhetoric to Reality*. New York: UNESCO.

Munslow, A. (1997) *Deconstructing History*. London: Routledge.

Munslow, A. (1999) *Routledge Companion to Historical Studies*. London: Routledge.

Murphy, P. and Elwood, J. (1998) Gendered experiences, choices and achievement – exploring the links, *International Journal of Inclusive Education*, 2(2): 85–118.

Naidoo, R. (2003) Repositioning higher education as a global commodity: opportunities and challenges for future sociology of education work, *British Journal of Sociology of Education*, 24(2): 249–59.

Naude, P. and Ivy, J. (1999) The marketing strategies of universities in the United Kingdom, *International Journal of Educational Management*, 13(3): 126–34.

Nead, L. (1992) *The Female Nude*. London: Routledge.

Nelson, J.A. (1993) The study of choice or the study of provisioning? Gender and the definition of economics, in M.A. Ferber and J.A. Nelson (eds) *Beyond Economic Man: Feminist Theory and Economics*. Chicago: University of Chicago Press, IL.

Newman, M. (2007) On track for a new battle of the sexes, *The Times Higher Education Supplement*, 25 May.

Newstead, S.E. (1996) The psychology of student assessment, *The Psychologist*, December: 543–7.

Newstead, S.E. and Dennis, I. (1990) Blind marking and sex bias in student assessment, *Assessment and Evaluation in Higher Education*, 15: 132–9.

Newstead, S.E. and Dennis, I. (1994) Examiners examined: the reliability of exam marking in psychology, *The Psychologist*, 7: 216–19.

Nietzsche, F. (1964) *Beyond Good and Evil*. New York: Russell and Russell.

Nightingale, P. (1988) Language and learning: a bibliographic essay, in G.E.A. Taylor (ed.) *Literacy by Degrees*. Milton Keynes: SRHE and Open University Press.

Nochlin, L. ([1971] 1988). Have there been no great women artists? in L. Nochlin (ed.) *Women, Art, and Power and Other Essays*. New York: Harper and Row.

O'Connor, P. (2003) 'Faculty women: making our mark . . .', in V. Batt, S.N. Fhaoláin and R. Pelan (eds) *Gender Matters in Higher Education: Proceedings of Conference in NUI Galway*, National University of Ireland, Galway, 8–9 November.

O'Leary, V.E. and Mitchell, J.M. (1990) Women connecting with women: networks and mentors in the United States, in S.S. Lie and V.E. O'Leary (eds) *Storming the Tower: Women in the Academic World*. London: Kogan Page.

O'Neill, A.-M. (1996) Privatising public policy: privileging market man and individualising equality through choice within education in Aotearoa/New Zealand, *Discourse: Studies in the Cultural Politics of Education*, 17(3): 403–16.

Odejidea, A. (2007) Being women in a Nigerian university, *Feminist Africa* (8).

www.feministafrica.org/index.php/what-can-a-woman-do   (accessed 3 April, 2008).

OECD (2007) *Education at a Glance 2007*. Paris: Organisation for Economic Co-operation and Development.

Olson, L. (2006) Few women professors in Sweden, *Swedish Secretariat for Gender Research*, www.genus.gu.se/News/News/2006/?articleId=668875 (accessed 3 April, 2008).

Osborne, H. (2007) Gender pay gap 'grows', *guardian.co.uk*, 7 October.

Osler, A. (1997) Black teachers as professionals: survival, success and subversion, *FORUM*, 39(2): 55–9.

Osman, H. (2008) Re-branding academic institutions with corporate advertising: a genre perspective, *Discourse and Communication*, 2(1): 57–77.

Ourliac, G. (1988) The feminization of higher education in France: its history, characteristics and effects on employment, *European Journal of Education*, 23(3): 281–93.

Owen, G. (2004) Women take the lead in the contest for top degees, *Timesonline*. www.timesonline.co.uk (accessed 4 November, 2004).

Oxford, E. (2008) Still second among equals, *The Times Higher Education Supplement*, 27 March–2 April: 30–5.

Pappu, R. (2002) Constituting a field: women's studies in higher education, *Indian Journal of Gender Studies*, 9: 221–34.

Parker, M. and Jary, D. (1995) The Mcuniversity: organization, management and academic subjectivity, *Organization*, 2(2): 319–38.

Parker, R. and Pollock, G. (1987) *Framing Feminism: Art and the Women's Movement 1970–1985*. London: Pandora.

Pateman, C. (1988) *The Sexual Contract*. Cambridge: Polity Press.

Pederson, O. (2003) *The First Universities: Studium Generale and the Origins of University Education in Europe*. Cambridge: Cambridge University Press.

Pereira, C. (2007) *Gender in the Making of the Nigerian University System*. Ibadan and Oxford: Heinemann Educational Books (Nigeria) and James Currey.

Pessl, M. (2006) *Special Topics in Calamity Physics*. London: Penguin.

Pirie, M. (2001) How exams are fixed in favour of girls, *Spectator*, 20 January.

Plummer, G. (2000) *Failing Working-Class Girls*. Stoke-on-Trent: Trentham.

Pollock, G. (1999) *Differencing the Canon: Feminism and the Writing of Arts Histories*. London: Routledge.

Powell, A., Bagilhole, B. and Dainty, A. (2006) The problem of women's assimilation into UK engineering cultures: can critical mass work? *Equal Opportunities International*, 25(8): 688–99.

Prichard, C. and Deem, R. (1998) Wo-managing UK further education: gender and the construction of the manager in the corporate colleges. Paper presented at Massey University College of Education Research Seminar Series.

Probert, B. (2005) 'I just couldn't fit it in': gender and unequal outcomes in academic careers, *Gender, Work and Organisation*, 12: 50–72.

Prosser, M. and Webb, C. (1994) Relating the process of undergraduate essay-writing to the finished product, *Studies in Higher Education*, 19(2): 125–39.

Purcell, K., Wilton, N. and Elias, P. (2003) *Older and Wiser? Age and Experience in the Graduate Labour Market*. www2.warwick.ac.uk/fac/soc/ier/research/completed/7yrs2/rp2.pdf (accessed 23 March, 2008).

Purnell, J. (2006) *Are Choice and Competition Labour?* http://eustonmanifesto.org/joomla/content/view/60/46/ (accessed 17 August, 2006).

Pyke, K.D. and Johnson, D.L. (2003) Asian American women and racialized femininities: 'doing' gender across cultural worlds, *Gender and Society*, 17(1): 33–53.

QAA (Quality Assurance Agency for Education) (2000) *Politics and International Relations Subject Benchmark Statements*. Gloucester: QAA.

Queiroz, M.D. (2004) Protests rage over sexist remarks by health authorities, *Inter Press Service*, www.newsbank.com (accessed 29 January, 2008).

Quinn, J. (2003) *Powerful Subjects: Are Women Really Taking over the University?* Stoke-on-Trent: Trentham.

Quinn, J. (2004) The corporeality of learning: women students and the body, in S. Ali, S. Benjamin and M. Mauthner (eds) *The Politics of Gender and Education: Critical Perspectives*. London: Palgrave Macmillan.

RAE (2008) *RAE 2008: Analysis of Panel Membership* www.rae.ac.uk/panels/members/equalops.pdf (accessed 23 March, 2008).

Rajan, R.S. (1993) *Real and Imagined Women: Gender, Culture and Postcolonialism*. London: Routledge.

Raloff, J. (1994) Are environmental 'hormones' emasculating wildlife? *Science News Online*. www.sciencenews.org/pages/sn_edpik/ls_7.htm (accessed 14 November, 2007).

Ramsay, K. and Letherby, G. (2006) The experience of academic non-mothers in the gendered university, *Gender, Work & Organization*, 13(1): 25–44.

Randle, K. and Brady, N. (1997) Managerialism and professionalism in the 'Cinderella service', *Journal of Vocational Education and Training*, 49(1): 121–39.

Rasmussen, B. (2001) Corporate strategy and gendered professional identities: reorganization and the struggle for recognition and positions, *Gender, Work & Organization*, 8(3): 291–310.

Read, B. (1996) Historical representations and the gendered battleground of the 'past', *European Journal of Women's Studies*, 3(2): 115–30.

Read, B. (2003) Speaking in the academy: the experience of women and men academics. Paper presented to the British Educational Research Association (BERA).

Read, B. (2005) Gender and the construction/'performance' of academic identities through speaking and writing in HE. Paper presented at the Gender and Education Conference, Cardiff, 29–31 March.

Read, B. (2006) Gendered constructions of cooperation and competition by pupils, in A. Ross, M. Fülöp and M. Pergar Kuščer (eds) *Teachers' and Pupils' Constructions of Competition and Cooperation: A Three-country Study of Slovenia, Hungary and England*. Ljubljana: University of Ljubljana Press.

Read, B. (forthcoming) 'The world must stop when I'm talking': gender and power relations in primary teachers' classroom talk, *British Journal of Sociology of Education*.

Read, B., Archer, L. and Leathwood, C. (2003) Challenging cultures? Student conceptions of 'belonging' and 'isolation' at a post-1992 university, *Studies in Higher Education*, 28(3): 261–77.

Read, B., Francis, B. and Robson, J. (2001) Playing safe: undergraduate essay-writing and the presentation of the student 'voice', *British Journal of Sociology of Education*, 22(3): 387–99.

Read, B., Francis, B. and Robson, J. (2002) 'Who am I to question all these established writers?' Gender and confidence in student essay writing. Changing Contexts for Teaching and Learning: Proceedings of the Writing Development in Higher Education Conference, Leicester.

Read, B., Francis, B. and Robson, J. (2004) Re-viewing undergraduate writing: tutors' perceptions of essay qualities according to gender, *Research in Post-compulsory Education*, 9(2): 217–38.

Read, B., Francis, B. and Robson, J. (2005) Gender, 'bias', assessment and feedback: analysing the written assessment of undergraduate history essays, *Assessment and Evaluation in Higher Education*, 30(3): 243–62.

Reay, D. (1997) The double bind of the working class feminist academic: the success of failure or the failure of success? in P. Mahony and C. Zmroczek (eds) *Class Matters: Working Class Women's Perspectives on Social Class*. London: Taylor & Francis.

Reay, D. (2000) 'Dim dross': marginalised women both inside and outside the academy, *Women's Studies International Forum*, 23(1): 13–21.

Reay, D. (2001) Finding or losing yourself?: Working-class relationships to education, *Journal of Education Policy*, 16(4): 333–46.

Reay, D. (2008) Learner identities in higher education. *SEHE Dissemination Event*. Institute of Education, London. http://education.sunderland.ac.uk/our-research/sehe.

Reay, D., David, M. and Ball, S. (2001) 'Making a difference? Institutional habituses and higher education choice', *Sociological Research Online*, 5(4). www.socresonline.org.uk/5/4/reay.html (accessed 8 February, 2002).

Reay, D., David, M.E. and Ball, S. (2005) *Degrees of Choice: Social Class, Race and Gender in Higher Education*. Stoke-on-Trent: Trentham Books.

Reay, D., Davies, J. David, M. and Ball, S.J. (2001) Choices of degree or degrees of choice? Class, race and the higher education choice process, *Sociology*, 35(4): 855–74.

Rendell, J., Penner, B. and Borden, I. (2003) *Gender Space Architecture: An Interdisciplinary Introduction*. London: Routledge.

Rich, A. (1980) Toward a woman-centered university, in A. Rich (ed.) *On Lies, Secrets and Silence: Selected Prose 1966–1978*. London: Virago.

Rich, A. (1986) *Compulsory Heterosexuality and Lesbian Existence*. London: Norton.

Richardson, D., McLaughlin, J. and Casey, M. (2006) *Intersections between Feminist and Queer Theory*. Basingstoke: Palgrave Macmillan.

Riddell, S. (2006) Disability, gender and identity: the experiences of disabled students in higher education in C. Leathwood and B. Francis (eds) *Gender and Lifelong Learning: Critical Feminist Engagements*. London: Routledge.

Robson, J., Francis, B. and Read, B. (2002) Writes of passage: stylistic features of male and female undergraduate history essays, *Journal of Further and Higher Education*, 26: 351–62.

Robson, J., Francis, B. and Read, B. (2004) Gender, student confidence and communicative styles at university: the views of lecturers in history and psychology, *Studies in Higher Education*, 29(1): 7–23.

Roper, B., Ross, A. and Thomson, D. (2000) Locked out, *The Education Guardian*. www.education.guardian.co.uk/ (accessed 12 April, 2007).

Rorty, R. (1979) *Philosophy and the Mirror of Nature*. Princeton, NJ: Princeton University Press.

Rose, G. (2001) *Visual Methodologies: An Introduction to the Interpretation of Visual Materials*. London: Sage.

Ross, A. (2003) Access to higher education: inclusion for the masses? In A. Archer, M. Hutchings and A. Ross (eds) *A Higher Education and Social Class: Issues of Exclusion and Inclusion*. London: Routledge/Farmer.

Rowse, R.C. (1936) The first university, in T.K. Barrett (ed.) *Psychology and Philosophy: The World of Thought*. London: Odhams Press.

Rubin, D. and Greene, K. (1992) Gender-typical style in written language, *Research in the Teaching of English*, 26(1): 7–40.

Ruddick, S. (1996) Reason's 'Femininity': a case for connected knowing, in N.R. Goldberger, J.M. Tarule, B.M. Clinchy and M.F. Belenky (eds) *Knowledge, Difference, and Power: Essays Inspired by Women's Ways of Knowing*. New York: Basic Books.

Rutledge Shields, V. (1990) Advertising visual images: gendered ways of seeing and looking, *Journal of Communication Inquiry*, 14: 25–39.

Ryle, S., Ahmed, K. and Bright, M. (2000) The war of Laura's rejection, *Observer*, 28 May.

Saunders, P. and Woodfield, R. (2003) *Explaining Gender Differences in Achievement in Higher Education: Preliminary Results from a Sussex Panel Survey*. www.sussex.ac.uk/ Units/TLDU/LM/LMissue10/article2.html (accessed 4 December, 2003).

Sax, L. (2003) The feminization of American culture: how modern chemicals may be changing human biology. *worldandi.com*: www.worldandi.com/public/2001/ October/sax.html (accessed 14 October, 2007).

Schick Case, S. (1990) Communication styles in higher education: differences between academic men and women, in L.B. Welch (ed.) *Women in Higher Education: Change and Challenges*. New York: Praeger.

Schiebinger, L. (1989) *The Mind Has No Sex? Women in the Origins of Modern Science*. Cambridge, MA: Harvard University Press.

Schuster, J.H. and Finkelstein, M.J. (2006) *The American Faculty: The Restructuring of Academic Work and Careers*. Baltimore, CA: JHU Press.

Scott, J. (2000) *Gender and the Politics of History*. Irvington, NY: Columbia University Press.

Seddon, T. (1997) Education: deprofessionalised? Or Reregulated, reorganised and reauthorised? *Australian Journal of Education*, 41(3): 228–46.

Sewell, B. (2008) Bluestocking blues, *The Evening Standard*, 4 April.

Shackleton, L., Riordan, S. and Simonis, D. (2006) Gender and the transformation agenda in South African higher education, *Women's Studies International Forum*, 29: 572–80.

Shanks, M. and Tilley, C. (1992) *Re-constructing Archaeology: Theory and Practice*. London: Routledge.

Shavarini, M.K. (2005) The feminization of Iranian higher education, *International Review of Education*, 51(4): 329–47.

Shepherd, J. (2006) Women's work gets less male attention, *The Times Higher Education Supplement*, 11 August.

Shore, C. and Wright, S. (2000) Coercive accountability: the rise of the audit culture in higher education, in M. Strathern (ed.) *Audit Cultures*. London: Routledge.

Siemienska, R. (2000) Women in academe in Poland: winners among losers, *Higher Education in Europe*, 25(2): 163–72.

Silova, I. and Magno, C. (2004) Gender equity unmasked: democracy, gender, and education in central/southeastern Europe and the former Soviet Union, *Comparative Education Review*, 48(4): 417–42.

Silver, H. (2003) *Higher Education and Opinion Making in Twentieth-Century England*. London: Woburn Press.

Silverman, D. (1993) *Interpreting Qualitative Data*. London: Sage.

Sims, S. (1999) Women advance but still face hardships. *Inter Press Service*, Global Newsbank, 19 November.

Singh, M. (2006) Universities and society: whose terms of engagement? in S. Srlin (ed.) *Knowledge Society vs Knowledge Economy: Knowledge, Power and Politics*. Gordonsville, VA: Palgrave Macmillan.

Singh, M., Kenway, J. and Apple, M.W. (2005) Globalizing education: perspectives from above and below, in M. Apple, J. Kenway and M. Singh (eds) *Globalizing Education: Policies, Pedagogies and Politics*. New York: Peter Lang.

Skeggs, B. (1994) Situating the production of feminist methodology, in M. Maynard and J. Purvis (eds) *Researching Women's Lives from a Feminist Perspective*. London: Taylor & Francis.

Skeggs, B. (1995) Women's studies in Britain in the 1990s: entitlement cultures and institutional constraints, *Women's Studies International Forum*, 18(4): 475–85.

Skeggs, B. (2004) *Class, Self, Culture*. London: Routledge.

Skelton, C. (2002) The 'feminization' of schooling or 're-masculinising' primary education, *International Studies in Sociology of Education*, 12(1): 77–96.

Skelton, C. (2005) The 'individualized' (woman) in the academy: Ulrich Beck, gender and power, *Gender and Education*, 17(3): 319–32.

Skelton, C., Francis, B. and Valkanova, Y. (2007) *Breaking Down the Stereotypes: Gender and Achievment in Schools*. www.eoc.org.uk (accessed 13 September, 2007).

Smith, D. (1992) Women's perspective as a radical critique of sociology, in M. Humm (ed.) *Feminisms: A Reader*. Hemel Hempstead: Harvester Wheatsheaf.

Smith, J. (2006) Watch out: the patriarchy is striking back, *The Independent* www.independent.co.uk/opinion/commentators/joan-smith/joan-smith-watch-out-the-patriarchy-is-striking-back-469018.html (accessed 11 October, 2007).

Sommers, C.H. (2000) *The War against Boys: How Misguided Feminism is Harming Our Young Men*. New York: Simon & Schuster Paperbacks.

Sommers, E. and Lawrence, S. (1992) Women's ways of talking in teacher-directed and student-directed peer response groups, *Linguistics and Education*, 4: 1–36.

Sones, B. with Moran, M. and Lovenduski, J. (2005) *Women in Parliament: The New Suffragettes*. London: Politicos.

Southgate, B. (1996) *History, What and Why? Ancient, Modern and Postmodern Perspectives*. London: Routledge.

Spear, M. (1984) Sex bias in science teachers' ratings of work and pupil characteristics, *European Journal of Science Education*, 6(4): 369–77.

Spender, D. (1982) *Invisible Women: The Schooling Scandal*. London: Writers & Readers Publishing Cooperative Society.

Spender, D. and Sarah, E. (1980) *Learning to Lose*. London: Women's Press.

Spivak, G.C. (1996) *A Spivak Reader*. London: Routledge.

Spivak, G.C. (2006) *In Other Worlds*. London: Routledge.

Spurling, A. (1990) *Women in Higher Education*. Cambridge: King's College Research Centre.

Spurling, A. (1997) Women and change in Higher Education, in H. Eggins (ed.) *Women as Leaders and Managers in Higher Education*. Buckingham: SRHE and Open University Press.

Stake, J. (2006) Pedagogy and student change in the women's and gender studies classroom, *Gender and Education*, 18(2): 199–212.

Stanley, C. (2006) Coloring the academic landscape: faculty of color breaking the silence in predominantly white colleges and universities, *American Educational Research Journal*, 43(4): 701–36.

Statistics Canada (2006) *2006 Census.* www12.statcan.ca/english/census06/analysis/ education/proportion.cfm (accessed 19 March, 2008).

Sternglanz, S. and Lyberger-Ficek, S. (1977) Sex differences in student-teacher interactions in the college classroom, *Sex Roles,* 3: 345–52.

Stewart, H. (2008) The glass ceiling isn't broken – in fact, it's getting thicker, *Observer: Business and Media,* 3 February.

Stewart, T. (2007) Vying for an unsustainable/inappropriate(d) organic queer space in higher education, *Journal of Curriculum and Pedagogy,* 4(2): 89–95.

Strassmann, D. (1993) Not a free market: the rhetoric of disciplinary authority in economics, in M.A. Ferber and J.A. Nelson (eds) *Beyond Economic Man: Feminist Theory and Economics.* Chicago, IL: University of Chicago Press.

Stromquist, N. (2001) Gender studies: a global perspective of their evolution contribution, and challenges to comparative higher education, *Higher Education,* 41(4): 373–87.

Suriya, M. (2003) Gender issues in the career development of IT professionals: a global perspective, *Map Asia 2003.* Kuala Lumpur, Malaysia, October 13–15.

Suspitsina, T. (2000) Mothers, bosses, and superwomen: the construction of identities of Russian woman administrators in higher education, *Higher Education in Europe,* 25(2): 207–12.

Swain, H. (1999) Social divisions traced in old binary divide, *The Guardian,* 12 February.

Swift, A. (2003) *How not to be a Hypocrite: School Choice for the Morally Perplexed Parent.* London: Routledge.

Tannen, D. (1990) *You Just Don't Understand: Women and Men in Conversation.* New York: Harper Row.

Thomas, K. (1990) *Gender and Subject in Higher Education.* Buckingham: SRHE & Open University Press.

Thomas, R. (1996) Gendered cultures and performance appraisal: the experience of women academics, *Gender, Work and Organisation,* 3: 143–55.

Thomas, R. and Davies, A. (2002) Gender and 'new public management': reconstituting academic subjectivities, *Gender, Work and Organisation,* 9(4): 372–97.

Thornham, S. (2000) *Feminist Theory and Cultural Studies: Stories of Unsettled Relations.* London: Arnold.

Tierney, W. and Bensimon, E. (1996) *Promotion and Tenure: Community and Socialization in Academe.* Albany, NY: State University of New York Press.

Tolley, J. and Rundel, J. (2006) *A Review of Black and Minority Ethnic Participation in Higher Education.* London: National BME Education Strategy Group, Action on Access.

Tomlinson, S. (2003) Globalization, race and education: continuity and change, *Journal of Educational Change,* 4: 213–30.

Trethewey, A. (1999) Disciplined bodies: women's embodied identities at work, *Organization Studies,* 20(3): 423–50.

Trowler, P. (1998) *Academics Responding to Change: New Higher Education Frameworks and Academic Cultures.* Buckingham: Open University Press.

Tyler, M. and Taylor, S. (2001) Juggling justice and care: gendered customer service in the contemporary airline industry, in A. Sturdy, I. Grugulis and H. Willmott (eds) *Customer Service: Empowerment and Entrapment.* London: Palgrave Macmillan.

Tyrer, D. and Ahmad, F. (2006) *Muslim Women and Higher Education: Identities, Experiences and Prospects. A Summary Report.* http://image.guardian.co.uk/sys-files/

Education/documents/2006/08/02/muslimwomen.pdf (accessed 15 March, 2008).

UNESCO (2008) *EFA 2008 Global Monitoring Report: Education for All by 2015: Will We Make It?* Oxford: UNESCO Publishing.

Vander Stichele, C. and Penner, T. (2005) Mastering the tools or retooling the masters? The legacy of historical-critical discourse, in C. Vander Stichele (ed.) *Her Master's Tools? Feminist and Postcolonial Engagements in Historical-Critical Discourse.* Atlanta, GA: Society of Biblical Literature.

Vázquez-Cupeiro, S. (2003) *Are Women the Creeping 'Proletariats' of British Academia?* http://csn.uni-muenster.de/women-eu/download/Vazquez_CupeiroTP02_01.pdf (accessed 22 Feb. 2008).

Vernant, J.P. (1987) *Myth and Thought among the Greeks.* London: Routledge.

Vishnevskii, I.R. and Shapko, V.T. (2002) The college student of the 1990s, *Russian Education & Society,* 44(3): 6–24.

Wakeling, P. (2005) *La Noblesse d'état Anglaise?* Social class and progression to postgraduate study, *British Journal of Sociology of Education,* 26(4): 505–22.

Walby, S. (1997) *Gender Transformations.* London and New York: Routledge.

Waldman, D. (1989) Film theory and the gendered spectator: the female or the feminist reader? *Camera Obscura,* 18: 80–94.

Walker, M. (1998) Academic identities: women on a South African landscape, *British Journal of Sociology of Education,* 19(3): 335–54.

Walkerdine, V. (1990) *Schoolgirl Fictions.* London, New York: Verso.

Walkerdine, V. (1994) Femininity as performance, in L. Stone (ed.) *The Education Feminism Reader.* London: Routledge.

Walkerdine, V. (2003) Reclassifying upward mobility: femininity and the neo-liberal subject, *Gender and Education,* 15(3): 237–48.

Walkerdine, V., Lucey, H. and Melody, J. (1999) Class, attainment and sexuality in late twentieth-century Britain, in C. Zmroczek and P. Mahony (eds) *Women and Social Class – International Feminist Perspectives.* London: UCL Press.

Walkerdine, V., Lucey, H. and Melody, J. (2001) *Growing up Girl: Psychosocial Explorations of Gender and Class.* Basingstoke: Palgrave.

Wang, R.-J. (2001) Gender barriers in higher education: the case of Taiwan, *Education Policy Analysis Archives,* 9(51). http://epaa.asu.edu/epaa/v9n51/ (accessed 2 August, 2001).

Warlaumont, H. (1993) Visual grammars of gender: the gaze and psychoanalytic theory in advertisements, *Journal of Communication Inquiry,* 17: 25–40.

Wartchow, K. (2001) Writing as a woman in graduate school: how female graduate students construct identities as academic writers (unpublished dissertation).

Waters, M. (1995) *Globalization.* London: Routledge.

Watson, D. and Bowden, R. (2002) *The New University Decade 1992–2002.* Brighton: Education Research Centre, University of Brighton.

Watts, R. (2005) Gender, science and modernity in seventeenth century England, *Paedagogica Historica,* XLI(1–2): 79–93.

Watts, R. (2007) Whose knowledge? Gender, education, science and history, *History of Education,* 36(3): 283–302.

Weber, R. (1985) *Basic Content Analysis.* London: Sage.

Weisman, L. (1994) *Discrimination by Design: A Feminist Critique of the Man Made Environment.* Chicago, IL: University of Illinois Press.

Wenneras, C. and Wold, A. (1997) Nepotism and sexism in peer-review, *Nature* 387: 341–3.

Wertsch, J. (1991) *Voices of the Mind: A Socio-Cultural Approach to Mediated Action.* Cambridge, MA: Harvard University Press.

Whelehan, I. (1995) *Modern Feminist Thought.* Edinburgh: Edinburgh University Press.

Whistleblower (2006) The war on fathers, *Whistleblower.* www.worldnetdaily.com/news (accessed 27 October, 2007).

White, M. (2006) *Body and the Screen: Theories of Internet Spectatorship.* Cambridge, MA: MIT Press.

Williams, J. (1997) The discourse of access: the legitimation of selectivity, in J. Williams (ed.) *Negotiating Access to Higher Education: The Discourse of Selectivity and Equity.* Buckingham: SRHE and Open University Press.

Williams, R. (2000) Being queer, being black: living out in Afro-American studies, in U. of. M. Social Justice Group at The Center for Advanced Feminist Studies (ed.) *Is Academic Feminism Dead?* New York: New York University Press.

Willmott, H. (1995) Managing the academics: commodification and control in the development of university education in the UK, *Human Relations,* 48: 993–1025.

Wilson, F. and Nutley, S. (2003) A critical look at staff appraisal: the case of women in Scottish universities, *Gender, Work and Organization,* 10(3): 301–19.

Wilton, T. (1995) *Lesbian Studies: Setting an Agenda.* London: Routledge.

Wisniewski, R. (2000) The averted gaze, *Anthropology & Education Quarterly,* 31.

Witz, A. (1992) *Professions and Patriarchy.* London and New York: Routledge.

Wolf, D. (1993) Assessment as an episode of learning, in R. Bennett and W.C. Ward (eds) *Construction Versus Choice in Cognitive Measurement.* Hillsdale, NJ: Lawrence Erlbaum.

Wolf-Wendel, L. and Ward, K. (2003) Future prospects for women faculty: negotiating work and family, in B. Ropers-Huilman (ed.) *Gendered Futures in Higher Education.* Albany, NY: State University of New York Press.

Wolff, J. (1981) *The Social Production of Art.* London: Macmillan.

Wolffensberger, J. (1993) 'Science is truly a male world': the interconnectedness of knowledge, gender and power within university education, *Gender and Education,* 5(1): 37–54.

Woodfield, R., Earl-Novell, S. and Solomon, L. (2005) Gender and mode of assessment at university: should we assume female students are better suited to coursework and males to unseen examinations? *Assessment and Evaluation in Higher Education,* 30(1): 35–50.

Woolf, V. (1992) *A Room of One's Own.* Oxford: Oxford University Press.

Young, M. ([1958] 1971) *The Rise of the Meritocracy.* Harmondsworth: Penguin.

Young, M. (2001) Down with meritocracy, *The Guardian,* 29 June.

Yuval-Davis, N. (1997) Ethnicity, gender relations and multiculturalism, in P. Werbner and T. Modood (eds) *Debating Cultural Hybridity: Multicultural Identities and the Politics of Anti-Racism.* London: Zed Books Ltd.

Zimmer, A. (2003) *Women in European Universities: Research and Training Network Final Report 2002–03.* http://csn.uni-muenster.de/women-eu/download/Final Report_Zimmer_20.11.2003.pdf (accessed 2 February, 2008).

Zimmer, A., Krimmer, H. and Stallmann, F. (2007) Women at German universities, in R. Siemienska and A. Zimmer (eds) *Gendered Career Trajectories in Academia in Cross National Perspective.* Warszawa: Wydawnictwo Naukowe Scholar.

Index

academic citizenship, 96–7
academic cultures, 128–38, 144
academic freedom, 96, 131
'academic literacies' approach, 144, 149
academic practices, 8, 141–74
  assessment, 8, 141, 152–6
  curriculum *see* curriculum
  language, 142–5
  speaking, 8, 126, 129–31, 145–8
  writing, 8, 142–3, 148–51, 153–6
academic staff, 8, 16, 22, 119–40, 178
  gender and marginalization, 124–8
  global overview and labour market,
    41–6
  objectivity and neutrality, 134–8
  representations on university websites,
    89–91, 94
  ruthlessness and competitiveness,
    128–34
  UK, 43, 44, 65–9
  women as the intellectual 'other',
    121–3
  see also academic practices
academic support, 16–17, 100–3
Academies of Art, 161
access to higher education, 3, 15, 26–9,
  48–9
achievement, 15–16, 31, 53–4
Acker, S., 127, 128, 134–5
'active' male students, images of, 87–9
activism, 177–9
Adkins, L., 17, 23, 74, 112, 136
advanced degrees, 32
advertising, images in, 72–5
Ahmad, F., 116, 117

Ahmed, S., 19, 74, 111
Aizenberg, J., 90
alternative academic identities, 139
Alverno College, 79, 92, 93
American studies, 169
Amis, K., 18
Anderson, M., 166, 169
Anthias, F., 4, 124
Appadurai, A., 106
Apple, M.W., 106, 174
appraisal, 137–8
Archer, L., 115, 146, 147
architecture, 85–6
Aristotle, 162
Armenti, C., 127, 134–5
art historians, 164
artists, 169
arts, 161, 163–4
Arts Council, 161
Arum, R., 37
ascribed identity, 125
assertions, 143, 148–9, 149–50
assertiveness, 128–9, 151
assessment, 8, 141, 152–6
  coursework, 16, 152, 153–6
  social construction of, 153–4
Assié-Lumumba, N.D., 40
Atkinson, H., 90
Australia, 29, 42, 44
autonomy, 5
  independent learner, 97–100
'avatar' student guides, 81–4

Bagilhole, B., 135, 137
Ball, S., 2, 105

Banerji, S., 42
Barata, P., 116
Barnett, R., 171–2
Barthes, R., 161
Bartholomae, D., 150
Bartky, S.L., 25, 111
Baudrillard, J., 107
Baxter, A., 109, 111
Baxter, S., 3
Becher, T., 119
benchmarking, 171–2
benefits of higher education
    global context, 39–41
    UK, 63–5
Berkeley University, 87
bias, 154–5
Bildung, 97
Bird, E., 167
Blackmore, J., 3, 4–5, 19, 29, 133, 172
'bluestockings', 5
Bodichon, B., 48
Bouchard, P., 15
Bourdieu, P., 126, 150
Bowden, R., 57
Bradley, C., 154–5
Brady, N., 120
brain, 11
Branthwaite, A., 143
Brecher, B., 170
'Bright Boys' project, 20
'Brilliant Women: 18th-century
    Bluestockings', 5
Brine, J., 2
Bristol University, 167
Britton, C., 109, 111
Broadfoot, P., 141
Broecke, S., 53
Brooks, A., 126
Brouns, M., 44–5
Brown, P., 63–4
Brown, R., 61
Brown, V.B., 21
Bryson, C., 66, 67
Buerk, M., 12
Burman, E., 54

Cambridge University, 48–9, 63–4, 101, 152
Canada, 34, 116, 117, 122
Canberra University, 79
Canterbury University, 83–4, 87
caring relationships, 134–5
caring work, 40, 135–6

Carter, J., 67
casualization, 44, 66–7, 122–3
Central Asia and the Caucasus, 29
Central and Eastern Europe, 28, 32, 33, 34, 166
Chanana, K., 29, 36, 38
Chesworth, K., 142
Chevalier, A., 63
children, 134–5
China, 45
choice, 105–6
    subject choice, 34–6, 54–6
Cixous, H., 159
Clark, L., 13–14
class, social *see* social class
Coate, K., 167
co-education, 21
Cohen, M., 18
Cohen, S., 19
Cohen, S. Baron, 11
colonialism, 28
Committee on Maximizing the Potential
    of Women in Academic Science and
    Engineering, 11, 44, 47
commodification of knowledge, 170–3
Commonwealth Secretariat, 176
communication, 129–31, 142–51
    academic language, 142–5
    speaking, 8, 126, 129–31, 145–8
    writing, 8, 142–3, 148–51, 153–6
competitiveness, 128–34, 137
computer science, 35
confidence, 147, 150–1
conforming, 115–16
Conlon, G., 63
Connolly, K., 12
consensus on existence of problem, 20
constructions of gender, 21–3
consumer, student as, 104–7
content analysis, 77
contract research, 122–3
corporatization, 72
counter-resistance, 177
coursework assessment, 16, 152, 153–6
Cronin, A., 91
cultural feminization, 10–11, 12, 22, 176
culture, academic, 128–38
curriculum, 8, 18, 157–74
    marginalization, 158–62, 169–70
    skills and employability, 170–3
    'traditional', 158–66
    women's studies, 26, 166–9
customer service 'avatars', 81

Czarniawska, B., 81

David, M., 105
Davies, B., 121
Davies, C., 131
Davies, E., 48
De Beauvoir, S., 123
Deem, R., 6, 134
deficit model, 54
Delamont, S., 27
democracy, 105–6
Denham, J., 20, 171
Dennis, I., 153, 155
Dent, M., 124
Derrida, J., 162
Descartes, R., 161
deskilling, 120
detraditionalization of gender, 23
devaluing of higher education, 18, 21,
    45–6
developing countries, 3–4
disability, 6
    disabled students, 52–3, 91
discourse analysis, 77
discourses, dominant, 124
disproportionality, 20–1
diversity mainstreaming, 176
division of labour, 5
Doherty, S., 131, 139
dominant discourses, 124
drop-out rates, 31–2
'dumbing down', 18, 21, 45–6
Dyhouse, C., 27, 48, 78

Eastern and Central Europe, 28, 32, 33,
    34, 166
Ecclestone, K., 17
economic factors, 28–9
education, 13–15
elite universities, 36–7, 56–62, 63–4, 67–8
Elwood, J., 155
emotion, 16–17
    'needy student', 100–3
emotional literacy, 17–18, 113–14
employability, 107–8, 170–3
employment prospects, 39–40, 63–5
    student as future graduate, 107–14
empowerment, 166
England, P., 46
Enlightenment, 158–9, 161, 164
entrepreneurship of the self, 108,
    109–13
Epstein, D., 19, 92, 116, 165

equality policies, 176–7
essays
    assessment of, 153–6
    writing, 142–3
ethnicity, 20
    and academic language, 144–5
    academic staff, 125, 136
    and employment prospects, 64
    feminist challenges to 'malestream'
        knowledge, 164–5
    images of students, 91
    and institutional diversity, 37–8, 58, 62
    participation in higher education,
        33–4
    and student identity, 115
    UK students, 52, 55, 58, 62
ethnocentrism, 5
European Commission, 104
European Network on Gender Equality
    in Higher Education, 178
European Union, 176
Evans, M., 106, 113–14, 169
examinations, 152–3
external examiners, 154–5

failure, fear of, 110–11
family responsibilities, 134–5
fear of feminization, 19
fees, tuition, 50–1, 61, 104
female students, images of, 78–87
feminism, 168–9
    challenges to 'malestream'
        knowledge, 163–6
    continuing marginalization of feminist
        research, 169–70
    future of higher education, 176–9
'Feminist Africa', 178
'Feminist Salon', 178
feminization thesis, 1–2, 7, 9–25, 175–6
    constructions of gender, 21–3
    contemporary discourses, 10–13
    education, 13–15
    feminization and devaluing of higher
        education, 15–18
    moral panic, 18–21
Fenton, S., 65
Ferber, M.A., 104
Ferguson, K.E., 114
Fisher, G., 122, 133
Fleming, J., 42
'folk devils', 19
Fordham, S., 125
former Soviet Union, 28, 32, 33, 34

Foucault, M., 74, 124, 127
France, 27
Francis, B., 14, 129, 152, 179
Fraser, N., 98
Frederickson, K., 169
freedom, 40–1
    academic, 96, 131
friendliness, 78–84
Fukuyama, F., 10
Fülöp, M., 128
Furedi, F., 16
further education, 62, 134
future graduate, student as, 107–14
'Future of Higher Education, The', 98
futuristic architecture, 86

Gadamer, H., 75, 76
gay students and academics, 92, 116, 125
gender, constructions of, 21–3
gender binary, 5, 12–13
    'traditional' curriculum, 158–66
gender essentialism, 10–11
gender mainstreaming, 176–7
gender neutrality myth, 5
gender transformation, 22–3
gendered organizations, 5
'Gendered Patterns in Undergraduate
    Writing in the Context of
    Achievement', 145
genius, 123
Germany, 12, 28, 45, 46, 96
Gilder, G., 16, 20
Gillborn, D., 62
'girl power', 12
Girton College, Cambridge, 48
Glasgow University, 91
'glass ceiling', 40
global context, 7, 26–47
    academic labour market, 41–6
    benefits of higher education, 39–41
    institutional diversity, 36–8
    subject choice, 34–6
    women students' participation in
        higher education, 29–34
globalization, 2–4
Goffman, E., 73
'good' feminized student, 84–7
Gordon, L., 98
Gqola, P.D., 178
Grant, B., 97, 148
Griffiths, M., 98
Guerrilla Girls, 164
guides, welcoming, 81–4

Gustavsson, E., 81

Hakim, C., 123
Hall, S., 4
Haraway, D., 165
Harding, S., 148
Harley, S., 133
Harris, P., 135
Hartley, J., 142
Harvard University, 79, 85, 87, 90, 91
Hatcher, R., 105
Hayes, D., 17, 101, 131
hedges and qualifiers, 148–9
Hefner, D., 34
Hekman, S., 159
Hesketh, A., 63–4
hetersexuality, naturalization of, 13
Hey, V., 101, 138
higher education (HE), 7
    academic labour market, 41–6, 65–9
    benefits of, 39–41, 63–5
    changing face of, 2–4
    feminization and devaluing, 15–18, 21,
        45–6
    feminization and moral panic, 18–21
    global context, 7, 26–47
    institutional diversity, 36–8, 56–62
    students' participation in HE, 29–34,
        49–54
    subject choice, 34–6, 54–6
    UK, 7, 48–70
    women's access to, 3, 15, 26–9, 48–9
Higher Education Funding Council for
    England (HEFCE), 66, 68, 172
Higher and Further Education Act 1992,
    56–7
Hill Collins, P., 74, 123
Hilton, M., 104
Hirsch, E., 75
history, 161–2
    essays, 149
    feminist challenges, 164
Holland, 44
Holmes, J., 149
hooks, b., 137, 164–5
hostility, 19–20
Howie, G., 133, 135
humanities, 163–4
Hunjan, S., 116
Husu, L., 140

identity construction, 4, 124
Illouz, E., 113

images
  of academics, 89–91, 94
  gendered in advertising, 72–5
  negated 'other', 91–3
  of students, 78–89, 93–4
independent learner, 97–100
India, 29, 33, 38, 167
individual, conceptualizations of the, 95–6
individualism, 134–6, 139
institutional diversity
  global context, 36–8
  UK, 56–62
institutional identities, 7, 71–94
  construction and reception of visual texts, 75–6
  gendered images in advertising, 72–5
  images of students, 78–89, 93–4
  negated 'other', 91–3
  representations of academics, 89–91, 94
  study of university websites, 7, 76–94
intellectual work, 96–7
intellectuals, 5
  women as intellectual 'other', 121–3
International Alliance of Research Universities (IARU), 36–7
internet, 10
Iran, 15, 28, 39, 40–1
Ivanic, R., 132

Jackson, S., 132, 169
Jacobs, S., 53–4
Jansen, W., 28, 32, 38, 39, 41
Jefferson, T., 129
Jenkins, R., 125
Jordan, 28, 32, 35–6, 38, 39, 41
Jordanova, L., 162

Kaba, A.J., 34
Kenway, J., 56
King, J.E., 20
knowledge, 8, 157–74
  as commodity, 170–3
  as 'truth', 158–66
Kohlberg, L., 100
Kupelian, D., 12

labour market
  academic staff, 41–6, 65–9
  employment prospects for students, 39–40, 63–5, 107–14

feminization of, 22–3
Lacan, J., 74
Lafferty, G., 42
Lakoff, R., 148–9
Lambert, C., 174, 178–9
language, academic, 142–5
  class, gender, ethnicity and, 144–5
  speaking, 8, 126, 129–31, 145–8
  writing, 8, 142–3, 148–51, 153–6
Le Feuvre, N., 22–3
Lea, M., 144
league tables, 37, 57–61
learner independence, 97–100
learning style, 54
Leathwood, C., 56, 98–9, 101, 125
Leggatt, J., 116
Leicester University, 87, 90, 91
Leitch Report, 171
lesbian, gay, bisexual and transgender (LGBT) students and academics, 92, 116, 125
Lester, J., 131
Letherby, G., 136, 168
Limerick University, 88
Lloyd, G., 95–6
loans, student, 51, 104
local context, 6–7
London Metropolitan University, 168
Longe Report, 32
Longitudinal Study of Students Learning and Experiences, 98
Lucey, H., 108
Lury, C., 112, 136
Lynch, C.M., 149

Mackinnon, A., 24
Maddock, S., 133
Magno, C., 6–7, 28, 29, 32, 33, 34
Maguire, M., 137
Mahony, P., 20
male bodies, feminization of, 11
'male gaze', 73–4
male students, images of 'active', 87–9
male teachers, 13, 14
'malestream' knowledge, feminist challenges to, 163–6
Malveaux, J., 39
management, 111–12, 133–4
Manchester Metropolitan University, 88, 92
Mann, C., 146–7, 152
Marcet, J., 160
Marchbank, J., 168

marginalization
  academics, 124–8
  subject disciplines, 158–62, 169–70
Marginson, S., 104
marketing, 72
Marshall, B., 14
Martin, M., 144
masculinity
  and academic support, 102–3
  women and performing, 22
masculinity politics, 16
'masculinized' disciplines, 158–62
'masculinized' tradition, 84–7
mass higher education system, 17
mature students, 50, 91, 117
maturity, 96
Mazon, P.M., 96–7, 99
McDowell, L., 23
McGann, J., 75
medicine, 10, 15
Melody, J., 108
members of parliament, 10
Mercer, I., 14–15
meritocracy, 62
Middlesex University, 82–3, 86, 91
Miller, J., 17, 19
Mirza, H.S., 32, 64, 84, 114–15, 125, 136
mobility of students, 38
Modood, T., 52, 62
modular courses, 170, 172
Mohanty, C., 3–4, 5
Moi, T., 123
moral panic, 18–21
Morley, L., 6, 18, 38, 43, 50, 68, 116,
    131–2, 133–4, 140, 171, 172, 177
Morrison, Z., 115–16
Munford, R., 43
Murphy, P., 155
Muslim countries, 166–7
Muslim students, 116, 117

Naidoo, R., 2, 61, 172
'needy student', 100–3
Nelson, J.A., 104
neo-liberalism, 2, 28–9, 104, 107–8
networking, 136–7
  women, 178–9
neutrality, 134–8
new managerialism, 2, 20, 141
  and academic identities, 119–20,
    132–3, 137–8
  and support for learning, 103
New Zealand, 178

Newnham College, Cambridge, 48
Newstead, S.E., 153, 155
Nicholls, T., 53
Nietzsche, F., 158, 160
Nigeria, 27, 28, 31, 32, 33, 39, 42–3, 177
non-academic staff, 41–2, 65–6
numbers of women, increasing, 10, 15,
    176
  academics, 121–2, 163
  students, 29–31, 49–50, 163
Nutley, S., 137–8

objectivity, 134–8, 148
occupational hierarchy, upper levels of,
    22–3, 42–3, 44, 66
O'Connell, P., 56
O'Connor, P., 177
OECD, 33, 104
oestrogens, environmental, 11
O'Neill, A.-M., 105
opinions, 150–1
oral communication, 8, 126, 129–31,
    145–8
other
  'negated' and university websites, 91–3
  women as the intellectual 'other',
    121–3
Ourliac, G., 27
'overweight' students, 91
Oxford University, 49, 63–4, 85–6, 89, 91,
    101

panopticon, 127
Pappu, R., 167
Parker, A., 174, 178–9
Parkin, D., 133
parliament, 10
part-time students, 50–1
participation in HE
  global context, 29–34
  UK, 49–53
passive images of women, 73–4
Pateman, C., 95
pay gap, 39–40, 64–5
  academics, 43–4, 67–8
people skills, 17–18, 108, 113–14
Pereira, C., 3, 5, 28, 31, 39, 42, 44, 177
Pereira, S., 15
performance
  academics, 127, 131–3
  student identities, 110–13
performativity, 2–3, 127, 132–3
Pessl, M., 157, 162

physical activity, 87–9
physical changes, 11
Pirie, M., 152
Plato, 27, 161
Poland, 28, 38, 42, 45, 46
political action, 92
political factors, 28–9
polytechnics, 56–7
Portugal, 15
post-1992 universities, 56–62, 68
postcolonialist feminism, 165
post-feminism, 177
poststructuralism, 165, 179
power, 124
  advertising images and, 73–4
  webs of power and university web
    pages, 77–91
Pratt, J., 121
pre-1992 universities, 56–62
presentations, 126, 130–1
Prichard, C., 134
primary schools, 13, 14
Probert, B., 135
professionalism, 119–20
professorial posts, 42, 43, 68
promotion, 45
Purnell, J., 105–6

qualifications, 62
Quality Assurance Agency (QAA), 171
quality audit, 132–3
queer theory, 165
question and answer sessions, 130–1
Quinn, J., 41, 107, 118, 169–70

racism, 116
Ramsay, K., 136
Randle, K., 120
Read, B., 126, 130, 131
reason, 95–6
reasoned argument, 143, 144
Reay, D., 105, 122–3, 125
refuge, 40–1
reinforcement of femininity, 25
reliability, 153–4
reputation, 136–7
research, 68–9
  contract research, 122–3
  grant applications, 44–5
Research Assessment Exercise (RAE),
  68–9, 132, 167
resources, 60–1
Rich, A., 1, 116, 141

Roma, 34
Roper, B., 57
Rorty, R., 159
Rose, G., 75, 77
Ross, A., 57
Royal Society, 160
Rumball, S., 43
Rundel, J., 52, 53
Russia, 33
  see also former Soviet Union
ruthlessness, 128–34
Rutledge Shields, V., 74, 75
Ryle, S., 63

Sachs, J., 3, 29
Saunders, P., 152–3
Sax, L., 11
Schick Case, S., 129, 154
Schiebinger, L., 163
science, 11, 29, 35, 56, 162
  exclusion of women from, 160–1
  feminist challenges, 163
  images of science students, 86–7
self-regulation of behaviour, 127
self-transformation, 108, 109–13
seminars, 146–8
senior academic posts, 22–3, 42–3, 44, 66
Sewell, T., 13–14
'sex war' discourse, 19–20
sexual harassment, 116, 177
sexuality, 6
  LGBT academics and students, 92,
    116, 125
  naturalization of heterosexuality, 13
Shavarini, M.K., 28, 40–1
Siemienska, R., 28, 42, 45, 46
Silova, I., 6–7, 28, 29, 32, 33, 34
Sims, S., 39
Singh, M., 170–1
Skeggs, B., 105, 109, 112
Skelton, C., 152
skills
  employability, 8, 170–3
  people skills, 17–18, 108, 113–14
smiling, 82, 84
Smith, J., 4
social class, 20, 33
  and academic language, 144–5
  institutional diversity and, 37–8, 58,
    59, 62
  and subject choice, 55–6
  and student identity, 115
  UK students, 34, 51–2, 55–6, 58, 59, 62

'Social Class and Widening Participation in Higher Education', 146
social movements, 177–9
Soemmerring, S.T. von, 163
Somerville, E., 160
Spanier, B., 168
speaking, 8, 126, 129–31, 145–8
Spender, D., 24
sports, 88
Stake, J., 167
Starkey, D., 61
Strassman, D., 105
Strauss-Noll, M., 149
Street, B., 144
student honour, 96
student loans, 51, 104
students, 7–8, 95–118, 178–9
    constructing the university student, 95–7
    as consumers, 104–7
    future graduates, 107–14
    gender and nature of students in UK, 49–53
    global overview of women's participation in higher education, 29–34
    images of on university websites, 78–89, 93–4
    independent learner, 97–100
    mobility, 38
    multiple possibilities for identity, 114–16
    'needy student', 100–3
subject disciplines, 157–70
    choice by students, 34–6, 54–6
    feminist challenges to 'malestream' knowledge, 163–6
    marginalization, 158–62, 169–70
    'masculinised', 158–62
    and pay gap, 40
    women's studies, 26, 166–9
support culture, 16–17, 100–3
support work, 135–6
Sutton, M., 40

Taiwan, 32, 36, 38
Tanzania, 33
Tauchert, A., 133, 135
teachers' attention, 24
texts, visual, 75–6
    see also university websites
Thompson, D., 57
threat, perceived, 19, 24–5

time, 162
Tolley, J., 52, 53
Tomlinson, S., 3
'tradition', masculinized, 84–7
'traditional' curriculum, 158–66
    feminist challenges, 163–6
    'masculinized' disciplines and marginalization of the 'feminine', 158–62
transnational organizations, 2, 104
Trethewey, A., 113
Trowler, P., 119
'truth', knowledge as, 158–66
tuition fees, 50–1, 61, 104
Turkey, 31
Tyrer, D., 116, 117

Uganda, 41
UNESCO, 176
    World Declaration on Higher Education for the Twenty-First Century, 26, 27
United Kingdom (UK), 3, 7, 15, 31, 34, 48–70
    academic labour force, 43, 44, 65–9
    benchmarking, 171
    differential benefits of HE, 63–5
    gender and student participation in HE, 49–53
    historical context, 48–9
    institutional diversity, 56–62
    Leitch Report, 171
    quality audit, 132–3
    RAE, 68–9, 132, 167
    student achievement, 31, 53–4
    subject choices, 36, 54–6
    women's studies, 167, 168
United States of America (USA), 34, 38, 39, 167
    female academic staff, 42, 43, 44
University College, Dublin, 79–81, 87
university league tables, 37, 57–61
'University Lecturers' Constructions of Undergraduate Writing', 145
university presidents, 43
university status, 42
    and academic pay, 67–8
    elite universities, 36–7, 56–62, 63–4, 67–8
    see also institutional diversity
university websites, 7, 76–94
    gender and webs of power, 77–91
    images of students, 78–89, 93–4

methodology, 76–7
'negated' other, 91–3
representations of academics, 89–91, 94

validity, women's studies and, 167, 168
vice-chancellors, 43
victims of feminization, 12
violence, 4, 116, 177
visual grammars, 74–5
visual texts
    construction and reception of, 75–6
    see also university websites
volatility, 21

Walby, S., 3
Walker, M., 127, 139
Walkerdine, V., 17, 53, 102, 108, 109, 112, 134
Wang, R.-J., 32, 36, 38
war, 28
Warlaumont, H., 72
Warwick Anti-Sexism Society (WASS), 174, 178–9
Warwick University 'Reinvention Centre', 174
Watson, D., 57
Watts, R., 160, 161

Webber, M., 128
websites, university *see* university websites
welcoming guides, 81–4
Wenneras, C., 69
West of Scotland, University of, 82, 92
Whistleblower, 12
Whitehead, S., 124
Wilson, F., 137–8
Wold, A., 69
Wolf, D., 156
Woolf, V., 71
Women in Higher Education Network (WHEN), 178
women's access to higher education, 3, 15, 26–9, 48–9
women's studies, 26, 166–9
Woodfield, R., 152–3
World Bank, 104
World Trade Organization, 2
Wright, D., 155
writing, 8, 142–3, 148–51
    essays, 142–3, 153–6
writing retreats, 178

Youdell, D., 62
Young, M., 62

Zimmer, A., 28, 45, 46